WORSHIP IN ISLAM

WORSHIP IN ISLAM

BEING A
TRANSLATION WITH COMMENTARY AND INTRODUCTION

OF

AL-GHAZZALI'S BOOK OF THE IHYA' ON THE WORSHIP

REV. EDWIN ELLIOT CALVERLEY

GYAN

Published by

GYAN

Gyan Publishing House
5, Ansari Road
Daryaganj, New Delhi-110002
Phone: 011-47034999, 9811692060
E-mail: books@gyanbooks.com

Distribution Network
gyanbooks.com
India, USA, Canada, UK, Australia, France

ISBN : 978-81-212-4229-5 (PB)
First Published, Madras, 1925

2nd Impression 2020

Printed at: Gyan Press, Delhi.

Worship in Islam
Author: Edwin Elliot Calverley

WORSHIP IN ISLAM

Being a Translation, with Commentary and Introduction

OF

AL-GHAZZALI'S BOOK OF THE IHYA ON THE WORSHIP

BY THE

REV. EDWIN ELLIOT CALVERLEY, PH.D.

THE CHRISTIAN LITERATURE SOCIETY
FOR INDIA

MADRAS ALLAHABAD RANGOON COLOMBO

1925

Dedicated

to

Duncan Black Macdonald,

Scholar, Teacher, Friend,

Master Missionary to Muslims

PREFACE

When a person unacquainted with the doctrines and exercises of the Christian religion attends a cathedral service or reads a Christian devotional book, he undoubtedly notices many acts and many phrases that are new and strange to him, and that require explanation before he understands them. Such a one might want to know just what thoughts and feelings pass over the heart and mind of the Christian worshipper as he performs his religious acts. He might inquire further about the recognized practices provided in Christianity for meeting the times of religious need common to mankind. He would have to investigate deeply and broadly before he could appreciate the background, recognize the allusions, comprehend the terminology and understand the attitude that are the common Christian possession.

Similarly, one who does not have a Muslim training finds it difficult to understand what he sees and hears when he observes a Muslim at worship alone or with others in a mosque. Al-Ghazzálí supplies the required information in his *Book of the Worship*, of which the present work is a translation. The Introduction brings together the acts and utterances which constitute the formal ceremony called 'the Worship', and gives an account of the times when this ceremony is used in the religious life of the Muslim. The annotations are an attempt to make clear the allusions and the technical terms, the knowledge of which al-Ghazzálí takes for granted because he wrote his description of the Worship for Muslims.

The work here presented was undertaken and carried on under the inspiring direction and with the grateful assistance of Professor Duncan Black Macdonald, D.D., and the late Professor M. H. Ananikian, S.T.M., of the Kennedy School of Missions of the Hartford Seminary Foundation, as an original investigation, to fulfil in part the School's requirements for the degree of Doctor of Philosophy. It is published in the hope that it will assist missionaries and others, with or without a knowledge of Arabic, tc understand the ideas and emotions which are expressed by the Muslim peoples in their most important religious ceremony.

Kuwait, Arabia. E.E.C.

CONTENTS

PART I. INTRODUCTION

PART II. TRANSLATION

APPENDICES

PART I

INTRODUCTION

INTRODUCTION

The Word Ṣalá and Its Meanings

The Muslims use the term *'ibáda* to express the relationship and attitude of a creature as slave to Allah his Lord, who formed him and therefore owns him. This relationship finds outward expression in acts of obedience, worship and devotion. Some of these acts are commanded; others are recommended; while still others are voluntary.

Chief among those that are commanded are fasting, pilgrimage to Mecca, payment of the quarter-tithe and the *ṣalá*. *Ṣalá* here means a specific ceremony of *'ibáda*, opened with the expression 'Allah is greater', and closed with the Salutation.[1] To designate this special ceremony the term 'Worship' will be used, rather than 'prayer', simply because it is a ceremonial service.

It is chiefly by means of the *ṣalá*, Worship, that the prayer and devotional life is expressed in Islam, both in public and private worship. Other expressions of worship and devotion consist in *al-tiláwa*, the Recital of the Qur'án; *al-du'á'*, the offering of Supplication; *al-dhikr*, the Invocation of the Names of Allah and the mentioning of His Qualities; *al-wird*, the Recital of a section of the Qur'án or other religious work; *al-ḥizb*, a Portion of the Qur'án or other devotional writing used as a petition, together with other forms of communion with Allah to be mentioned later.

It is the *ṣalá*, the Worship, which is to be considered first in this Introduction. As to the word itself, the lexicographers have had difficulty in explaining both its form and its meaning. Some held that it was originally *ṣalawa*, and others that it was *ṣalwa*.[2] But in nouns of the form *fa'ala* from verbs with *wáw* for the third radical, the *wáw* is changed to long *alif*, but the (etymologically more correct) orthography *ṣalawt* is often found.[3] The *Diction-*

[1] SM iii. p. 99. [2] *Táj al-'Arús*, x. p. 213.
[3] Wright, *Grammar*, ii. pp. 121C, 12A.

second stem has the sense of 'stretching out', and also of 'praying'.[1]

The word seems also to be known in Assyrian in the sense of 'begging', although, apparently, not begging of the gods.[2]

This bending and inclining, merely physical in the first stem, intensified, that is, repeated, in the second stem, may very well express the spiritual idea accompanying the repeated physical act, and thus mean the ceremonial acts of bowing in worship and the accompanying supplication of favour by the creature. It is in this sense of ceremonial acts of worship, consisting of the standing, bowing, prostration and sitting, together with the accompanying utterances, that the word is technically and chiefly used. The people of Arabia, at least the foreigners, in the time of Muhammad, used the word in the sense of ceremonial worship and supplication. One of the Arab authorities stated that it was also used by the Arabs in that sense. The Muḥammadans apparently took it over and applied it to their special form of Worship, while at the same time they recognized that the word was used for simple prayer or supplication as well. The other meanings of 'magnifying', 'asking forgiveness' and 'blessing', which the lexicographers give to the word, would be simply explanations of the content of the ceremony.

The further development of the use of *ṣallá ʿalá* for Allah would then be explained as the response of Allah to His creatures: the creature's physical inclination expresses his request for Allah's inclination towards him in mercy and favour. The expression *ṣallá ʿalá* is also used of both angels and men, and is understood as 'intercession', 'asking forgiveness on behalf of another'. This is more likely to be a development from the standpoint of the creature of the idea of supplication for the sake of another, than a development from the standpoint of Allah of inclination towards the creature.

[1] Payne Smith, *Thesaurus Syriacus*, ii. p. 3399; Dalman, *Aramäisch-Neuhebräisches Wörterbuch*, p. 347.

[2] Schrader, *Keilinschriften*, 3rd edit., p. 610 f.

There is a claim on the part of some of the lexicographers and commentators that the expression *ṣallá ʿalá* should be used only on behalf of Muḥammad, and then in the sense of Allah's magnifying him. But there are too many instances and traditions of its use for his family and for others for this restricted use to be generally accepted.[1] This formula of blessing also occurs used ironically, and hence becomes an imprecation and a curse.[2]

The Performance of the Worship

The performance of the Worship is preceded by certain necessary acts. These include the cleansing of the body, clothing and place of worship. Book Three of the First Quarter of the *Iḥyá'* describes the proper performance of these operations. After them follows the covering of the person from the navel to the knees, when the worshipper is a man. These acts are the pre-requisites of the Worship.

When they are finished the man is ready for the Worship. He assumes 1 (the same numbering of the parts of the Worship will be repeated in the Analytical Table, pp. 16-18), the Standing Position, facing the *qibla*[3] with his feet apart, his head preferably inclined, and his gaze upon his place of worship.

Then he says 2, the *Basmala*:[4]

> 'In the name of Allah, the Merciful and Compassionate One.'

He says immediately after it 3, the *Taʿawwudh*, Seeking for Refuge:[5]

> 'Say: I seek refuge in the Lord of mankind,
> the Possessor of mankind,
> the God of mankind,
> from the evil of the Whisperer,[6]

[1] Cf. Goldziher, *Die Eulogien der Muhammedaner*, *Zeitschrift der Deutschen Morgenländischen Gesellschaft*, vol. 50, pp. 97-128.

[2] *Ibid.*, p. 123. [3] Note 1, p. 63.

[4] SM 33A; all references similar to this are to the *Itḥáf al-Sáda*, vol. iii. See note 2 of Translation, p. 37

[5] SM 33A; see note 3, p. 64. [6] Note 2, p. 77.

the one who goes back,
who whispers in the breasts of mankind,
of the jinn and mankind.'[1]

Then, if he expects anyone to worship behind him, he says 4, the Call to Worship:[2]

'Allah is greater! Allah is greater!
I witness, There is no god but Allah!
I witness, Muḥammad is the Messenger of Allah!
Come to the Worship! Come to prosperity!
Allah is greater! Allah is greater!'

Instead of the two phrases, 'Come to the Worship! Come to prosperity', called the *Ḥaiʿalatain*. the follower says:

'There is no might and no strength but in Allah!'

In the Morning Worship the *mu'adhdhin* adds, after the *Ḥaiʿalatain*, the *Tathwīb*:[3]

'The Worship is better than sleep!'[4]

The follower thereupon responds:

'You have spoken truly! You have acted rightly! You have given good advice!'[5]

After the Call to the Worship, the *mu'adhdhin*, or the worshipper himself if he is alone, says 5, the Institution:[6]

'The Worship is instituted!'

The follower responds:

'May Allah institute it and continue it as long as the heavens and the earth continue!'[7]

He also adds:

'O Allah! By the right of this complete Call and Worship instituted, grant Muḥammad mediation and excellence, and elevate him to the praiseworthy station which Thou didst promise him: Thou dost not violate a promise!'[8]

[1] Qur'án, cxiv.
[2] SM 33B; note 3, p. 41.
[3] Note 4, p. 42.
[4] SM 6C.
[5] SM 6C.
[6] SM 33B; note 3, p. 42.
[7] SM 6C.
[8] SM 6D.

These items, except the Standing Position, constitute the Introduction to the Worship, and are not considered to be parts of the Worship itself. The Worship proper begins with 6, the Intention:[1]

> 'I perform at its proper time the Prescribed Noon Worship to Allah.'

The statement of Intention must be appropriate to the Worship presented; cf. p. 65 of Translation. The Intention is made in the heart, according to al-Ghazzálí.[2] As soon as it is present in his heart, the worshipper 7, Raises the Hands, until the tips of the fingers are opposite the tops of the ears, with the palms toward the *qibla*.[3] Resting them there a moment,[4] he begins 8, the *Takbír*, and then lowers his hands, placing the left just above the navel, and the right on the left, with the index and next finger along the left forearm, and the others grasping the wrist.[5] This *Takbír* is called the *taḥarrum*,[6] and also the *takbírat al-iḥrám*,[7] because it forbids to the worshipper what was previously allowable,[8] that is, he enters upon a time sacred to Allah, when only certain words and acts are allowable, and all others, at other times permissible, are now forbidden. The *Takbír* consists of the words:

> 'Allah is greater!'[9]

It is said by the follower only audibly enough for himself to hear, and it is said after the *imám* finishes saying it.[10] It is immediately followed by 9, the Opening Supplication, which is so called because it is the supplication with which the Worship is begun after the *Takbír*.[11] It is as follows:

> 'Allah is greater indeed!
> Much praise belongs to Allah!
> O the praise of Allah, early and late!

[1] SM 33B. [3] SM 36. [5] SM 37. [7] Note 3, p. 51.
[2] SM 36. [4] SM 37. [6] SM 103D. [8] SM 100B.
[9] 'Than any other' is understood; SM 141 f.
[10] SM 181. [11] SM 142B.

I have turned my face to Him who divided the heavens and the earth, as a Ḥaníf, and I am not one of the associators ;
My Worship and my devotion, my time of living and of dying belong to Allah, the Lord of the worlds, who has no associate: and that I am commanded, and I am one of the Muslims.'[1]

More may be added to this.[2] In the same position he says 10, the *Ta'awwudh*, the Seeking for Refuge:[3]

'I seek refuge in Allah from the Pelted Saṭan!'[4]

Then he recites 11, the *Fâtiḥa*, beginning with the *Basmala*:[5]

'In the name of Allah, the Merciful and Compassionate One.
Praise belongs to Allah, the Lord of the worlds,
The Merciful Compassionator, Possessor of the Judgement Day!
Thee do we worship and of Thee do we ask aid!
Guide us into the Straight Way,
The Way of those on whom Thou hast bestowed favour,
Not of those against whom there is anger,
Nor of those going astray!'

It is recited audibly when alone, in the Morning, Sunset and Evening Worships.[6] This is followed by the audible utterance of 12, the *Ta'mín*:[7]

'Ámín!'

Then he recites 13, the *Súra*, consisting of three or more verses of the Qur'án.[8] At the Noon Worship the Eighty-fifth *Súra* may be used, as follows:[9]

'By the sky having towers!
By the Day promised!
By a Seeing One, and one seen!' etc.

[1] SM 142-45.
[2] SM 42.
[3] SM 46.
[4] SM 46, 145.
[5] SM 47.
[6] SM 49.
[7] SM 49.
[8] SM 50.
[9] SM 51.

That finishes the Recital. The Bowing comes next. This he does by 14, Raising the Hands,[1] and simultaneously saying 15, the *Takbīr* :[2]

'Allah is greater!

At the same time he performs 16, the Bowing, placing his palms on his knees, which are kept straight, and making his back, neck and head to be in line, level.[3] In this position he recites, three times, or, if alone, seven or ten times, 17, the *Tasbīḥ*, or Praise :[4]

'O the praise of my great Lord!'

Then 18, he Rises to the Standing Position ;[5] 19, Raising his Hands ;[6] and says 20, the *Tasmī'* :[7]

'Allah hearkens to anyone who says His praise!'

He remains quiet a moment in this standing position.[8] The remaining quiet or composed is called the *tuma'inna*. While in this position he adds to the *Tasmī'* :[9]

'O our Lord!
Thine is the praise to the fullness of the heavens and the earth,
And to the fullness of whatever else Thou wilt!'

This may be lengthened still more in the Worships of the *Tasbīḥ*, the Praise,[10] and of the *Kusūf*, Eclipse,[11] and of the Prescribed Morning Worship.[12] Then he lowers himself to the ground, saying 21, the *Takbīr* :[13]

'Allah is greater!'

until he completes 22, the Prostration, by placing his knees, hands and face on the ground.[14] In this position he says, three or more times, 23, the *Tasbīḥ* :[15]

'O the praise of my Lord, the Most High!'

Then he, 24, Raises his Head, saying 25, the *Takbīr* :[16]

[1] SM 53. [5] SM 60. [9] SM 61. [13] SM 67.
[2] SM 53. [6] SM 60. [10] p. 222 f. of the Translation. [14] SM 67.
[3] SM 59. [7] SM 60. [11] pp. 211 ff. of the Translation. [15] SM 69.
[4] SM 59. [8] SM 60. [12] SM 61. [16] SM 70.

'Allah is greater!'

He then sits on his left foot,[1] with his hands on his thighs, and makes 26, Seven Supplications:[2]

> 'O my Lord! Forgive me! Have mercy on me! Apportion provision for me! Guide me! Help me! Preserve me in health and pardon me!'

Then he lowers himself again, saying 27, the *Takbîr*:

> 'Allah is greater!'

and completes 28, a Second Prostration like the first,[3] and repeats three times 29, the *Tasbîḥ*:

> 'O the praise of Allah, the Most High!'

Then he raises his head, saying 30, the *Takbîr*:

> 'Allah is greater!'

until he comes to the Sitting Position, sitting briefly in each *rak'a*, Cycle, not followed by the Witnessing,[4] and then rises,[5] prolonging his *Takbîr* to the middle of his standing.[6]

This is the end of the First *Rak'a*, or cycle or acts and utterances in the Worship, and he follows it with a second, precisely like it, beginning with the Seeking Refuge.

At the end of the Second Prostration of the Second *Rak'a*, instead of rising, the worshipper continues in 31, the Sitting Position,[7] sitting on his left foot, with his hands on his thighs, with the index finger of the right hand extended and the others folded. Then he says 32, the First Witnessing:[8]

> 'The greetings belong to Allah!
> Peace be upon thee, O Prophet,
> And the mercy and blessing of Allah!
> Peace be upon us,
> And upon the righteous creatures of Allah!
> I witness: There is no god but Allah!
> I witness: Muḥammad is the Messenger of Allah!'[9]

[1] Note 2, p. 72.
[2] SM 71, 157.
[3] SM 71.
[4] SM 72.
[5] SM 73.
[6] SM 74.
[7] SM 31B.
[8] SM 75.
[9] SM 75, 158 f.

In the same position he says 33, the Blessing upon the Messenger of Allah and upon his family:[1]

> 'O Allah! Bless the Messenger of Allah!
> And the family of Muhammad!'[2]

Then he changes his position, and 34, sits on his left thigh,[3] and says 35, the Last Witnessing:[4]

> 'I witness: There is no god but Allah!
> I witness: Muḥammad is the Messenger of Allah!'[5]

This is followed by 36, the Blessing upon the Prophet:[6]

> 'O Allah! Bless the Messenger of Allah!'

After this 37, the Traditional Supplication, is said.[7]

The worshipper may make any supplication he will for anything of this life or the next.[8] The Murtaḍa says the best supplication is:[9]

> 'O Allah!
> I seek refuge in Thee from the punishment of the grave!
> I seek refuge in Thee from the testing of the Anti-Christ!
> I seek refuge in Thee from the testing of the time of life and of death!
> O Allah! I seek refuge in Thee from sin and obligation!'

Then the worshipper turns his head to the right for 38, the First Salutation:[10]

> 'Peace be upon you, and the mercy of Allah!'

He then turns to the left for 39, the Second Salutation:[11]

> 'Peace be upon you, and the mercy of Allah!'

At the same time he has 40, the Intention of withdrawing from the Worship with the Salutation.[12]

[1] SM 77.
[2] SM 78B.
[3] SM 83; see note 2, p. 72.
[4] SM 81, 160.
[5] SM 160B.
[6] SM 81.
[7] SM 81.
[8] SM 82B.
[9] SM 161B.
[10] SM 83.
[11] SM 83.
[12] SM 84.

The Parts of the Worship

In the preceding description of the performance of the Worship it has been noticed that the Worship consists of acts and utterances of varying importance and prominence.

There are two preparatory operations. The first is the *wuḍú'*, 'ablution', or *ghusl*, 'bathing'. This includes the cleaning of the body, clothing, and place of worship. Precise directions are given for the kind of water that may be used for the cleansing and for the *tayammum*, the use of *turab*, 'clean earth', when water is not available. The other is the clothing of the person. The minimum is covering the body from the navel to the knees, for men and slave women, but the putting on of the turban is also included. The free woman covers herself as completely as she does when she is to be seen by any other people than those of her own family.

There are three other pre-requisites of the Worship, which really indicate those upon whom the Worship is obligatory. These are *al-islám*, that is, acceptance of the Muslim faith, the attainment of puberty, and the possession of intelligence.[1]

When these preliminaries are completed the Worship may be begun. There are four introductory parts: the *basmala*, i.e. saying, 'In the name of Allah'; the *ta'awwudh*, the Seeking for Refuge; the *ádhán*, the Call; and the *iqáma*, the Institution. These are called the *shurúṭ*,[2] 'stipulations', of the Worship. This term *sharṭ* is also applied to the inner qualities or states of the heart, such as humbleness, magnifying, fear, awe, hope and shamefacedness, which, it is stipulated, with varying degrees of emphasis, are to accompany the outward acts and utterances of the Worship.

These *shurúṭ*, Stipulations, of the Introduction are all performed by the worshipper in the Standing Position, which is the first of the *faráʼiḍ*,[3] Prescribed, parts of the Worship. Another term also used by al-Ghazzálí interchangeably with *faráʼiḍ* for the Prescribed Elements is

[1] Al-Bájúrí, *Commentary on Abú Shujá'*, i. p. 157 f.

[2] Singular, *sharṭ*. [3] Singular, *farḍ*.

arkán,[1] which is the term used most by his commentator. The word *faráʼiḍ* includes both the *arkán* and the *shurúṭ*, but it is the outward acts and utterances which are the *arkán* that determine the validity of the Worship, rather than the *shurúṭ*, the inner Stipulations. In this work al-Ghazzálí includes the Intention among the Prescribed Elements, although in his *Wajíz* he places the Intention among the Stipulations.

The Prescribed Elements are those upon which the validity of the Worship normally depends. Modifications are allowed or required in certain performances of the Worship. For instance, the Standing Position is not an absolute requirement in the *náfl*, Supererogatory, Worship, nor in the *farḍ*, Prescribed, Worship in the case of inability.

In addition to the Prescribed Elements there are *sunan*,[2] Usage, acts and utterances in the Worship. They are of hardly less importance than the Prescribed Elements, for, while the Worship is valid, it is not complete without them. Some of these Usages are indeed so important that if they are omitted through forgetfulness they should have an extra prostration called *al-sujúd al-sahú*, Prostration of Forgetfulness or Oversight, to be performed before the Salutation, to make up for them. The four Usage Parts that should have the Prostration of Forgetfulness are called *abʻáḍ*,[3] Parts.

Both the Prescribed Elements and the Usages include both *afʻál*, Acts, and *adhkár*, Utterances, which are enumerated in the Text. Each one of these acts and utterances, of both the Elements and Usages, is done in certain recommended manners, which are called *ádáb*, Proprieties, and *haʼiát*, Forms. The Standing is done with the head, hands and feet in specified positions. The *takbír* is recited in a specified manner, with special care given to the vowelling of the consonants and with the utterance of the letters done while in certain positions.

The enumeration of the parts of the Worship is not fixed in Islam. The authors differ in the parts they

[1] Singular, *rukn*. [2] Singular, *sunna*. [3] Singular, *baʻḍ*.

consider to be separate elements, and consequently in the enumeration of the parts. Al-Ghazzálí, for instance, considers the Bending down from the Standing Position until the worshipper comes to rest, with his palms on his knees and his back and head level, all as the Bowing, and counts it as one single Element. Others consider the Bending down to be the Bowing, and the *mutma'inna*, the Coming to Rest, in the bowing position to be a separate Element. Al-Ghazzálí considers the Coming to Rest to be a Form of the Bowing, and only to that extent admits it to be a distinct part of the Worship. The situation is the same in the case of the Prostration.

Because of this variance in the differentiation of the parts of the Worship, some authors give the number of the Elements to be eleven, twelve, thirteen, up to eighteen, and the case is similar with the *sunan*, Usages, of the Worship.

Another difficulty of enumeration arises through the fact that some authors count a part of the Worship only once in their list of the Elements or the Usages, although that same part will be repeated two or more times in the Worship. For instance, each *rak'a* of the Worship contains two Prostrations, but in the enumeration of the Elements they are counted as one, and similarly the Rising from the position of Prostration is counted as one Element.

A further development of this enumeration is that the parts are counted as if the Worship consisted of a single *rak'a*, Cycle, that is, as if it were a *witr*, Odd, Worship of only one *rak'a*, although the five Prescribed performances of the Worship have two, three or four *rak'as*, with a consequently varying number of times of occurrence of each Element and with also a varying total number of Parts.

In the following table the Worship is analyzed into the component parts, although not all the *ha'iát*, Forms, that al-Ghazzálí mentions in connection with each Element or Usage are given.

ANALYTICAL TABLE OF THE *ARKÂN*, ELEMENTS, *SUNAN*, USAGES, AND *HAI'ÂT*, FORMS OF THE WORSHIP

ARKÂN				SUNAN			
af'âl, Acts	*hai'ât*	*adhkâr*, Utterances	*hai'ât*	*af'âl*	*hai'ât*	*adhkâr*	*hai'ât*
1 Standing,	Facing *qibla* ; Feet paired ; Knees straight ; Head lowered.						
						2 *Basmala*. 3 Seeking Refuge. 4 Call. 5 Institution.	
		6 Intention.					
				7 Raising hands,	Palms out ; Lowers hands ; Puts right on left ; Two fingers extended ; Others grasp wrist.		
		8 *Takbîr*,	Begins *alif* ; Ends *râ'*.				
						9 Opening Supplication. 10 Seeking Refuge.	
		11 Recites *al-Fâtiḥa*,	Perfects the letters.				
						12 Says *âmîn*,	Audibly ; Prolongs it ; Separates it from *al-Fâtiḥa*
						13 Recites the *Sûra*,	Three verses, Long in morning ; Short in evening.

	14 Raises hands.	
		15 *Takbîr*.
16 Bowing, Head and back level ; Hands on knees.		
		17 *Tasbîḥ*, Three, seven or ten times.
18 Straightening, Stands briefly ; Stands long in morning.		
	19 Raises hands.	
		20 *Tasmî‘*.
		21 *Takbîr*.
22 Prostration, Knees on ground ; Hands ,, Forehead on ground ; Hands opposite shoulders.		
		23 *Tasbîḥ*.
24 Straightening, To sitting position ; As he raises head, Sits on left foot ; Right foot is straight ; Hands on thighs ; Fingers extended.		
		25 Says *Takbîr*.
		26 Seven Supplications.
		27 *Takbîr*.
28 Second Prostration, Like 22.		
		29 *Tasbîḥ*, Like 23.
		30 *Takbîr*, Like 25.
Straightening (a component part of 1b or 31), Sitting briefly at close of each *rak‘a* not followed by Witnessing.		

Arkān				Sunan			
af'āl, Acts	*nai'āt*	*adhkār*, Utterances	*hai'āt*	*af'āl*	*hai'āt*	*adhkār*	*hai'āt*
1b Straightening,	Standing, for Second *Rak'a*, with						
				7b Raising hands, etc.			Or, instead of
1b,				31 Sitting for First Witnessing,	Sits on left foot ; Folds right fingers ; Extends index finger.		
						32 First Witnessing. 33 Greeting and Blessing on Prophet.	
34 Sitting	for Last Witnessing, Left foot on ground.						
		35 Last Witnessing. 36 Blessing on Prophet,					
						37 Supplication.	
		38 First Salutation,	Turns to right ; Cheek seen from behind ; Salutes angels and Muslims.			39 Second Salutation,	Turns to left.
						40 States Intention to stop.	

The Kinds of the Worship

Passing from the consideration of the content of the Worship to the description of the kinds of the Worship, it is found that there are two divisions, the *faráʼiḍ*, Prescribed, and *nawáfil*,[1] Additional, Supererogatory. It is noticed that the same word *farḍ* is used in connection with both the parts of a single performance of a Worship and with the Worship as a whole. Similarly, the word *sunna*, Usage, is applied to some of the acts and utterances of the Worship, and to one of the kinds of the *náfl*, Supererogatory, Worship. The word *farḍ* is in common use among Muslim authors to mean the same performances that al-Ghazzálí includes under that name. These are the five daily performances, consisting of the morning, noon, mid-afternoon, sunset and evening Worships. These are prescribed, required or obligatory. If they are omitted for any reason they need to be made up. If they are abandoned intentionally the penalty is death, or, among Ḥanafites, imprisonment until compliance.

The number of the *rakʻas*, Cycles, in the five daily performances of the Worship is fixed. The Morning Worship has two, Sunset has three, Noon, Mid-afternoon and Evening have four each. On Friday the Congregational Worship takes the places of the Noon Worship, but if it is missed, the Noon Worship must be performed. The three performances of Noon, Afternoon and Evening may have two *rakʻas* each, instead of four, during a journey.

Al-Ghazzálí calls all the performances of the Worship that are not Prescribed *nawáfil*, Supererogatory, meaning 'extra, additional'. Other authors use other classifications, using the words *taṭawwuʻ*, 'voluntary', *wájib*, 'behoving', *muʼakkada*, 'confirmed', *mustaḥabb*, 'liked', *manḍúb*, 'recommended', *marghúb fíhi*, 'desired', *sunna*, 'usage', *ḥasan*, 'beautiful', *adab*, 'proper', *fáḍila*, 'excellent', *haʼia*, 'form', and *náfl*, 'additional'. Al-Ghazzálí has simply chosen certain of these words to label his classifications of the Worship, and states that there is no objection to the use of a different nomenclature on the part of others.

[1] Singular, *náfila*.

The important thing is to understand his use of the terms.

The *náfl*, Supererogatory, performances of the Worship then include all those that are not Prescribed. The religious law pronounces the doing of all these performances to be preferable to the omitting of them, and says that they secure reward, although the omitting of them is allowable, and not punished.

There are two concurrent classifications of them. The first classification relates to their excellence, and the second to the time of their occurrence.

Classified according to their excellence, the Supererogatory Worships are of three kinds, depending respectively upon the more or less consistent and constant performance of them by Muḥammad, and upon the general excellence of performing Worship even when there is no definite example or special command of the Prophet to be followed.

The first of these classes is the *sunna*, Usage or Customary, performances of the Worship. They are those that the Prophet usually performed and did not omit except for some cause. His consistent performance of them is known through traditions. Traditions of course vary in reliability, and that fact has bearing upon the question of the Prophet's continual performance of any specified Worship. For that reason the term *mu'akkada*, Strengthened, Confirmed, is also used by al-Ghazzálí and others for these *sunna* performances, sometimes instead of, and sometimes in addition to, the term *sunna*. As in the case of the word *farḍ*, the term *sunna* is thus used to designate certain parts of each individual Worship and also a certain class of whole performances of the Worship.

The second class of the *náfl* Worship is the *mustaḥabb*, Liked. These are those that the Prophet performed sometimes and omitted sometimes, and which therefore it would be wrong to abandon entirely. To this class belong chiefly, although not entirely, the performance of the Worship by the individual alone, while the congregational performances are for the most part of the *mu'akkada*, Confirmed, class.

The third class is the *taṭawwu'*, Voluntary, Worship. Concerning these there is no specific command or example of the Prophet except in traditions that are of weak authority. Their basis is rather the general principle that Worship is a good thing, and therefore it is good to do as much of it as possible, and, further, one may show true zeal by performing voluntary Worship that he is not required or even definitely recommended to do.

The second classification is according to the time and the occasion of the performances of the *náfl* Worship. These are in four sub-divisions: the Daily, Weekly, Yearly and Occasional Performances, varying, as has been said, in their authority and excellence.

The first sub-division is the Daily performances. These, considered as to their time, are eight in number. Five of them consist of Worships of a varying number of *rak'as*, Cycles, performed before or after, or both before and after, the regular Prescribed Worship. Al-Ghazzálí uses the term *rátiba*, Fixed, Established, in naming them, in connection with each of the five Prescribed performances. The object of an extra Worship immediately before or after the required Worship is, in the first case, to prepare one by preliminary practice to be in the right state of mind and body for the more important Worship to come; and in the second case, to make up, by the additional performance, for any possible defect or deficiency in the preceding Prescribed Worship.

The number of *rak'as* to be performed in these *rátiba* Worships is not certain, nor is it certain in the case of some of them, as for instance, the Sunset *rátiba*, whether the particular Worship is to be performed before or after the Sunset Prescribed Worship. The uncertainly, in both instances, is, of course, due to conflicting traditions mentioning different numbers of *rak'as* and different times of performance for the same Worship.

In the case of the Noon *rátiba* six *rak'as* are recommended, four of them to be performed in a Worship before, and two in another Worship after, the Prescribed performance. Furthermore, in this case, because there is a separate tradition mentioning two *rak'as* to be performed before the Prescribed Worship, it is said that two of the four *rak'as* in the *rátiba* Worship, before the *farḍ*, Prescribed, Noon Worship, are of the *mu'akkada*, Confirmed, class, while the other two *rak'as* of the same performance remain simply *mustaḥabb*, Liked.

In addition to these five *rátiba*, Fixed, performances, connected with the five Prescribed performances, there are three other daily *náfl* Worships. These are the *witr*, Odd, Worship, the *ḍuḥá*, Forenoon, Worship, and the *iḥyá'*, Enlivening, Worship.

The *witr*, Odd, Worship is a Worship of one, three, five or other odd number of *rak'as*, up to thirteen, or even seventeen. It may be performed any time after the Sunset Worship up to the time for the Morning Worship. It is preferably performed in connection with, or after, the *táhajjud*, Night, Worship, because there is a tradition that the *witr* is the last Worship of the night. Indeed, al-Ghazzálí says that it is this night Worship, that is, Worship performed in the night after one has been asleep.

The *ḍuḥá* Worship is a Confirmed Worship of four, six or eight *rak'as*, and, according to al-Bájúrí, of from two to twelve *rak'as*, performed in the early, mid or late forenoon, according to different understandings of the word.

The third is the *iḥyá'*, Enlivening, the cultivation or bringing into use, of the time between the two evening performances of the Worship, i.e. between the Sunset and the Evening Worships. Six is the number of *rak'as* al-Ghazzálí quotes for it, and he classes it as Confirmed in excellence.

The second class after the Daily *náfl* Worship is the Weekly *náfl* Worship, i.e. Worship that is performed once each week. It is in two sub-divisions, the first containing Worship to be done in the day-time, and the second Worship to be done at night.

Al-Ghazzálí's treatment of this class is simply to repeat a tradition mentioning Worship on each day and night of the week. The traditions usually state the number of *rak'as* to be performed, the time they are to be done, and the particular reward attached to the Worship.

The third or Yearly class of *náfl* Worship includes four different performances, although the number of occasions exceeds that amount. The four are the two Feasts of *al-fitr*, the Breaking of the Fast of Ramaḍán, on the first day of Shawwál, the tenth month of the Muslim year, and of *al-aḍḥá*, the Sacrifice on the 10th of the month of Dhú al-Ḥijja, the last of the Muslim year, at the conclusion of the Pilgrimage Ceremonies; the *taráwíḥ*, Rest-giving, Worship of Ramaḍán; the Worship of Rajab, and the Worship of Sha'bán.

The Feast Worships are both of the Confirmed class in degree of excellence and have two *rak'as*, and are similarly performed, except as to time, for the first is delayed towards noon to allow for the distribution of alms, and the second is hastened so that the sacrifice may be slaughtered early. Both these performances are additional to the Daily Prescribed Worship and they differ from the usual Worship in a number of particulars. For instance, except at Mecca, it is more excellent to perform this Worship outside the city, although on rainy days the usual congregational mosque is the preferred place. Further, the Worship of the Feasts differs from the regular Worships in that the usual *ádhán*, Call, and *iqáma*, Institution, are not given. Al-Ghazzálí prefers the phrase 'The Worship is gathering!' as the Feast Call to Worship, while other authors add other phrases.

The *taraḥwíḥ*, Rest-giving, Worship is so called because a brief rest is taken after every four *rak'as* which constitute a *tarwíḥa*. Each *tarwíḥa* consists of two complete Worships of two *rak'as* each, and five *tarwíḥas* constitute the complete *taráwíḥ* Worship. It is a Confirmed Worship, performed every night of Ramaḍán after the Evening Prescribed Worship. It is recommended to perform a complete recital of the Qur'án by reciting ten or more verses in each of the 580 or 600 *taráwíḥ rak'as* performed in the twenty-nine or thirty days of that month.

Al-Ghazzálí adds here a note to the effect that in the last half of the month it is liked that *witr*, Odd, Worship, performed after the *taráwíḥ* Worship, should include the *qunút*, Supplication, a special petition recited in the Standing Position.

The Worship of Rajab occurs on the first Thursday of that month, the seventh of the Muslim year. It is a

Worship of twelve *rak'as*, with special invocations. A fast is to be observed the whole day. The reward specified is forgiveness for all sins and the right of intercession for 700 relatives, for which reason it is also called *ṣalát al-raghá'ib*, 'Worship for which a large recompense is desired'.[1] The Worship is of the *mustaḥabb* class, and al-Ghazzálí only adds it because the people of Jerusalem seemed to favour it. His commentator gives what purports to be an account of its origin, showing that it is a late addition to the performances of the Worship, and one that met much opposition.[2]

The Worship of Sha'bán occurs on the eve of the 15th of that month, the eighth of the Muslim year. It consists of fifty separate Worships of two *rak'as* each, or, as it is usually expressed, a hundred *rak'as* with fifty Salutations. It is of the *mustaḥabb* class, and sometimes was performed as a Congregational Worship. Because of the reward attached to its recital, consisting of the fulfilling of seventy needs with each of seventy glances of Allah at the Worshipper, the Worship is also called *ṣalát al-khair*, the Good Worship.

In his fourth class of the *náfl*, Supererogatory, Worship, al-Ghazzálí enumerates nine particulars, although in the rest of the *Iḥyá'* he mentions others belonging to this class. They are called Occasional Worships, because they are connected, not with specified times, but with particular occasions. Those that he enumerates are as follows:

The Worship of *al-kusúf*, or Eclipse of the Sun. This is a Congregational Worship of two *rak'as*, differing from the usual *rak'as*, in that each contains two *ruku's*, Bowings, instead of one, as a special Sháfi'ite feature. The Worship begins with the beginning of the eclipse and ends with its conclusion, and the first four long *súras* are recommended to be recited.

The Worship of *al-khusúf*, or Eclipse of the Moon. This, among Sháfi'ites, is similar to the former, except that the recital is to be done audibly instead of inaudibly.

[1] Lane, *Lexicon*, p. 1111C. [2] SM iii. p. 422 f.

Both *kusúf* and *khusúf* are used of each luminary, although the more approved usage, and that of the astronomers, is that used by al-Ghazzálí here.[1]

These Worships are among those that may be performed in the Disliked times, although they are what al-Ghazzálí calls less *mu'akkada* than the Feast Worships. Al-Bájúrí calls them *masnún.*

The second is the Worship of the Request for Rain. It is a Congregational Worship, like that of the Feast, in that it is held outside the city, and has a similar Call to Worship, without the Institution formula. But it is unlike the Feast Worships in that poor clothes are to be worn, old people, children, women, and cattle are taken along. Jews and Christians subject to Muslim rule may also attend, according to al-Ghazzálí, although al-Sháfi'í considers that to be Disliked. The Worship is to be observed after a three-day fast has been proclaimed. Two *rak'as* are performed similar to those of the Feast Worship, except that, according to two texts, there are no *takbírs*, while the commentator emends and says that there is no difference. The underlying traditions differ. Another difference is that in this Worship the outer cloaks are to be worn up-side down, the addresses have requests for forgiveness, in place of the *takbírs*, and in the second address the *imám* turns his back on the people.[2] In turning the cloaks up-side down, the right side is to be on the left, and the cloak is not to be inside out, although al-Ghazzálí mentions that in the *Wajíz*,[3] forgetting that the right side cannot then be on the left.

The Funeral Worship, more properly, the Worship connected with the death of a person, differs from all the other performances of Worship in that it does not contain any *rak'a.* It is for that reason the *ṣalát al-janáza*, or *jináza*, is used in grammars to illustrate the *iḍáfat al-náqiṣa*, 'the incomplete connection', because its subject-matter is not complete.[4] The word *janáza* is applied to both the

[1] SM iii. p. 427CD; Lane, *Lexicon*, p. 738B.

[2] See also article by Bel in the *Ency. of Islam*, ii. p. 562 f.; and *Dict. of Tech. Terms*, p. 726.

[3] i. p. 44. [4] SM iii. p. 427C.

dead person and the bier on which he is placed. The Worship is performed for all Muslims, except the *shahíd*, 'martyr', killed in the course of battle with unbelievers. When Muslims and unbelievers are indistinguishable among the dead in battle all are to be buried, and the Muslims are to be singled out in the Worship.

The Funeral Worship is of the *farḍ kifáya* class, i.e. the requirement for its performance is satisfied when one or more of the Muslims take it upon themselves to fulfil it as a duty.[1] It has, according to al-Ghazzálí, seven essential Elements, consisting of (1) statement of Intention; (2) the Standing Posture; (3) four *takbírs*, or possibly five. After the first comes (4) the *Fátiha*; (5) the Blessing upon the Prophet after the second *takbír*; (6) the Supplication for the dead after the third *takbír*,[2] and (7) the Salutation.[3]

Besides this Worship there is a Greeting bestowed upon the dead people of the cemetery when the company arrives there, and another Supplication offered when the body is lowered into the grave

The fourth is the Worship of the Greeting of the Mosque. It is a Confirmed Usage and is performed upon entering the mosque even if that happens to be when the *imám* is lecturing, although it should not then be a separate, distinct Worship of its own, but may be Prescribed or Substitution Worship due from him. Its object is to occupy with Worship the beginning of the time one enters the mosque. It may, therefore, be performed in the five Disliked times for Worship.[4]

The fifth is the Worship after the Ablution. It consists of two *rak'as* and is of the *mustaḥabb*, Liked, class. Al-Ghazzálí states that the Intention is to be omitted from this Worship while al-Nawawí says that it may be made.[5]

The sixth is the Worship of two *rak'as* to be performed upon Entering or Leaving the House. Under this head come all the performances of Worship that are

[1] *Wajíz*, i. p. 47A.
[2] Al-Ghazzálí gives in his text an example of the Supplication.
[3] SM iii. p. 450. [4] SM p. 459. [5] SM p. 463D.

recommended to be performed upon the beginning of each occurrence of importance, such as the wearing of the *iḥrám* when nearing Mecca for the Pilgrimage, and the beginning of the *ṭawáf*, or Encircling of the Ka'ba while on Pilgrimage, and upon starting and returning from a journey. The invocation of 'In the name of Allah', uttered upon eating and drinking, comes under this sub-division, for it may be extended to become a full performance of the Worship. Likewise the marriage contract, and the giving of advice, may be prefaced with the *basmala*, and Invocations of Praise and Blessing upon the Prophet. The most important events, such as journeys, are recommended to have two full *rak'as*.

Under this sub-division may be mentioned also the modifications of the *náfl*, Supererogatory, Worship allowed to one on a long journey, for these may be performed walking and riding upon an animal or ship. The traveller faces the *qibla* only when stating the Intention, and he nods his head for the Bowing and the Prostration. Al-Murtaḍá says that unless it is easy even the facing of the *qibla* is not obligatory.[1]

The seventh is the Worship of the Request for Prospering. It is a Worship of two *rak'as*. When it is finished the matter of anxiety is named and then the Supplication, which is the request for the blessing, prospering and favour of Allah, is presented with uplifted hands in the traditional words as given in the Text. When this has been done the man goes away to that for which his bosom becomes dilated, i.e. to that which is made to seem acceptable to him.[2] The Request for Prospering is to be offered for any matter of concern. Saiyid Murtaḍá records that he made the request for prospering in the matter of giving his commentary on the *Iḥyá'* the name of the 'Gift of the God-fearing Masters'.[3] Corruptions of this Worship and Supplication, consisting of the casting of lots and chance opening of the Qur'án and other books and magic, are strongly condemned in Sunni Islam.[4]

[1] SM vi. p. 435 f. [2] SM p. 469A ; cf. Qur'án, xcv. 8.
[3] SM i. p. 3, l. 11.
[4] See *Ency. of Islam*, ii. p. 561 f.; Goldziher.

The eighth is the Worship of Need. It is a Worship of twelve *rak'as* with specified Recitals and is followed by the Supplication of Need, offered in the attitude of Prostation. The need may be any pressing necessity, religious or worldly. The text of the request includes the phrase 'I ask Thee by Thy greatest Name', which has found so large a place in magic in Islam. It is recommended that this Supplication should not be taught to the foolish, lest they encourage one another in antinomianism.

The ninth is the Worship of Praise. This is a special Worship unconnected with any set time or circumstance. It has four *rak'as* with specified Recitals in them, and specified Invocations during each of the four attitudes in each *rak'a*, so that the same Invocation is repeated 300 times during the Worship.

This is the last of the performances of the Worship mentioned by al-Ghazzálí in the Book of the Mysteries of the Worship. In addition to them three modifications of the Prescribed Worship are recommended, and three special Prostrations are prescribed or recommended.

The first of the modifications of the Prescribed Worship is that allowed to the traveller, for he may perform two instead of four *rak'as* in the Noon, Afternoon and Evening Worships, performing the Morning and Sunset Worships as usual.

The second modification is that the uniting of the Noon with the Afternoon, and the Sunset with the Evening Worship is allowable, for the traveller, and for the one accustomed to worship with the congregation, when it is raining. The Noon Worship would be performed before the Afternoon, and separated from it only by the length of time it takes for the *iqáma*, Institution, of the Worship.

The third is the Worship of Fear, that is, of the one who is in fear. The Qur'ánic basis is iv. 103. It is, according to al-Bájúrí,[1] of sixteen varieties, of which al-Ghazzálí mentions four in his *Wajíz*,[2] and in his *Iḥyá'*.

The variations are according to the stress of danger and the number and position of the enemy. In the circum-

[1] Op. cit., i. p. 288. [2] i. p. 40 f.

stance of utmost fear, if it is impossible to leave the battle when the time for the Prescribed Worship comes, the Worship may be performed on foot or riding, with or without facing the *qibla*, with nodding of the head in the place of the Bowing and the Prostration, with the guarding against crying out and giving unnecessary blows.

This Worship may also be performed by one fleeing from fire, drowning and ferocious beast, just as it is permissible to wear silk, or the skin of a dog or pig, in case of sudden fear.[1]

The special Prostrations, which may be considered as partial Worships, are the *sajdat* or *sujúd al-sahú*, the Prostration of Forgetfulness, and the *sajdat al-tiláwa*, Prostration of the Recital of the Qur'án, and the *sajdat al-shukr*, the Prostration of Thanksgiving.

The Prostration of Recital is required to be performed when, in the course of the reading, i.e. reciting of the Qur'án, the Muslim reaches one of the fourteen Verses of Prostration. These verses are given in a note to the Text.[2] This Prostration has the same preliminary requirements as the usual Worship. The least Prostration is simply placing the forehead on the ground, while the most complete includes the Standing Posture and a *takbír* with the Raising of the hands; then a *takbír* while going down for the Prostration, and then a Supplication appropriate to the portion just read, followed by a *takbír* on rising, and then the Salutation.[3] Saiyid Murtaḍá says *al-tálí*, 'the reciter', is a *muṣallí*, 'worshipper', that is a *munájí*, 'one who is communing' with Allah.[4]

In the *Wajíz* al-Ghazzálí states that this Prostration is incumbent upon both the *imám* who is reciting and the hearer of the verse.[5]

The Prostration of Forgetfulness or Oversight is a *sunna*, Usage, that may or may not be performed whenever any of the four *ab'áḍ*, Parts, of the *sunna*, Usage, items of the Worship are unintentionally omitted. These are the First Witnessing, the *qunút*, the Blessing upon the

[1] *Al-Wajíz*, i. p. 42. [2] Note 1, p. 53. [3] SM iv. pp. 482, 488.
[4] *Ibid.*, p. 485D. [5] i. p. 32.

Messenger of Allah in the First Witnessing and the Blessing on his family in the Last Witnessing. It is performed at any of six places before the Salutation.

Any of the other *sunan*, Usages, of the Worship, according to al-Ghazzálí, may be made up by a Prostration,[1] although al-Bájúrí, calling these other *sunan*, Usages, by the name of *hai'át*, Forms, says they are not.[2]

If the *arkán*, Prescribed Elements, of the Worship are unintentionally omitted they are repeated. This is called *tadáruk*, 'supplying' what was omitted through inadvertence.[3]

Any *rukn*, Element, if omitted, is to be performed before engaging in the next Element; otherwise, either the Worship is invalid, or he supplies the omission and performs the rest of the Worship over again, together with an Oversight Prostration.[4]

The Prostration of Thanksgiving is a *sunna*, Usage, performed on the occasion of the receipt of some unusual favour, or the warding off of some misfortune. It is liked to be performed also before an evil person out of thankfulness for the warding off of disobedience and as a warning to him.[5] The Second Book of the Fourth Quarter of the *Iḥyá'*[6] deals with the subjects of Patience and Thanksgiving.

Other Expressions of the Devotional Life

Except for the Prostrations of the Recital of the Qur'án and of Thanksgiving, all the preceding forms of devotion consisted of the particular ceremony called the Worship, comprising special elements and known utterances, accompanied by certain stipulations, restricted within specified times,[7] or else of modifications of that ceremony. The two exceptions above mentioned consist in parts of that ceremony and are included by al-Ghazzálí

[1] *Al-Wajíz*, i. p. 30. [2] Op. cit., i. p. 200.
[3] *Al-Wajíz*, i. p. 30; Lane, *Lexicon*, p. 874D.
[4] Al-Bájúrí, op. cit., i. p. 224 f.
[5] *Al-Wajíz*, i. p. 32. [6] SM ix. pp. 46 ff.
[7] Jurjání, *Ta'rífát*, p. 139.

in his treatment of the Worship in his book on Fiqh, called *al-Wajíz*.

Of the recommended and voluntary methods of *'ibáda*, 'religious service', paid by the tongue, to use al-Ghazzálí's phrase,[1] the first in importance is *al-tiláwa*, the Recital of the Qur'án. It is the subject of Book viii of the First Quarter of the *Iḥyá'*.[2]

He presents first the excellence of the Qur'án and the recital of it. Then he describes the proper method of its outward recital, which includes ten items, some of which are as follows: (1) The reader should be ceremonially clean and should stand or sit sedately, although the last two points are not absolutely required. (2) The amount recited may vary. Some have finished the Qur'án twice in a day and night, and others once a month. (3) The Qur'án is usually divided into seven sections, although divisions into five, ten, thirty and other numbers of parts, are mentioned or allowed. (4) The recital should be prefaced by the Seeking Refuge formula. (5) The rites of the Verses of Prostration should be observed. (6) The recital should be at least loud enough for the reciter himself to hear.

There are ten inward acts of the heart and understanding that accompany the recital, such as causing the heart to be present, and the understanding to appreciate what is read, and for the reciter to attend as if he were hearing speech from Allah and not from himself.

Next in importance to the Recital of the Qur'án, according to al-Ghazzálí, is the *dhikr*, Invocation. He devotes Book ix of the First Quarter of the *Iḥyá'* to the consideration of *al-adhkár* and *al-da'awát*, Invocations and Supplications.[3] He presents first the evidence of the excellence of the Invocations and the gathering for reciting them from the Qur'án, Traditions and Records. Then he shows the excellence of the various invocations, such as *al-tahlíl*, 'There is no god but Allah', with several additional phrases; *al-tasbíḥ*, 'O the Praise of Allah';[4]

[1] SM v. p. 3D. [2] SM iv. p. 460 to end. [3] SM v. pp. 1-117.

[4] For the meaning assigned in this term, see Lane, *Lexicon*, p. 1289; Baiḍ., i. p. 49, 1.2.

al-taḥmíd, 'The praise or thanksgiving belongs to Allah'. The names of Allah are also used. The number of repetitions of these and other phrases and the amount of reward the repetitions bring are both recorded.

The reason for the superiority of the *dhikr* over the forms of religious service involving hardship can be revealed only by the 'unveiled knowledge', he says, but this much may be mentioned, that the beneficial effect is the constant remembrance of Allah, along with the presence of the heart. For the connection of the *dhikr* with the darwish fraternities, and bibliography, see article by Macdonald in the *Ency. of Islam*, i, p. 958.

The *du'á'*, Supplication, is another of the methods of communion with Allah. It includes the asking for forgiveness and the blessing upon the Prophet as well as requests for needs. Al-Ghazzálí mentions ten proprieties that are to be observed in offering supplications, among which are the observance of the Day of 'Arafa in the Pilgrimage ceremonies, the month of Ramaḍán and Friday of every week; the offering of Supplications after the Prescribed Worship, when fasting, when facing the *qibla*, repeating the request at three times, meanwhile being hopeful of an affirmative reply and repentant towards Allah.

Al-Ghazzálí gives three chapters of Traditional Supplications—the prayers of the Muslim saints—for all times and occasions. Then he discusses the value of Supplications in view of the immutability of predestination. His answer is that the Supplication for the Warding Off of Evil and the Bringing of Mercy is among the things predestined. He who decreed the good decreed it by a cause, and He who decreed the evil decreed its being warded off by a cause. Further, supplication is the marrow of religious service, and it requires the presence of the heart with Allah.[1]

The Tenth Book of the First Quarter of the *Iḥyá'* is the *Kitáb Tartíb al-Awrád*.[2] Al-Ghazzálí uses the word *wird* as a 'portion' of the day and night. He divides the day into seven *wirds*: one between dawn and sunrise; two

[1] See also *Ency. of Islam*, i. p. 1077. [2] Singular, *wird*.

each between sunrise and noon, noon and *'aṣr*, 'mid-afternoon', *'aṣr*, and sunset. The night has, including the period of sleep, five *wirds*, two before and two after the sleep *wird*. These times are to be occupied by the four devotional exercises: Invocation, Supplication, Recital of the Qur'án and Meditation. The last he discusses in Book ix of the Fourth Quarter of the *Iḥyá'*. His object in the *Book of Wirds*, Portions, is simply to set forth the manner of the previously mentioned Supplications and the method of spending the day and night in pious occupation. *Wird* then means the portion of time used in devotional recitation, or the devotional recitations themselves, including portions of the Qur'án, devotional phrases, and, nowadays, also commentaries on the Qur'án.

A word of similar meaning to *wird* is *ḥizb*.[1] It is that recital of the Qur'án or performance of the Worship which a man imposes on himself. So, in the *Táj al-'Arús*, i. p. 208. This is a development of the original meaning of the word, which is 'party', 'division'. It was early applied to divisions of the Qur'án. The darwish fraternities applied the term to their special services. Then special supplications, prepared by individuals, were used as *ḥizbs*, so that now *ahzáb* for the days of the week are in common use.[2]

The *hirz*, 'protection', is a petition for protection and refuge, and is simply a *du'á'*, 'supplication', of a special character. Similarly the *istighátha*, 'cry for help', is a petition for aid and succour. The term *waẓá'if*, 'offices', 'duties', is also used to cover the directions and recitals for spending set times at Worship.

There are still other forms of expression of devotion that need only brief mention. These are the Poems of Petition, which are a kind of hymns of Allah's praise, and also the declarations of the praise of Allah, and descriptions of His qualities, usually in *saj'*, 'rhymed prose', at the beginnings of books.

Additional to these methods of expressing devotion, it is necessary to note several other general customs. The

[1] Plural, *aḥzáb*.

[2] See the article by Macdonald, *Ency. of Islam*, ii. p. 322 f.

first is the *mawlid*, 'birthday anniversary'. There is a large and increasing *mawlid* literature of petitions and poems of praise for the celebration of the birthday anniversaries of Muhammad and noted saints of Islam. Lane gives a full account of Egyptian celebrations in his *Modern Egyptians.*[1]

The second is the *i'tikáf*, 'retreat' within a mosque, for a day, preferably Friday, or longer, in order to spend the time between the Prescribed Worships in quiet performances of the *náfl* Worship and the four other devotional exercises.[2] The last third of Ramaḍán is a favourite time for the Retreat.

Another is the *ziyára*, 'visit', to some special place, usually the tomb of a saint, for the offering of the Worship, supplications and invocations, in the name of the saint.

This concludes the survey of the devotional exercises of the Muslims and indicates the paramount importance of the ceremony of the Worship in all private and public religious service.

[1] By index under 'moolid'.
[2] See Juynboll, *Ency. of Islam*, ii. p. 564.

PART II

TRANSLATION

[1]INTRODUCTION[2]

In the name of Allah, the Merciful and Compassionate One[3]

PRAISE belongs to Allah, who overwhelms His creatures with His favours, and fills their hearts with

[1] Abú Ḥámid Muḥammad bin Muḥammad bin Muḥammad al-Ghazzálí (A.H. 450-505 ; A.D. 1058-1111). For his biography, see D. B. Macdonald, *Life of al-Ghazzálí*, in the *Journal of the American Oriental Society* for 1899, vol. xx. pp. 71-132, and his article in the *Encyclopedia of Islam*, ii. pp. 146 ff. To the references in the latter should now be added, *A Moslem Seeker after God*, by S. M. Zwemer, New York, 1920, and *Al-Ghazálí*, by W. R. W. Gardner, in *The Islam Series* of the Christian Literature Society for India, Madras, 1919.

For the spelling of the *nisba*, al-Ghazzálí, with one or two z's, see Macdonald's *Note*, added to his article on 'Emotional Religion in Islam', *Journal of the Royal Asiatic Society*, 1902, pp. 18-22, and, Zwemer, *Moslem Seekers after God*, p. 64.

The *Kitáb Asrár al-Ṣalá* is the fourth of the ten books of the *'ibádát*, 'religious services', which form the First Quarter of the forty books of the *Iḥyá' 'Ulúm al-Dín*, 'The Vitalizing of the Religious Sciences'. It forms Part Three of Saiyid Murtaḍá's ten-volume Commentary, and was completed by him in A.H. 1197.

[2] The translation is made from the text in the *Itḥáf al-Sáda al-Muttaqín*, 'The Precious Gift of the God-fearing Masters', the Commentáry on the *Iḥyá'* by the Saiyid Murtaḍá (Brockelmann, i. p. 422 ; ii. 287 f.). References are also made to the text on the margin, and to the text of the *Iḥyá'* published by the *Dár al-Kutub al-'Arabíya al-Kubrá* Press, Cairo, 1334. The Commentary is referred to hereafter as SM.

Abú al-Faiḍ al-Saiyid Muḥammad bin Muḥammad bin 'Abdal-Razzáq al-Murtaḍá al-Ḥusainí al-Zabídí (A.H. 1145-1205 ; A.D. 1732-91). Al-Jabártí gives the record of his early travels, his studies and teachers, his moving to Cairo and trips in Egypt, his welcome and position among the learned there, his preparation of the Commentary on the *Qámús al-Muḥíṭ*, of Fairúzabádí, which he called the *Táj al-'Arús*, and for a copy of which he received a hundred thousand dirhams, his knowledge of Arabic, Turkish, Persian and some Georgian, his increasing reputation and wealth, his other works besides the *Táj* and the Commentary on the *Iḥyá'* and his death in 1205, as well as the disgraceful scramble for his possessions afterwards (*'Ajá'ib al-Áthár fí al-Tarájim w'al-Akhbár*, by 'Abdalraḥmán bin al-Shaikh Ḥasan

the lights and duties of religion, whose descent[1] from the throne of majesty to the nearest heaven[2] is, of the degrees of mercy, one of His kindnesses.[3] He differs from kings, for all His unique majesty and grandeur, in inspiring His creation to ask and supplicate, for He
(1) says:[4] 'Is there any who supplicates? I will answer him!' and, 'Is there any who asks forgiveness? I will forgive him!' He differs from sultans in opening the door and lifting the veil, and permitting His creatures confidential communion, by the performances of Worship, however their circumstances may change,

al-Jabártí (d. 1236), vol. ii. pp. 196-210; see also, Lane, *Lexicon*, Preface, xviii ff.).

³ In the Qur'án, Raḥmán is a proper name for God, but for Islam it has become an epithet noun (cf. Article by Macdonald, *Emotional Religion*, etc., p. 198, note 2). Al-Ghazzálí is not concerned with the distinctions in the epithets in his remarks on the *basmala* on p. 113 of this book (SM p. 149). Modern commentators, e.g. Muḥammad 'Abduh, *Tafsír al-Qur'án al-Ḥakím* (Cairo, 1330, vol. i. p. 29), reject the position of al-Jalálain that Raḥmán and Raḥím have one meaning and that the second merely corroborates the first. *Raḥmán* is said to denote that active quality from which the evidences of mercy come, while *raḥím* denotes the permanent inherent quality which originates that mercy.

¹ The descent of Allah from the highest heaven to that nearest earth takes place in the last third of the night. The tradition is part of the one immediately following. It is an encouragement to the *taḥajjud*, Night Worship, one of the most excellent of the acts of religious service. The descent, the SM says (p. 3D), is not to be understood literally.

² On the Arabian system of Cosmography, see note 2 to the Introduction to Lane's *Arabian Nights*. The allusion here is probably to Qur'án lxv. 12. The Qur'án references throughout are to Flügel's text.

³ The allusion may be to the following tradition of Abú Huraira's, wherein the same word is used for 'kindness': 'Allah has one hundred mercies; of them He has sent down one among mankind and jinn, cattle and serpents, in which and by which they are kind to one another and by which the wild beast is kind to its offspring. He reserved ninety-nine mercies by which He will be merciful to His creatures on Resurrection Day.' *Mishkát al-Maṣábíḥ*, Cairo, 1309 (vol. iii. bk. x. chap. iv. division 1).

⁴ The traditions are numbered to facilitate repeated references. This one has Qur'ánic basis in xl. 62.

whether in congregations or solitary places. Moreover, He does not limit Himself to permission, but rather shows favour and kindness by inspiring desire and by calling. Any other than He is of the weak kings, who do not freely grant private audience, except after the presentation of a gift or a bribe. So—O His praise! How great is His state, and strong His authority and complete His kindness and general His beneficence!

May blessing and peace indeed be upon Muḥammad,[1] His elect Prophet and His chosen intimate, and upon his family and his companions, keys of guidance[2] and lamps in darkness!

(2) 'Worship is the support of the religion' and the handle[3] of certainty, the chief of good works, and the most conspicuous of the acts of obedience. In the department of canon law,[4] we have investigated,[5] in

[1] On the translation and Muslim use of this formula, see Goldziher's article in *Z.D.M.G.*, vol. l. 1896, pp. 97 ff., and the Introduction to the present translation. The SM's discussion of its meaning is on p. 158 f.

[2] The phrase is unusual. It is the city-dweller who thinks of keys and lamps in connection with guides, for with them he enters the locked and dark rooms of palaces, mosques and other places.

[3] The 'handle' is the strap by which the water-skin is carried about, and the 'certainty' is vision face to face by the power of faith, not by argument and proof; so comments the SM.

[4] In SM i. 231 ff., is the discussion by al-Ghazzâlî and al-Murtaḍâ of the original meaning of *fiqh*, as simply 'understanding', and 'knowledge' (based on Qur'ân ix. 123 and vii. 178), and of the development of its application to religious matters. In SM i. p. 153, *'ilm al-fiqh* is contrasted with *'ilm al-dîn*, 'science of religion', to which it is complementary, for it deals with mundane matters of political authority and civil protection. It had become the business of the *amîr*, his vice-regent and the one who assumed its responsibility. The companions avoided its problems, although they readily replied to questions of faith and the next abode. There is a long article by Goldziher in the *Ency. of Islam*, ii. pp. 101 ff. *Fiqh* is 'jurisprudence. . . . All aspects of public and private life and business should be regulated by laws recognized by religion; the science of these laws is *fiqh*.'

[5] These works are mentioned in the SM's list of al-Ghazzâlî's books, vol. i. pp. 41, 43; Brockelmann, *Arabische Litteratur*, i. p. 424.

Basîṭ al-Madhhab,[1] 'The Wide Way', *Al-Wasîṭ*, 'The Medium', and *Al-Wajîz*, 'The Brief', the Worship's trunks and branches, expending abundance of care upon its rare ramifications and exceptional occurrences, that they may be a treasure-store for the *muftî*,[2] canon lawyer, from which he may seek help, and may be something reliable for him, to which he may flee for aid and refer.

We now, in this book, limit ourself to what the devotee must needs have of canon law, consisting of the Worship's external acts and its inner mysteries, while revealing refinements of the inner qualities hidden in the qualities of humbleness, singleness of devotion and intention which it has not been customary to mention in the department of canon law.

We are arranging the book in seven chapters: I. The Excellences of the Performances[3] of the Worship. II. The Particulars[4] of the External Acts of the Worship. III. The Particulars[4] of the Inward Acts thereof. IV. The Leadership by the *imâm* and the Imitation [by the Worshipper]. V. The Friday Worship and its *âdâb*, Proprieties. VI. The Various Problems from which Trouble Commonly Arises, and which the Devotee Needs to Know. VII. The Voluntary Performances of the Worship, etc.

[1] Al-Ghazzâlî was a Shâfi'î. For the origin and position of this school, and of those of Abû Ḥanîfa, Mâlik and Ibn Ḥanbal, see, by index, Macdonald, *Development of Muslim Theology, Jurisprudence and Constitutional Theory*. For Abû Ḥanîfa and the Ḥanafites, see also *Ency. of Islam*, i. p. 91 f.; ii. p. 256; for Ibn Ḥanbal, *vide ibid.*, i. pp. 188 ff.

[2] The *muftî* is the canon lawyer of standing who delivers *fatwâs*, 'formal legal opinions'. See 'fatwa', *Ency. of Islam*, ii. p. 92, and 'faqih', *ibid.*, ii. p. 45 (both by Macdonald).

[3] The other texts have *ṣalâ*, singular, instead of plural.

[4] The 1334 text reads *tafḍîl* 'superiority', instead of *tafṣîl*, as here.

CHAPTER I

THE EXCELLENCES OF THE WORSHIP, PROSTRATION, CONGREGATION, CALL TO WORSHIP, ETC.

THE EXCELLENCE OF THE CALL TO WORSHIP

HE (may Allah bless him and give him peace[1])
(3) said, 'Three there will be on Resurrection Day upon a hill of black musk whom no accounting will frighten and whom no fear will reach, until there is surcease from what is [happening] among men: (1) a man who recited the Qur'án, out of desire for the Face[2] of Allah (who is almighty and exalted), and led [in Worship] a people well-pleased with him; (2) a man who gave the Call[3] to Worship in a mosque and summoned to Allah, out of desire for the Face of Allah; and (3) a man who was tested by slavery[4] in this life,[5]

[1] The eulogia will be translated once, upon their first occurrence.

[2] For al-Ghazzálí's explanation of the word 'face', as applied to man, and meaning 'the self', or, more closely, 'the consciousness', see p. 109 f. of the present translation (SM 142). The SM says, 'face' means 'the essence of the man' and 'the whole of his body' (p. 104A). The meaning of 'the Face of Allah' belongs to 'the unveiled knowledge' (SM i. p. 164). Its meaning as 'the self', 'the essence of Allah', and 'the only real existence' is discussed in Macdonald, *Aspects of Islam*, pp. 186 ff.; 201 f.

[3] The SM adds that the noun *ádhán* is from *adhana*, 'to inform', and then was applied to a particular giving of information at a particular time. His treatment of it is at p. 132. He says it is a *sunna kifáya* for the congregation, i.e. a Usage fulfilled if some perform it, and a *sunna 'aín* for the individual worshipping alone, i.e. he may do it himself, or omit it. See also *Ency. of Islam*, i. p. 133 f. (Juynboll).

[4] The SM reads *riqq*, 'slavery', instead of *rizq*, 'apportioned provision', which the other texts have, to make the tradition accord with the other versions of it which he quotes. On slavery see the article by Juynboll in the *Ency. of Islam*, under '*Abd*, i. pp. 16 ff.

[5] *Al-dunyá* is used in the Qur'án alone or with *al-ḥaiá*, as 'the nearer life', and consequently 'this world' and it is contrasted with *al-ákhira*, used alone or with *al-dár*, as 'the other, or last, abode', hence, 'the next world'.

but that did not make him too busy for the work of the next life'.

(4) Muḥammad said, 'No *jinní*,[1] or man, or thing hears the Call of the *mu'adhdhin* but he will bear witness for him on Resurrection Day'. Muḥammad
(5) said, 'The hand of the Compassionate One is upon the head of the *mu'adhdhin* until he finishes
(6) his Call'. It is said in exposition of the saying of Allah, 'And who speaks better words than he who summons to Allah and does what is right?' (Qur'án xli. 33) that it was sent down concerning the *mu'adh-*
(7) *dhins*. Muḥammad said, 'Whenever you hear the Call say the like of that which the *mu'adhdhin* says'; and that is desirable[2] except when he gives the *hai'alatain* [i.e. 'Come for Worship! Come for prosperity!'] for in their case he says, 'There is no power or strength but in Allah!' And when he says, 'The time for the Worship has come!'[3] he says, 'May Allah institute it and may He continue it as long as the heavens and the earth continue!' At the *tathwíb*,[4] what he says is, 'You have spoken the

[1] On the *jinn*, see Lane, *Arabian Nights*, *Introduction*, note 21, the article by Wensinck, on Iblís, in *Ency. of Islam*, ii. p. 351, and Macdonald's article, 'From the Arabian Nights to Spirit', in *The Moslem World*, vol. ix. 1919, pp. 336 ff.

[2] Maḥbúb is used in a technical sense, and is the SM's synonym for *mustaḥabb*, found in the other texts. It is applied to something for the doing of which there is reward, without any blame for the occasional omission of it.

[3] The phrase *qad qámat al-ṣalá* is elliptical for *qáma 'l-násu lil-ṣalá*, or *qámú 'l-muṣallún*, 'the men stood up for the Worship', or, 'the worshippers stood up' (SM p. 180). It may be translated, 'The Worship is instituted or begun', and *iqáma* is then, 'the institution or beginning' of the Worship. On Iqáma see also *Ency. of Islam*, ii. p. 457 f.

[4] Lane, *Lexicon*, p. 361, gives five uses of *tathwíb*: calling to worship and other things; repeated call; a special phrase in the call of the *mu'adhdhin* (*a*) 'Prayer! May Allah have mercy on you! Prayer!' (*b*) 'Prayer is better than sleep!' the chanting of the Iqáma by those who arrive on time; supererogatory prayer. Al-Ghazzálí uses it here as the special phrase 'The Worship is better than sleep' in the morning Call to the Worship.

truth, you have acted rightly, you have given good advice!' And at the finish he says, 'O Allah, Lord of this complete Call and instituted Worship, give Muḥammad mediation and excellence and raise him up to the praiseworthy station which Thou didst promise him: "Thou dost not break a promise!"' (Qur'án iii.
(8) 192). Sa'íd bin al-Musaiyab[1] said, 'Whoever worships in a desert place has an angel worship on his right and an angel worship on his left, but, if he gives the Call and the *iqáma*, Institution, there worship behind him the likenesses of mountains consisting of angels'.

The Excellence of the Prescribed Worship

Allah (who is exalted in and of Himself) said, 'The Worship was prescribed and timed for the believers' (Qur'án iv. 104).

(9) Muḥammad has said, 'Five performances of the Worship has Allah prescribed upon His creatures. So, whoever brings them, and does not miss anything of them by slighting their right, has a compact with Allah that He will make him enter the Garden. And whoever does not bring them does not have a compact with Allah: if He will, He will punish him, or if He will, He will make him enter the Garden.'

(10) Muḥammad said, 'The five performances of the Worship are like a river, fresh and deep, beside the door of any of you, into which he plunges five times every day, and what do you think that leaves of his uncleanness?' They replied, 'Not anything!' He said, 'So the five performances of the Worship remove offences as water removes dirt'.

(11) Muḥammad said, 'The performances of the Worship are an atonement for whatever small sins occur

[1] Abú al-Qásim Sa'íd bin al-Musaiyab (he himself preferred Musaiyib), the chief of the first series of Successors, and son-in-law of Abú Huraira; A.H. 15 or 16-91 or 95; the SM says 94 (i. 116D); De Slane, *Ibn Khallikán*, i. p. 568 f.; ii. p. 210; iii. p. 673.

between them, so long as you have avoided the great'.[1]

(12) Muḥammad said, 'Between us and the hypocrites[2] there is the attendance of the Night and of the Morning [Worships], which they are not able to do'.

(13) Muḥammad said, 'Whoever meets Allah as a misser of the Worship [will find that] Allah will not pay attention to any part of his good works'.

(2) Muḥammad said, 'The Worship is the support of the religion, so whoever abandons it has thrown over the religion'.

(14) Muḥammad was asked, 'Which of the works is most excellent?' He replied, 'The Worship at its appointed times'.

(15) Muḥammad said, 'Whoever perseveres in the five [Worships] along with complete observance of their purification and their times, will have light, and, on Resurrection Day, proof. Whoever misses them will be assembled with Pharaoh and Hámán'.[3]

(16) Muḥammad said, 'The key of the Garden is the Worship'.

(17) He said, 'Allah has not prescribed upon His creatures, after the confession of the unity, anything more beloved to Him than the Worship. If there were anything more beloved to Him than it, His

[1] A 'great' sin is something clearly prohibited, for which punishment, in this life and the next, is clearly laid down in the religious law. *Ta'rífát*, p. 192. The small sins are expiated by the Worship, notes the SM. See also Lane, *Manners and Customs*, p. 530.

[2] The 'hypocrites' are *munáfiqún*, those who pretend to be Muslims but are inwardly unbelievers (*Dictionary of Tech. Terms*, p. 1422). One who testifies and works but does not believe is a hypocrite; one who testifies and does not work, but believes, is a transgressor, *fásiq*; one who stops short with testifying is an unbeliever, *káfir* (*Ta'rífát*, p. 41). For the historical 'Hypocrites' or disaffected of al-Madina, see the lives of Muḥammad and the Commentaries on Qur'án lxiii.

[3] According to Qur'án xxviii. 38, xl. 25, Hámán is grand vizier of Pharaoh, and, along with Korah (Qárún) is on his council. 'That Muḥammad places Hámán in this period betrays his confused knowledge of history, of which many other examples may be found in the Qur'án,' *Ency. of Islam*, ii. p. 244 f.; cf. Esther iii. 1; Numbers xvi. 1).

angels would devote themselves by means of it, but some of them bow, some of them prostrate, and some stand and sit.'

(18) The Prophet said, 'Whoever abandons the Worship intentionally, has become a *káfir*, unbeliever', that is, one near to being removed from the faith by the loosening of its handle and the falling of its support, as it is said of one who draws near to a village,[1] 'he has reached it and entered it'.

(19) He also said, 'Whoever abandons the Worship intentionally has become free of the protection of Muḥammad'.

(20) Abú Huraira[2] (Allah be pleased with him) said, 'Whoever performs the ablution, but does his ablution well, and then goes out, making for the Worship, is in worship as long as he is making for the Worship, and there is written for him with one of his footsteps one good work, and there is erased for him with the other one evil deed. So, whenever one of you hears the *iqáma*, Institution, it is not fitting for him to hang back, for the one of you who gets the greatest reward is the one whose house is the most distant.' They asked, 'Why, O Abú Huraira?' He replied, 'On account of the large number of the footsteps'.

(21) It is related that the first of the work of the creature that is looked into on Resurrection Day is the Worship. Then, if it is found to be complete, it is accepted from him, along with the rest of his work. If it is found to be deficient, it is returned to him, along with the rest of his work.

(22) Muḥammed said, 'O Abú Huraira! enjoin the

[1] This a favourite illustration, used in opposite senses, to avoid an undesirable situation. It is quoted in the *Lisán*, iv. 472, to show that *al-wurúd*, 'coming to' or 'into', is not *al-dukhúl*, 'entrance' in explanation of Qur'án xix. 72, 'There is not any of you but is coming to it', i.e. the Fire.

[2] Abú Huraira, 'the father of Little Cat' (his proper name is uncertain) was a Companion and the most prolific traditionist, as well as sometime governor of al-Baḥrain. He died A.H. 57 or 58. *Ency. of Islam*, i. p. 93 f. (Goldziher); see also the account of him in Goldsack, *Tradition in Islam*.

Worship upon your family, for Allah will bring you provision[1] from a place you do not reckon upon'.

(23) One of the learned said, 'One who worships is like a merchant to whom no profit results until his capital is secure, and likewise no *náfila*,[2] Supererogatory Worship is accepted for the one who worships until he makes a proper payment[3] of the Prescribed Worship'.

[1] *Rizq* is the apportioned provision or allowance which Allah creates and supplies to all His creatures, for their bodies and minds. *Lisán*, xi. p. 405. Some limited the definition to food for the animal kingdom. But the 'Ashariya, orthodox Muslims, accept the fuller definition, and add that the provision may be both allowed and prohibited things. The Mu'tazila denied that prohibited things, such as wine and pig, could be Allah's provision, and were answered that then a man could live all his life without *rizq* from Allah, which was contrary to Qur'án xi. 8. The question whether some one's *rizq* could be eaten by another was answered in the negative, and they explained Qur'án ii. 2, 'From the *rizq* we gave them they expended' by saying the expenditure is itself a *rizq*, as it is possible for the giver to be benefited by it as well as the receiver who eats it. *Dict. of Tech. Terms*, pp. 580 ff.; Baiḍáwí, *al-Tanzíl*, on Qur'án ii. 2; Macdonald, *Development*, p. 298 f., 311.

[2] Al-Ghazzálí divides all the performances of the Worship into two classes: *farḍ*, Prescribed, and *náfl*, Additional, Supererogatory. The latter class has three sub-divisions: *sunna*, Usage, or *mu'akkada*, Confirmed, *mustaḥabb*, Liked, and *taṭawwu'*, Voluntary. See Introduction, p. 20.

[3] *Al-adá'* is the payment of an obligation itself at its divinely enjoined time. The term may be applied to both Prescribed and Supererogatory acts which have times appointed by the divine law, when those acts are performed within, but not before or after, their time limits. *Dict. of Tech. Terms*, p. 100. It is of three classes: (1) The 'perfect', *kámil*, payment, such as is performed by the *Imám* and one who is on hand in the mosque for all the Worship. (2) A 'defective', *náqiṣ*, payment is, for instance, a Worship performed by one who worships alone, or who arrives at the mosque somewhat late. (3) Payment 'resembling the substitution performance', *shibh al-qa'á'*, is performed by one who arrives after the *imám* finishes, because, in respect of the time, it is an *adá'*, but in respect of the fact that he was under obligation to perform the Worship along with the *imám*, it is a *qaḍá'*. Further, it is distinguished from *al-i'áda*, 'the repetition' of the performance within the appointed time, by being called the 'first' performance. The *i'áda* is required, when, for some reason, the first performance is defective. *Ta'rífát*, p. 14; *Ency. of Islam*, i. p. 122; Lane, *Lexicon*, p. 38B; see also note on *al-qaḍá'*, p. 65.

(24) Abú Bakr[1] used to say, 'Whenever the Worship-time comes, stand up to the fire which you have ignited, and put it out!'

The Excellence of Performing Completely the Essential Elements[2]

Muhammad said, 'The Prescribed Worship is like
(25) a balance: whoever pays is repaid in full'.

(26) Yazíd al-Raqáshí[3] said, 'The Worship of the Messenger of Allah was symmetrical, as though it were measured in a balance'.

(27) Muhammad said, 'Two men of my people will perform the Worship and their bowing and their prostration will be one [= the same], but between their two Worships there will be what there is between heaven and earth'. He referred to humbleness [towards Allah].

(28) He said, 'On Resurrection Day, Allah will not look at the creature who does not straighten up his backbone between his bowing and his prostration'.

(29) He also said, 'Does he, who turns his face round in the Worship, not fear that Allah will turn his face into the face of a donkey?'

[1] Abú Bakr al-Ṣiddíq, the first khalífa, (d. A.H. 13). He received the surname of 'the Very Veracious' on account of his asserting the truth of the Prophet's miraculous night-journey (Lane, *Arabian Nights*, chap. xxvi. note 8). *Al-Ṣiddíq* its used of a man who is truthful in his speech and belief, and who has verified his truthfulness by his act (*Mufradát*, p. 278; cf. also Bauer, *Über Intention*, p. 75, note 1). For Abú Bakr see also *Ency. of Islam*, i. pp. 80 ff.; Muir and Weir, *The Caliphate*, pp. 1-81.

[2] Al-Ghazzálí divides the component parts of the Worship into *faráʼiḍ*, Prescribed Elements, *sunan*, Usage, Customary, Parts, *ádáb*, Proprieties, and *haiʼát*, Forms (SM p. 99). The *faráʼiḍ* include *arkán* (singular, *rukn*), which are acts and utterances, and (*shurúṭ*), (singular, *sharṭ*), which are stipulated inner states. Because of this connection, *rukn* is often used interchangeably with *farḍ* (SM p. 109A). The Murtaḍá defines *rukn* as an 'essential part', 'that of which a material is composed', and also 'that by which a thing exists' (SM 102D).

[3] Yazíd bin Abán al-Raqáshí, pious traditionist. SM i. pp. 123A, 233 f., 243A; Veth, *As-Soyuti, de Nominibus Relativus*, p. 118; Fischer, *Aḍ-Ḍahabí, Biographien von Gewährsmännern des Ibn Isḥáq*, p. xi; De Goeje, *Annales at-Tabari*, i. p. 569.

(30) He said, 'Whoever performs the Worship for its appointed time and does its ablution and performs completely its bowing, its prostration and its humbleness [for him] it ascends, white and shining, saying, "May Allah keep you as you have kept me!" And whoever performs the Worship for its unappointed time, and does not do its ablution, and does not perform completely its bowing, its prostration and its humbleness, [for him] it ascends, black and dark, saying, "May Allah neglect you as you have neglected me!" until, when it is in the place where Allah wills it to be, it is folded up as a shabby garment is folded up, and his face is struck with it.'

(31) He also said, 'The most evil of mankind, as regards stealing, is the one who steals from his Worship'.

(32) Ibn Mas'úd[1] and Salmán[2] said, 'The Worship is a measure: so, whoever gives full measure is fully repaid, and whoever gives light measure—well, he knows what Allah said about those giving light measure!' (Qur'án lxxxiii. 1).

The Excellence of the Congregational Worship

(33) Muḥammad said, 'Worship in the congregation is more excellent than Worship alone by twenty-seven degrees'.

(34) Abú Huraira relates that Muḥammad missed some men at the Worship. So he said, 'I surely was anxious to order a man to conduct the Worship with the people, and then [myself] to turn away after men who remain away from it, and burn up their houses for them!'

(35) In another narrative [it is said], 'Then I would go after the men who remain away from it and give

[1] 'Abdalláh bin Mas'úd b. Gháfil, a Companion of the Prophet (d. A.H. 32 or 33), *Ency. of Islam* (ii. p. 403 f.).

[2] Abú 'Abdalláh Salmán al-Fárisí al-Khair, *mawlá*, 'manumitted slave', of the Messenger of Allah (d. 34, 35 or 36). SM i. p. 400C; Wüstenfeld, *el-Nawawi, Tahdhíb al-Asmá'*, pp. 292 ff.; 'Alí bin Athír, *Tajríd Asmá' al-Ṣaḥába*, No. 2306; Túsí, *Fihris*, No. 329, p. 158.

orders about them, so that their houses should be burnt for them by means of a bundle of firewood. If any of them knew that he would find a fat bone, or two trotters,[1] he would be present at it', meaning the evening Worship.

(36) 'Uthmán[2] has reported a *marfú'*[3] statement of the Prophet's: 'Whoever is present at the evening Worship, it is indeed [for him] as if he stood half a night [in Worship], and whoever is present at the morning Worship, [for him] it is as if he indeed stood a night'.

(37) Muḥammad said, 'Whoever performs a Worship in congregation has filled his chest with divine service'.[4]

(38) Sa'íd bin al-Musaiyab said, 'The *mu'adhdhin* has not given the Call to Worship for twenty years except while I was in the mosque'.

[1] The treatment of *mirma*, sometimes *marma*, is fuller in the *Lisán*, xix. p. 53 f., than in al-Murtaḍá's *Táj al-'Arús*, x. 156. About ten meanings are listed, centered around 'arrows', 'hoofs', and 'trotters', of which the last seems to fit the context best. The tradition is in al-Bukhárí, *Ṣaḥíḥ*, *Kitáb al-Aḥkám*, ed. with commentary of al-Qasṭallání, vol. ii. p. 25. The word is used in the plural in the sense of 'thunderbolts' in Baiḍáwí on xviii. 38.

[2] Abú 'Amr 'Uthmán bin 'Affán, the third khalífa (d. 35); Muir and Weir, *The Califate*, pp. 193-233.

[3] A *marfú'* tradition is a statement from the Messenger of Allah, reported by a Companion (*Ta'rífát*, p. 224). In the article on Ḥadíth by Juynboll, *Ency. of Islam*, ii. p. 119B, it is designated simply 'the tradition which contains a statement about the Prophet'.

[4] *'Ibáda* is an infinitive noun for the first stem of *'abada*, which is used only of the relation and service of an *'abd* (plural, *'ibád*) to Allah his Lord, while *khadama* is the word for the service of an *'abd*, slave (plural, *'abíd*), to his master, with *'ubúdíya* for one of its infinitives. The *'ábid* (plural, *'ábidún*), is the *muwaḥḥid*, one who singles out Allah for his sole attention in life. The form of the noun for 'idolators is *'abada*. *Lisán*, iv. p. 259 f. So, an *'abd* is primarily a creature who belongs to Allah, and secondarily one who serves Him. Then, *'ibáda* is the relationship of a slave to his Lord, generally expressed in religious service. The word is used for one of the services ordained by the divine law in Qur'án xxi. 19, as explained by the SM iii. p. 165, and it is in this technical sense that the word is used in the plural in canon law (*Dict. of Tech. Terms*, p. 947).

(39) Muḥammad bin Wási'[1] said, 'I desire only three things from this life: a brother who, if I become crooked, will straighten me; some sustenance from the apportioned provision that is lawful and needs no claim, and Worship in congregation, in which forgetfulness is removed from me, and the reward of which is recorded for me' (cf. Qur'án lxxxii. 10-12).

(40) It is related that Abú 'Ubaida bin al-Jarráḥ[2] was *imám* [leader in Worship] for a people on one occasion, and when he departed he said, 'Satan kept at me just now until I thought I had superiority over anyone else: I will never act as *imám* again!'

(41) Al-Ḥasan[3] said, 'Do not worship behind a man who does not follow the learned!'

(42) Al-Nakha'í[4] said, 'The one who acts as *imám* for men, without knowledge, is like the one who measures the water in the sea—he does not know its increase from its decrease'.

(43) Ḥátim the Deaf[5] said, 'The Worship in the congregation escaped me, and Abú Isḥáq al-Bukhárí[6] alone condoled with me. But, had a child of mine died, more than ten thousand would have condoled with me, for religious misfortune is lighter with men than this life's misfortune.'

[1] Muḥammad bin Wási' al-Azdí al-Baṣrí (d. 120; the SM here says 127). Flügel, *Fihrist*, p. 183; De Goeje, *Annales at-Tabari*, ii. 1326).

[2] Abú 'Ubaida bin al-Jarráḥ (d. 18). *Ency. of Islam*, i. p. 112.

[3] Abú Sa'íd al-Ḥasan bin Abí al-Ḥasan Yasár al-Baṣrí, prominent and learned traditionist (d. 110). *Ency. of Islam*, ii. p. 273; De Slane, *Ibn Khallikan's Biographical Dictionary*, i. pp. 370 ff.

[4] When the *nisba* '*al-Nakha'í*' is used alone, says the SM here, it usually refers to Abú 'Imrán and 'Ammár Ibráhím bin Yazíd b. al-Aswad b. 'Amr b. Rabí' b. Ḥáritha b. Sa'd b. Málik b. al-Nakha'í, jurisprudent (d. 95-96), De Slane, *Ibn Khallikan*, i. p. 5; or, the reference may be to Ibráhím's maternal uncle, al-Aswad bin Yazíd, also a jurisconsult (d. 75), *ibid.*, p. 5, note.

[5] Abú 'Abdalraḥmán Ḥátim bin 'Alwán (or 'Anwán) the Deaf, ascetic, SM i. pp. 371, 379 ff.; *Abú al-Maḥásin Ibn Ṭagri Bardii, Annales*, i. p. 719 f.

[6] Abú Isḥáq Ibráhím bin Ismá'íl al-Ṣaffár al-Bukhárí (not the author of the *Ṣaḥíḥ*) (d. 534). Flügel, *Ḥaji Khalfae Lexicon*, ii. p. 399.

(44) Ibn 'Abbás[1] (may Allah be pleased with both 'Abbás and his son!) said, 'Whoever hears the call and does not respond, does not mean good and good is not meant for him'.

(45) Abú Huraira said, 'Truly, that the ear of a son of Adam should be filled with molten lead would be better than that he should hear the Call and then not respond!'

(46) It is related that Maimún bin Mihrán[2] came to the mosque, and then it was said to him, 'The men have left!' So he said, 'We are Allah's, and to Him are we returning ones! (Qur'án ii. 151). Truly, the favour of this Worship is more dear to me than the governorship of al-'Iráq!'

(47) Muḥammad said, 'Whoever does the performances of the Worship forty days in the congregation, with no *takbîrat al-iḥrám*[3] [saying of "Allah is greater" at the beginning of the Worship], escaping him, has Allah ascribe to him two immunities, one from hypocrisy and one from the Fire'.

(48) It is said, 'On Resurrection Day there will be assembled a people whose faces are like the bright star, so the angels will say to them, 'What were your works?' and then they will answer, 'We were [people who] whenever we heard the call to Worship, rose for the purification, nothing else preoccupying us'. Then there will be assembled also a group whose faces will be like moons, and they will say, after inquiry, 'We used to perform the ablution before the time [of the Worship]'. Then there will be assembled a group

[1] 'Abdalláh bin al-'Abbás, cousin of the Prophet (d. 68, 69, or 70). *Ency. of Islam*, i. p. 19.

[2] Abú Aiyúb Maímún bin Mihrán al-Jazarí (d. 116 or 117). Wüstenfeld, *Ibn Qutaiba, Kitáb al-Ma'árif*, p. 228; *Ibn Ta..ri Bardii*, i. pp. 291, 308; Wüstenfeld, *Yácút Geographisches Wörterbuch* (Index).

[3] The *takbîrát al-iḥrám* is so called because its utterance marks the prohibition to the worshipper of what was before permitted to him (SM 100B). The special garment put on by the pilgrim when nearing Mecca on the *ḥajj* is called the *iḥrám* for a similar reason. See Introduction, p. 8.

whose faces are like the sun, and they will say, 'We used to hear the call to Worship in the mosque'.

(49) It is related that the Fathers[1] used to condole themselves three days whenever the first *takbír* ['Allah is greater'] escaped them, and they condoled seven days whenever the Congregational Worship escaped them.

The Excellence of the Prostration

(50) The Messenger of Allah said, 'A creature does not draw near to Allah by anything more excellent than by hidden prostration'.

(51) The Messenger of Allah said, 'There is no Muslim who prostrates before Allah but Allah raises him a degree by it, and by it puts away from him an evil deed'.

(52) It is related that a man said to the Messenger of Allah, 'Supplicate Allah that He may make me one of the people of your intercession, and that He may apportion to me fellowship with you in the Garden' He replied, 'Help me with numerous prostrations'.

(53) It is said, 'The nearest a creature is to Allah is when he is prostrating, and that is the meaning of the saying of Allah: "And prostrate thyself and come near!"' (Qur'án xcvi. 19).

Allah said, 'Their mark is on their faces from the imprint of their prostration' (Qur'án xlviii. 29).

(54) It is said, 'It is the light of humbleness, for it shines from within on the surface', and that is the
(55) soundest meaning. It is also said, 'It is the brightness that will be in their faces on Resurrection Day from the trace of the ablution'.

(56) It is said, 'It is that which clings to their faces from the earth when they prostrate'.

[1] *Salaf*, Fathers, in the divine law is applied to every one whose tenets, *madhhab*, are transmitted and whose way, *athar*, is followed, such as Abú Ḥanífa and his companions, and their *salaf*, who were the *ṣaḥába*, Companions of the Prophet, and the Successors, *tábi'ún*. *Dict. of Tech. Terms*, p. 676 f. Muḥammad is the *muqaddam*, Head, of the *salaf*. Lane, *Lexicon*, p. 1408C. See also note on 'Traditions and Records', No. 1, p. 61.

(57) Muḥammad said, 'Whenever a son of Adam recites a verse of prostration[1] and then prostrates, Satan moves away, weeping and saying, "Woe is me! This man was commanded to prostrate and he did so, so he has the Garden; while I was commanded to prostrate[2] [to Adam] but I disobeyed, and so I have the Fire"'.

(58) It is related from 'Alí bin 'Abdalláh bin 'Abbás[3] that he used to perform a thousand prostrations every day, and they used to call him 'the Prostrator'.

(59) It is related that 'Umar bin 'Abdal'azíz[4] was wont not to prostrate except on bare earth.

(60) Yúsuf bin Asbáṭ[5] used to say, 'O company of young men, make use of your health before illness comes, for there does not remain anyone whom I envy except a man who performs completely his bowing and his prostration, since some hindrance has come between me and that'.

[1] Al-Ghazzálí gives a brief treatment of the Prostration of the Recital in the Seventh Section of the Second Chapter of *Kitáb Ádáb Tiláwat al-Qur'án*, 'The Book of the Proprieties of the Recital of the Qur'án', Book viii of the First Quarter of the *Iḥyá'*, SM iv. pp. 480 ff. He says the 'verses of prostration' are fourteen in number, with two in *Súrat al-Ḥajj* (xxii), and none in *Súrat Ṣád* (xxxviii). The SM gives them as follows: vii. 205; xiii. 16; xvi. 52; xvii. 108; xix. 59; xxii. 18, 76; xxv. 61; xxvii. 25; xxxii. 15; xli. 38 (or 37 or 3); liii. 62; lxxxiv. 21; xcvi. 18. The SM substitutes xxxviii. 23 for xxii. 76, and objects to liii. 62 and xcvi. 18, because they are commands, as he accepts the rule that the prostration is to be made only when the verses are statements. On this subject see Sell, *Faith of Islam*, pp. 338 ff. (2nd edition), and also Introduction, p. 29.

[2] For the story of Iblís's refusal to prostrate before Adam, see Wensinck's article in the *Ency. of Islam*, ii. p. 351 f. It occurs first in the Qur'án at ii. 32, where Baiḍáwí explains the strict theological aspect of it as a prostration to Allah with Adam as *qibla*.

[3] Abú Muḥammad and 'Abdalláh 'Alí bin 'Abdalláh b. 'Abbás b. 'Abdal-Muṭṭalib b. Háshim al-Qarashí al-Hátimí, the ancestor of the Abbasides (d. 117 or 118). *Ency of Islam*, i. p. 282 f.

[4] 'Umar bin 'Abdal'azíz al-Umawí, eighth Umaiyad khalífa (d. 101). Muir and Weir, *The Caliphate*, pp. 318, 369 ff.

[5] Abú Muḥammad Yúsuf bin Asbáṭ (d. after 190). SM i. p. 447; *Abú al-Maḥasin Ibn Ṭagri Bardii, Annales*, i. p. 413; *Fihrist*, p. 184.

(61) Sa'íd bin Jubair[1] said, 'I do not mourn over anything of this life except the prostration'.

(62) 'Uqba bin Muslim[2] said, 'There is no quality of a creature more beloved with Allah than [that of] a man who loves meeting with Allah, and there is no hour when a man is nearer to Allah than when he kneels in prostration'.

(63) Abú Huraira said, 'The nearest a creature is to Allah is when he prostrates: so, do much supplication then'.

The Excellence of Humbleness

Allah said, 'And perform the Worship for remembrance of Me' (Qur'án xvii. 80; xx. 14; cf. xi. 116).

Allah said, 'And do not be [one] of the unmindful!' (Qur'án vii. 204).

He also said, 'Do not offer the Worship while you are intoxicated, so that you may know what you are
(64) saying!' (Qur'án iv. 46). It is said, 'Intoxicated from
(65) the great amount of care', and it is said, 'from love of
(66) this life'. Wahb[3] said, 'The thing meant by it is its literal meaning'. Anyway, there is a warning in it against being intoxicated with this life, since He shows the defect in it for He said, 'so that you may know what you say', and how many a worshipper there is who has not drunk wine, and yet does not know what he says in his Worship!

(67) The Prophet said, 'Whoever performs [a Worship of] two *rak'as*,[4] without having polluted himself in them with anything of this life, has his previous sinning forgiven him'.

[1] Abú 'Abdalláh Sa'íd bin Jubair b. Hishám al-Asadí, a Successor (d. 95 or 94), De Slane, *Ibn Khallikan*, pp. 564 ff.

[2] 'Uqba bin Muslim al-Tujíbí, Imám of the congregational mosque of Cairo (d. 243). Sometime governor of Egypt. *Abú al-Maḥásin Ibn Ṭagri Bardii, Annales*, i. p. 278.

[3] Wahb bin Munabbih, Successor (d. 110; SM says here, 116); *el-Nawawi*, p. 619.

[4] The word *rak'atain* is elliptical for a Worship of two *rak'as*, Cycles. *Ruba'iya* is the parallel term for a Worship of four *rak'as*. The Noon, Afternoon and Evening Worships each have four *rak'as*.

(68) The Prophet said, 'The Worship is verily humbling and abasing yourself, intercession, crying-out and repenting, while you put down your hands and say, "O Allah, O Allah," for the worship of one who does not do so is a thing defective'.

(69) It is related about Allah (Oh, His praise!), in the former books that He said, 'Not from every worshipper do I accept the Worship. I accept the Worship only of him who humbles himself before My greatness and does not exalt himself over Me, and feeds the hungry needy for the sake of My Face.'

(70) Muḥammad said, 'The Worship was prescribed and the Pilgrimage and the Circumambulation [of the Ka'ba] commanded and the pilgrimage ceremonies were enacted as law only to institute remembrance of Allah, so, whenever you do not have any exaltation or awe in your heart for the One Remembered, who is the One to be sought and desired, of what value is your remembrance?'

(71) He said to the one to whom he gave an admonition, 'And whenever you perform the Worship, make it the Worship of one bidding farewell, i.e. of one bidding farewell to his passions, bidding farewell to his life, and journeying to his Lord, as Allah said, "O man, you are toiling on toward your Lord indeed, for you are one who shall encounter Him!"' (Qur'án lxxxiv. 6).

Allah said: 'And fear[1] Allah, and Allah will give you knowledge' (Qur'án ii. 282). He also said, 'And fear Allah, and know that you shall encounter Him!' (Qur'án ii. 223).

(72) Muḥammad said, 'Whosoever Worship does not

[1] The original form of *taqwá* is *wiqwá*, sometimes *waqwá*, from *wiqáya*, the *wáw* being changed to *tá'*, as in *turáth*, 'inheritance', and *tukhama*, 'indigestion'. It means 'putting the self on guard against what it fears', i.e. self-preservation. In the divine law it is 'obeying the commandments and avoiding the prohibitions'. Another interpretation is 'preserving the self from sins and the like'. *Dict. of Tech. Terms*, p. 1527. *Ittaqú al-qaṣṣáṣ*, 'beware of the story-teller', occurring in tradition (SM i. p. 241D), shows the force of the word. The same idea should be included in its translation as 'fear'. On the attitude toward story-tellers see Traditions Nos. 286-93.

prohibit him from the excessive and the disapproved, has no increase from Allah except of distance'.

(73) 'The Worship is confidential communion', so how does it exist along with unmindfulness?

(74) Bakr bin 'Abdalláh[1] said, 'O son of Adam! Whenever you will to enter the presence of your Lord without leave and address Him without an interpreter, you enter.' He was asked, 'And how is that?' He replied, 'You complete your ablution and enter your worship-niche, and behold! you have come before your Lord without leave, and then you address Him without an interpreter'.

(75) From 'Á'isha[2] [is this tradition]; she said, 'The Messenger of Allah used to talk to us and we to him, and when Worship-time came, it was as if he did not know us and we did not know him, so engrossed were we in the greatness of Allah'.

(76) Muḥammad said, 'Allah does not look at the Worship in which a man does not present his heart along with his body'.

(77) Whenever Ibráhím the Friend[3] rose for the Worship, the palpitation of his heart used to be heard two miles away.

(78) It happened whenever Sa'íd al-Tanúkhí[4] worshipped, tears did not cease to drop from his cheeks to his beard.

(79) The Messenger of Allah saw a man who was playing with his beard in the Worship, so he said, 'If this one's heart were humble, his members would be'.

(80) It is related that al-Ḥasan looked at a man who was playing with pebbles and saying, 'O Allah, marry

[1] Bakr bin 'Abdalláh b. 'Amr b. Hilál al-Muzaní al-Baṣrí (d. 108). Wüstenfeld, *Ibn Coteiba's Handbuch der Geschichte*, pp. 36, 232.

[2] 'Á'isha bint Abú Bakr, the favourite wife of Muḥammad (d. 58). *Ency. of Islam*, i. p. 216.

[3] Ibráhím al-Khalíl, the Biblical Abraham. For Muslim account and references, see *Ency. of Islam*, ii. p. 431 f.

[4] Sa'íd bin Abú Muḥammad Sa'íd bin 'Abdal'azíz b. Yahyá al-Tanúkhí al-Dimashqí, jurisconsult (d. 168 or 167). Wüstenfeld, *al-Dahabi, Kitáb Ṭabaqát al-Haffáẓ*, i. p. 47.

me to the *ḥúr*!'[1] so he said, 'A fine suitor you are! Asking in marriage the *ḥúr* while you are playing with stones!'

(81) Khalaf bin Aiyúb[2] was asked, 'Do not flies annoy you in your Worship, so that you chase them away?' 'I do not accustom myself to anything that corrupts my Worship.' He was asked, 'How do you have patience for that?' He replied, 'I have heard that criminals exercise patience under the lashings of the sultan, so that it may be said, "Such a one is patient!" and they boast about that. Now, I stand before my Lord: shall I, then, move for a fly?'

(82) It is related about Muslim bin Yasár[3] that he, whenever he wanted to perform the Worship, said to his family, 'Go on talking, for I do not hear you'.

(83) It is related also about him that he was worshipping in the mosque at al-Baṣra one day and a side of the mosque fell. Thereupon the people gathered

[1] The *Ihyá'* contains the usual frankly carnal descriptions of the *ḥúr*, the maidens of Paradise, and the Garden. (Chapters, *Sifát al-Ḥúr*, SM iii. p. 542; iv. p. 462; *Sifát al-Janna*, iv. p. 457; x. pp. 521 ff.) For the *ḥúr* see also the article in the *Ency. of Islam*, ii. p. 337. Al-Baiḍáwí on ii. 23, however, is not presenting a non-sensual view of the 'foods, wives and other circumstances of the Garden', but states that they are partners with their earthly likenesses in only some qualities and respects, and are called by their names by way of metaphor and comparison, and are not partners with them in the completeness of their reality, so that they should require all that holds good for earthly beings; that is, the production of children and the avoidance of hunger are not purposes necessarily inferred from the existence of wives and foods in the Garden. There are, of course, in Islam, non-sensual aspects of life in the next world, but they are found in connection with the ideas of the Beatific Vision, for which see the article by Macdonald on 'Blessedness (Muḥammadan)', in the *Ency. of Religion and Ethics*, vol. ii. pp. 677 ff.; based on SM ix. pp. 544 ff.; cf. SM x. p. 553. For a discussion of the two recompenses in Paradise, carnal with the literalists, and spiritual with the *ṣúfís*, see Massignon, *La Passion d'al-Hallaj*, ii. pp. 689 ff.

[2] Al-Khalaf bin Aiyúb al-'Ámirí al-Balkhí *muftí* (d. says SM here, 209; others say 205, 215 or 220). Flügel, *Ibn Kuṭlúbuga's Ṭabakát der Ḥanefiten*, pp. 20, 108.

[3] Abú 'Abdalláh Muslim bin Yasár al-Baṣrí, a Successor, and canon lawyer (d. 100). Wüstenfeld, *el-Nawawi's Tahdhíb al-Asmá'*, p. 553.

together, but he was not cognizant of it until he withdrew from the Worship.

(84) 'Alí bin Abú Ṭálib[1] (may Allah honour his face!), whenever Worship-time came, used to shake, and his face used to change colour. So he was asked, 'What is the matter with you, O Commander of the believers?' And he would say, 'There has come the time of "trust"[2] which Allah "offered to the heavens and the earth and the mountains, but they refused to bear it and shrank from it" (Qur'án xxxiii. 72) and I have borne it'.

(85) It is related about 'Alí bin al-Ḥusain[3] that it was the case that, whenever he performed the ablution, he became yellow in colour. So his family would say to him, "What is this which befalls you during the ablution?" and so he would reply, "Do you know before whom I wish to stand?"'

(86) It is related from Ibn 'Abbás that he said, 'Dáwud[4] said [in his devotional communion], "O my God! who will dwell in Thy house, and from whom wilt Thou accept Worship?" And Allah revealed to him, "O Dáwud! only he shall dwell in My house and have his Worship accepted who is humble before My greatness, cuts up his day with remembrance of Me and withdraws himself from fleshly appetites for My sake, giving food to the hungry, sheltering the stranger and showing mercy to the unfortunate. For he it is whose light shall shine in the heavens as the sun. If

[1] Abú al-Ḥasan 'Alí bin Abú Ṭálib 'Abd Manáf b. 'Abdal-Muṭṭalib b. Háshim, cousin and son-in-law of Muḥammad and fourth khalífa (d. 40). *Ency. of Islam*, i. pp. 283 ff.; Muir and Weir, *The Caliphate*.

[2] Lane, *Lexicon*, p. 102A, brings together from the commentaries the explanations of what the 'trust' in this passage means, as (1) obedience; (2) intelligence; (3) tasks; (4) recommended acts of worship; (5) the obligatory statutes, all as things committed by Allah to man to be kept faithfully.

[3] 'Alí bin al-Ḥusain Zain al-'Ábidín, one of the twelve Shí'ite *imáms* (d. 94). *Ency. of Islam*, i. p. 288.

[4] The Biblical David. For the Muslim account of him see *Ency. of Islam*, i. p. 927 f.

he call upon Me, I will respond; if he ask of Me, I will give; I will give him, in ignorance, intelligence; in heedlessness, remembrance; and, in darkness, light; and truly he shall be among men like Paradise in the Gardens,[1] whose rivers do not run dry and whose fruit does not change." '

(87) It is related about Ḥátim the Deaf that he was asked about his Worship, so he said, 'Whenever Worship-time comes I complete the ablution and I go to the place I wish to worship in, and sit there until my members are composed. Then I rise for the Worship, and place the Ka'ba between my eyebrows and the Bridgeway[2] under my feet with the Garden on my right and the Fire on my left and the Angel of Death behind me and I think it to be my last Worship. Then I stand, between hope and fear, and repeat a *takbír* with precision and recite a recitation that is distinct and bow a bow with humility and make a prostration with self-abasement, and sit on the left thigh and spread on the ground the top of its foot and set the right foot on its great toe; then I follow it up with singleness of devotion, and then—I do not know whether it has been accepted or not!'

(88) Ibn 'Abbás said, 'A Worship of two *rak'as* that are purposed in thought are better than standing a night with the heart heedless'.

The Excellence of the Mosque and the Place of Worship

Allah said, 'Only he repairs[3] to the mosques of Allah

[1] The other texts, i.e. that on the margin and the Cairo edition of 1334, read 'in the highest of the Gardens'.

[2] The *ṣirâṭ* here is the bridgeway over the Fire, sharper than a sword and thinner than a hair, over which the people of Paradise will pass, while the people of the Fire will slip. In the Qur'án the word in most cases refers to 'The Straight Road', meaning Islam. It is one of the foreign words of the Qur'án, and is derived from the *via strata*, 'the straight road', of the Romans (from Prof. Macdonald).

[3] This verse has commonly two interpretations among commentators. The meaning of 'visit, repair to', is derived by them

who believes in Allah and the Last Day' (Qur'án ix. 18).

(89) Muḥammad said, 'Whoever builds Allah a mosque, even though it be as the nest of a partridge, will have Allah build a palace for him in the Garden'.

(90) He said, 'Whoever becomes familiar with a mosque, will have Allah become familiar with him'.

(91) He also said, 'Whenever any of you enters a mosque, let him perform two *rak'as* before he sits down'.[1]

(92) Muḥammad said, 'There is no Worship for the neighbour of a mosque except in the mosque'.

(93) He said, 'The angels intercede[2] for any one of you as long as he is in the place of worship in which he is worshipping, saying, "O Allah! have mercy[3] on him! O Allah! be merciful to him! O Allah! forgive him as long as he does not do anything polluting or go out from the mosque!"'

(94) He also said, 'There shall come, in the last time, men of my people who will come to the mosques and sit in them in circles with their thought being of this life and of the love of this life: do not sit with them, for Allah has no need of them!'

(95) Muḥammad said, 'Allah said in one of the Books, "My houses on the earth are the mosques, and My visitors in them are those who repair to them, so, blessed is the creature who purifies himself in his house

from *'umra*, 'a visit', and, hence, 'a minor pilgrimage' to the Ka'ba. The other meaning is 'to keep in repair' by, primarily, improving the building, and then its furniture, and even using the building for improvement in knowledge (Baiḍáwí). This meaning is connected with the root meaning of 'inhabit, dwell upon and build up' the land. *'Amr* and *'umur*, 'mortal life', is the period during which the spirit inhabits the body, and contrasts in length of time with *al-baqá'*, 'continuance, immortality', the opposite of which is *al-faná'*, 'passing away', which term has also a mystical sense.

[1] This tradition refers to the Worship of the Greeting of the Mosque, for which see Introduction, p. 26.

[2] The phrases in both cases are *ṣallá 'alaihi*, and are translated in accordance with the definitions discussed in the Introduction, p. 5.

[3] The other texts read, 'What is his right?'

and then visits Me in My house, for there is a duty upon a host to honour his guest"' (cf. Baiḍ, on Qur'án ix. 18).

(96) Muḥammad said, 'Whenever you see a man accustomed to the mosque, testify to his faith'.

(97) Sa'íd bin Musaiyab said, 'Whoever sits in a mosque truly has fellowship with his Lord, so, how right it is for him not to say anything but good!'

(98) It is related in the Records[1] or the Traditions, 'Talking in the mosque devours good works as cattle devour grass'.

(99) Al-Nakha'í said, 'They used to think that walking to the mosque on a dark night was something that makes the Garden obligatory [as a reward]'.

(100) Anas bin Málik[2] said, 'Whoever lights a lamp in a mosque, has the angels and the bearers of the throne ceasing not to ask forgiveness for him as long as its light remains in that mosque'.

(101) 'Alí said, 'Whenever a creature dies, the place of his Worship on the earth and the place of heaven where his work ascends weep over him'; thereupon he recited, 'Then the heaven and the earth wept not for them and they were not granted respite' (Qur'án xliv. 28).

(102) Ibn 'Abbás said, 'The earth weeps for him forty mornings'.

(103) 'Aṭá' al-Khurásání[3] said, 'There is no creature who makes a single prostration to Allah in any one of the places of the earth but will have it testify for him on Resurrection Day and weep for him the day he dies'.

[1] The SM's distinction between *khabar* and *athar* is given in his Introduction to the *Itḥáf*, vol. i. p. 48. The *akhbár* are traditions from the Prophet, while the *áthár* are from the Companions and from the Successors and their Successors and the early Fathers after them. See note, p. 52.

[2] Abú Hamza Anas bin Málik, prolific traditionist (d. 91-93). *Ency. of Islam*, i. p. 345.

[3] Abú Aiyúb (*et al*, 'Aṭá' bin Abú Muslim 'Abdalláh al-Azdí al-Khurásání al-Balkhí (d. 133; SM says 135). Wüstenfeld, *el-Nawawi, Kitáb Tahdhíb al-Asmá'*, p. 423 f.

(104) Anas bin Málik said, 'There is no place in which Allah is mentioned in Worship or Invocation[1] but it boasts over the places around it, and they rejoice in the mention of Allah to their uttermost limit, consisting of seven lands, and there is no creature who stands up for the Worship but has the earth embellished for him'.

(105) It is said, 'There is no place in which people alight but that place begins to intercede for them or curse them'.

[1] The *dhikr*, Invocation, has always two aspects, 'remembrance in in the heart or mind', and 'mention by the tongue'. It is discussed in the Introduction, pp. 31, 32.

CHAPTER II

THE MANNER OF PERFORMING THE OUTWARD ACTS OF THE WORSHIP

Beginning with the Takbīr and what Precedes it

It is fitting that the one performing the Worship, when he finishes the ablution and the cleansing from the uncleanness of body, place and clothing, and the covering of his nakedness from the navel to the knee, should rise, standing facing the *qibla*[1] outwardly [and the Divine Presence inwardly[2]], and pair[3] his feet together without joining them, for that is one of the things by which they [the Fathers[4]] used to infer a man's legal knowledge.

(106) Muḥammad prohibited *ṣafn*,[5] 'the raising of the

[1] For the account of the change of the *qibla* or 'direction' towards which the Worship is performed, from Jerusalem to the Ka'ba in Mecca, see the biographies of Muḥammad and histories of Islam. Facing the *qibla* is a stronger preliminary Stipulation than the Standing Posture, for the latter may be dispensed with in the *náfl*, Supererogatory, Worship (Al-Bájúrí, *Commentary on Abú Shujá'*, i. p. 174), while the former may be dispensed with only in permissible battle and in parts of the Worship while travelling. In congregation and on pilgrimage it is a *farḍ kifáya* to learn to tell where the *qibla* is, but at other times it is obligatory. The discussion of the subject in the SM is at iii. p. 135 f.

[2] This is an addition in the SM's text.

[3] In this instance the other texts have been translated. The SM reads *yuráwiḥa*, 'to stand alternately upon' the feet. But the Cairo 1334 text, and still another Cairo text (of the Maṭba'a 'Ámira, 1326), both read *yuzáwija*, 'to pair', which reads much better, although it is said that Abú Ḥanífa used to stand alternately upon his feet, *taráwaḥa* (vi stem) in his famous long-continued performances of the Worship. But they were *náfl*, Supererogatory, performances, which do not have strict requirements as to posture.

[4] This is supplied by the SM's explanation.

[5] The action referred to in the *ḥadíth al-ṣáfin* (the noun of action is *sufún*) has two interpretations: (1) joining the feet together, and (2) turning up one foot behind the other as a horse does when it stands upon three feet (*Lisán*, xvii. p. 116).

(107) foot', and '*ṣafd*, 'fettering', in the Worship. 'Fettering' is the uniting of the two feet, and this is the meaning of the saying of Allah, 'Bound together in fetters' (Qur'án xiv. 50). *Ṣafn* is the lifting of one of the feet, and this is the meaning of the saying of Allah, 'Raising the foot, fleet' (Qur'án xxxviii. 30). This is what he is to be mindful of as regards his feet when he stands.

He is to be mindful of straightness in his knees and waist, the place of tying his girdle. As for his head, if he will he may keep it erect, and if he will, he may incline it: to incline it appears more humble and more abasing. So let his gaze be fixed on the mat he worships on. If he has no worshipping-mat[1] let him draw near to the encircling wall, or let him draw a line, for that cuts off the extent of his gaze and prevents the scattering of the thought. Let him restrain his gaze from exceeding the edges of his worshipping-mat or the bounds of the line. Let him continue so standing until the Bowing is to be done, without turning. This is the *adab*, Proper Manner, of the *qiám*, Standing Posture.

Then, whenever his standing and his direction and his extremities are made symmetrical,[2] after this fashion, let him recite,[3] 'Say, I take refuge with the Lord of mankind' (Qur'án cxiv), fortifying himself by it against Satan. Then let him proceed with the Institution of the Worship. If he should hope for the presence of those who would follow his leadership,

[1] See further Tradition No. 120 and 'seggadeh' in Lane, *Modern Egyptians* (Everyman's edition, p. 73).

[2] *Istawa* is one of the important and fateful words of the Qur'án and of the origin and history of Islam. The root idea is 'symmetry'. Lane, *Lexicon*, pp. 1476 ff., gives translations of the Qur'án passages. These show that Muḥammad was tremendously impressed by the congruous and balanced character of creation. See further, Macdonald, *Development*, pp. 186 ff.

[3] The last two *súras* are called *al-mu'awwidhatán*, because the word *a'údh*, 'I take refuge', occurs at the beginning of them. It is a Qur'ánic injunction (xvi. 100) to begin its recital with such a formula, of which other examples are ii. 63; xi. 49; xix. 18; xxiii. 99, 100.

let him give the Call to Worship first. Next, let him cause the Intention to be present. This means to state an intention, at noon, for instance, and say in his heart, 'I perform at its proper time the Prescribed Noon Worship to Allah', in order to distinguish it from the *qaḍá'*,[1] 'substitute performance', by his saying, 'I perform at its proper time', *adá'*; and from the *náfl*, 'supererogatory Worship', by saying, 'the prescribed', and from the Afternoon or any other Worship, by saying, 'noon'. Let the meanings of these utterances be present in his heart, for that is the Intention, while the utterances themselves are reminders and causes of its presence.

He strives that that should continue until the end of the *takbír*, so that it may not go away. Then, when that is present in his heart, let him raise his hands opposite his shoulders in such a way that his palms will be opposite his shoulders and his thumbs opposite the lobes of his ears [and the tips of his fingers opposite the tops of his ears], so that he may combine the traditions which have come down concerning it. He turns his palms and thumbs towards the *qibla*, and opens up his fingers, not folding them and not taking pains to separate them or to keep them together, but he lets them be as they naturally are, since there is handed down in tradition both the spreading and the closing [of the fingers], and this is between the two, and so is preferable.

When the hands have come to rest in their position he begins the *takbír* at the same time letting them descend and causing the Intention to be present. Next he places his hands on what is above the navel

[1] *Al-qaḍá'* is setting up one thing in place of another (*Dict. of Tech. Terms*, p. 1234). It is the payment, for cause, of something similar to what was obligatory, *Ta'rífát*, p. 185 ; cf. *Dict. of Tech. Terms*, p. 100. Among Sháfi'ites, *adá'* and *qaḍá'* apply especially to the services of worship which have appointed times, and *adá'* is not applied to any performance which may not have a *qaḍá'*, e.g. the Worship of the Feasts and the Friday Congregation (*Dict. of Tech. Terms*, p. 100). See also note 3, p. 46.

and below the chest and places the right hand on the left, out of honour for the right hand in that it is the one to be borne. He extends the index and middle fingers of the right hand on the length of the forearm, and takes hold, by the thumb and the little and ring fingers, of the wrist of the left arm.

(108) It has been related that the *takbîr* comes along
(109) with the raising of the hands, and with their remain-
(110) ing[1] [at the ears] and with their descent. There is nothing wrong with any of these, but I think that it is more suitable that it should be combined with the descent of the hands, for it is the word of binding, since the placing of one of the hands on the other is a form of binding, its beginning being the lowering, and its ending being the placing of them in position. The *takbîr*, 'Alláhu akbar', begins with the 'A' and ends with the 'r', so it is suitable that there should be regard for the correspondence between the action and the binding. The raising of the hand is, as it were, preliminary to this beginning. Further, it is not fitting that he should raise his hands pushing them forward, nor move them back behind his shoulders, nor shake them to the right or left when he finishes the *takbîr*. He lowers them quickly and easily, and commences to place the right one on the left after the lowering.

(111) In one of the narratives it is related that whenever Muḥammad said the *takbîr*, he would lower his hands, and whenever he wished to recite, would place the right on the left. If that is sound,[2] it is preferable to what we have mentioned.

As for the *takbîr*, it is fitting that he should vocalize the 'h' of 'Allah' with a light *dhamma* [the vowel 'u'], without emphasis, and not insert

[1] The SM adds the explanation 'they are raised'.

[2] Among traditionists, *ṣaḥîḥ*, 'sound', means that the tradition is traced all the way back to Muḥammad, is handed down by an unbroken line of honest people, is accurate in imposing or discharging (a duty), and is not exceptional (*Dict. of Tech. Terms*, p. 817 ; article on Ḥadíth, *Ency. of Islam*, ii. p. 191B).

between the 'h' and the 'a' any resemblance to a *wáw* [the consonant 'w'], that being the tendency of emphasizing, nor insert between the 'b' and the 'r' of the 'akbar' an 'á', saying '*akbár*'. He leaves unvowelled the 'r' of the '*akbar*', not vowelling it with *dhamma.* This is the Form of the *takbír* and what accompanies it.

The Recital

Thereupon he begins the Introductory Supplication.
(112) It is well that he should say, after saying, 'Allah is greater', 'Allah is much greater! Praise belongs to Allah many times over! Oh, the praise of Allah, early and late! I have turned my face to His word,
(113) and I am one of the Muslims!' Then he says, 'Praise is Thine, O Allah!' and 'By Thy praise! Blessed of itself is Thy name, and exalted is Thy majesty, and sublime is Thy praise, and there is no god but Thee!' that he may combine the variations that have come down in the traditions. If he is behind an *imám*, he is brief, if the *imám* does not have a long pause, in which he recites [the Fátiḥa[1]].

Then he says: 'I seek refuge in Allah from Satan the Stoned'.

Next he recites the Fátiḥa, beginning it with, 'In the name of Allah, the Merciful and Compassionate One', giving full value to its doubled and other letters, and striving to differentiate between the ḍád and the ẓá',[2] and He says '*amín*' at the end of the Fátiḥa. He prolongs it considerably and does not at all join the '*amín*' to the words, 'and not of those going astray'. He makes the Recital audible in the morning, at sunset and in the evening, unless he is a follower.[3] He says the '*amín*' audibly.

[1] This is added by the SM as merely a measure of the length of the recital.

[2] These are two letters of the Arabic alphabet whose pronunciations among the Arabs of Arabia proper are very similar, but are nevertheless distinguishable.

[3] That is, he is worshipping behind an *imám*.

Next he recites the *súra*,[1] or as much as three verses[2] of the Qur'án, or more, not joining the last of the *súra* with the *takbír* of the bending, but keeping them apart as long as he takes to say, 'Oh, the praise of Allah!' He recites in the morning one of the long *súras* of the *mufaṣṣal*,[3] and at sunset one of the short ones; also at noon and in the afternoon and evening, such as, 'By the sky, possessor of the towers!' (lxxxv) and those near it; and in the morning on a journey, 'Say, "O unbelievers!"' (cix), and, 'Say, "He is Allah, One!"' (cxii); and likewise

[1] Both the spelling and origin of the word *súra* have a number of explanations, leaving the matter inconclusive. The term is applied to a part of a recital which has opening and closing verses, or, differently expressed, a portion (of the Qur'án) given a (special) name. It is also defined as part of revealed speech, whether Qur'ánic or not, since the terms *súrat al-zabúr* (Psalms) and *súrat al-injíl* (Gospel) are used (*Dict. of Tech. Terms*, p. 658C). In the performance of the *ṣalá*, Worship, the *sunna* utterance called the *súra* may be a chapter or a portion consisting of three or more verses. A list of the various names of the *súras* is given in the *Dict. of Tech. Terms*, p. 660 f.

[2] Áia, the form and derivation of which are uncertain, occurs also only as a noun in Hebrew and Syriac, with the meanings of 'sign', 'letter character' and 'written document' (Dalman, Gesenius-Buhl and Payne-Smith). In Arabic it means 'sign', really applying to some evident thing, necessarily connected with something else not evident in itself, whether things of sense or mind, i.e. it is an 'evidential sign'. It is applied to a high building, a part of the Qur'án, whether *súra* sections or a section of a *súra*, and sometimes to every separate expression, and hence to the verses into which the *súra* is divided. The skies and earth, Mariam together with 'Isá, and other matters, are all *áiát*, 'evidential signs' from Allah to mankind (*Mufradát*, p. 32 f.; Lane, *Lexicon*, p. 135).

[3] One of the divisions of the Qur'án (cf. Sell, *Faith of Islam*, p. 335) is into four parts, as follows: (1) *al-ṭiwál*, 'the long', consisting of seven *súras*, ii to ix (which includes viii because there is no *basmala* between them), or, others say, ii to vii, to which are added either x or xviii (*Dict. of Tech. Terms*, p. 656 f.; cf. further, Lane, *Lexicon*, p. 1897C, and *Táj al-'Arús*, vii. p. 424C, both of which give the form, *al-sab' al-túál*, 'the seven longer' *súras*). (2) Next to them are *al-mi'ún*, 'the hundreds', having nearly 100 verses, or more. (3) Next are *al-mathání*, 'the duplications', having less than 100 verses. (4) Then come *al-mufaṣṣal* (a term derived from Qur'án xlii. 2), 'the divided', because it has numerous sections, or, 'the manifest' (and therefore also called *al-muḥkam*), because it has few or no abrogated verses in it. This is said to be 'the seventh seven' (SM iii.

in the two *rak'as* of the Dawn[1] and of the Circumambulation[2] of the Ka'ba, and of the Greeting—with him, during all that, continuing to stand and placing his two hands as we have described at the first of the Worship.

The Bowing and Its Accompaniments

Next he bows, and in the Bowing he observes certain things. These are that he says a *takbîr* for the Bowing; and that he raises his hands with the *takbîr* of the Bowing; and that he prolongs the *takbîr* considerably (up to the end of the bow); and that he places the palms of his hands on his knees in the Bowing, with his fingers spread out towards the *qibla*, on the length of the fore-leg; and that he straightens his knees (not doubling them); and that he stretches out his back evenly; and that his neck and head are in line with his back, as one surface, his head not being lower or higher; and that he turns away his elbows from his sides (but a woman

p. 51C), 'the last seven' (*al-Mufradât*, p. 388), and 'the seven of the finals' (SM iv. p. 480, l. 2 from bot.). Here the word 'seven' refers to the seven-fold division of the Qur'ân into portions to be recited; the word is used as a verb in that sense (*Tâj*, v. 375A). The *mufaṣṣal* is said by most to begin with *sûra* xlix, but nine others are mentioned, from xlv to xciii.

The *mufaṣṣal* itself has three sub-divisions, also variously enumerated: (*a*) *al-ṭiwâl*, 'long', xlix-lxxviii, or xlvii-lxxxv, or xlix-lxxx, etc.; (*b*) *al-awsaṭ*, 'medium', to xc, or xciii, or xcviii, etc.; (*c*) *al-qiṣâr*, 'short', to the end (*Dict. of Tech. Terms*, p. 659; SM iii. 51; cf. Lane, *Lexicon*, p. 2407 f.).

[1] This is the morning *sunna* Worship, not the prescribed one, which has long *sûras*.

[2] The *ṭawâf* is the ceremony of encircling the Ka'ba seven times. It is enjoined in the Qur'ân (xxii. 27). It is one of the four prescribed acts of the *ḥajj*, the others being the wearing of the *iḥrâm*, or special garment (see note 3, p. 51), the standing upon 'Arafa, and the running between al-Ṣafâ and al-Marwa (Al-Bâjûrî, *Commentary on Abû Shujâ'*, i. 3 p. 325 f.). In his *Wajîz* (pp. 71 ff.) al-Ghazzâlî enumerates six elements and five usages of the *ṭawâf*. The distinction is not maintained in the *Iḥyâ'* (Quarter i. Book vii. Chapter ii. SM iv. pp. 23, 345 ff.). Burton gives a description in his *Pilgrimage to al-Madinah and Meccah* (Memorial Edition, ii. pp. 165 ff.).

keeps her elbows at her sides); and that he says, 'Oh, the praise of my mighty Lord!' three times or more, up to seven (or to ten is good, if he is not an *imám*). Next he rises from the Bowing to the Standing Posture, and raises his hands and says, 'Allah hears whoever says His praise'. He remains at rest in the erect position and says, 'Our Lord, Thine is the praise to the fullness of the heavens and the earth and of whatever Thou willest of anything more!' He does not prolong this Standing Posture except in the Worship of the Praise,[1] and of the Eclipse of the Sun,[2] and of the Morning. He recites the *qunút*,[3] in the morning in the second *rak'a* with the traditional words, before the Prostration.

The Prostration

Next he goes down for the Prostration, saying the *takbír*, and then places his knees on the ground and places his forehead, nose and palms [on the ground], uncovered. He says the *takbír* while lowering himself, but he does not raise his hands in anything but the Bowing. It is fitting that his knees should be the first to be placed on the ground, and after them his hands, and after them his face; and

[1] This is the ninth of the Occasional *náfl*, Supererogatory, Worships described by al-Ghazzálí. See Introduction, p. 28; SM p. 473.

[2] The Worship of the Eclipse of the Sun is the first of the Occasional *náfl* Worships described by al-Ghazzálí. Introduction, p. 24; SM p. 427.

[3] For the numerous explanations of *qunút*, as it occurs in the Qur'án and Tradition, and as meaning 'obedience', 'submission', 'supplication', 'supplication of evil upon enemies', 'standing long', 'being silent', and 'the performance of the Worship, pilgrimage or warfare', see Lane, *Lexicon*, p. 2566 f., where also the *qunút* Supplication is given. As used by al-Ghazzálí, it is a special supplication, in traditional phrases, added while standing, after the Bowing, in the Prescribed Worship of the Morning, and in the *taráwíḥ* Worship of the latter half of Ramaḍán. Others, however, say there is no *qunút* Supplication except in the morning. Al-Bájúrí, op. cit., i. p. 128D. The SM's discussion is at iii. pp. 61 ff.

that he should place his forehead and his nose on the ground; and that he should turn his elbows away from his sides (but a woman should not do that); and that he should keep his feet apart (but a woman should not do that); and that in his Prostration he should leave an open space on the ground (but a woman should not leave a space);—'leaving a space' means raising the stomach from the thighs and separating the knees;—and that he should place his hands on the ground opposite the shoulders, without separating the fingers but rather joining them and joining the thumb to them (but, if he were not to join his thumb, it would not matter); and without extending his arms on the ground, as a dog does, since that is forbidden; and that he should say, 'O the praise of my Most High Lord!' three times (but if he increases the number, it is well, unless he is acting as *imám*).

Next he rises from the Prostration, and rests himself a moment in a straight sitting position. So he raises his head, saying the *takbír*, and sits on his left leg and sets up his right foot, and places his hands on his thighs, with the fingers extended, not taking care to close or to separate them. He says, 'O Lord, forgive me! Have mercy on me! Provide for me! Guide me! Restore me! Preserve me in health and pardon me!' He does not prolong this Sitting[1] except in the Prostration of [the Worship of] the Praise. He makes the second Prostration similarly, and straightens up after it, sitting briefly for the rest in each *rak'a* not followed by the Witnessing.

Next he stands up: to do so he places his hand on the ground but he does not put either of his legs forward while getting up. He prolongs the *takbír* so that it takes up all the time between the middle of his rising from the Sitting Position to the middle of his rising to the Standing Posture, in such a manner that the 'h' of the word 'Allah' will come while he

[1] See further on this Sitting, pp. 79, 80.

is sitting straight, and the 'k' of the 'akbar' will occur while he is leaning on his hand for the rising, and the 'r' of the 'akbar' will occur in the middle of his rising for the Standing Posture, so that the *takbîr* may fall in the middle of his transition, and only the two extremities [beginning and end of the transition] be free from it [the *takbîr*]. This is the most inclusive [application of the varying traditions].

He performs the second *rak'a*[1] just like the first, and repeats the words 'I seek refuge' as at the beginning.

Ṭhe Witnessing

Next he gives the First Witnessing in the second *rak'a*. Then he says the Blessing for the Messenger of Allah and for his family. He places his right hand on his right thigh, folding his right fingers, except the index finger, there being no harm in letting loose the thumb also. He points with only the finger of his right hand as he says, 'but Allah', not as he says, 'There is no god'. He sits during this Witnessing on his left foot, as he does between the two Prostrations. In the Last Witnessing he perfects the Ṣupplication mentioned in Tradition for the Prophet. Its *sunan*, Usages, are like the Usages of the First Witnessing, but he sits, in the Last, on his left hip,[2] because he

[1] The *rak'a* consists of the cycle of all the acts and utterances of the Worship from the Seeking Refuge to and including the Second Prostration. See the Description of the Content of the *ṣalâ* in the Introduction, pp. 6-12. The Funeral Worship has none; the *witr* may have one; all the other Worships have two or more *rak'as*. Of the five Prescribed Worships, the Morning has two, the Sunset has three, and the others have four *rak'as*. So every day has seventeen prescribed *rak'as*, except Friday which has fifteen, as the Congregational Worship takes the place of the Noon Worship on that day, and it has two *rak'as*. On a journey, the Worships of four *rak'as* have two instead, making the total for the day eleven.

[2] *Al-iftirâsh* is placing the left lower leg on the ground and sitting on it, with the right foot made to stand up, with its toes towards the *qibla*. *Al-tawarruk* is the same except that the left foot extends

is not ready for the Standing, but rather is to continue there. He places the left foot out from under him [from behind], and sets up the right one. He places the tip of the great toe in the direction of the *qibla*, if it should not be difficult for him.

Then he says, 'The peace is upon you, and the mercy of Allah', and he turns to the right so that his right cheek may be seen from behind on the right side. He turns to the left similarly and gives the Salutation a second time. He has the Intention to leave off the Worship with the Salutation. He has in mind in his Salutation those angels and Muslims who are on his right in the First Salutation, and he has a similar intent in the Second. He makes the Salutation short, and does not prolong it to any extent, as that is the *sunna*, Usage. This is the Form of the individual Worship.

He raises his voice in the *takbîrs*, but he does not raise his voice louder than for himself to hear.

He [the *imâm*] states the Intention to do the leading, in order to receive reward. But if he does not state the Intention, the Worship of the people is valid when they state the Intention of imitating him and they will receive the reward of Worship in a congregation.[1]

He says, inaudibly, the Introductory Supplication and the Seeking Refuge, as in the individual Worship, and says, audibly, the Fátiḥa and the *súra* in each of the Morning, and the first two of the Evening and Sunset *rak'as*, and also in the individual Worship. He says the *âmîn* audibly at the end of the audible[2]

out from under him towards the right and the left hip is over the ground.

The SM notes here (p. 83A) that Aḥmad bin Ḥanbal held that if the Worship had two *tashahhuds*, the *tawarruk* is the *sunna*, Usage, in the last, and if it had but one, then the *iftirâsh* is the *sunna*. Abû Ḥanífa declared for the *iftirâsh* in them both and Málik said that both sittings should have the *tawarruk*.

[1] See Tradition No. 33, and the chapter on the 'Excellence of the Congregational Worship', pp. 144-46.

[2] The audible Worships are those of the morning, sunset and evening.

Worship, and so does the follower. The follower also says '*ámín*' simultaneously with the *imám's ámín* not after him.

The *imám* remains silent after the Fátiḥa in order that his breath may return to him. The follower recites the Fátiḥa in the audible Worship during this silence, so that he may be enabled to listen when the *imám* recites. The follower does not recite the *súra* in the audible [Worship], except when he does not hear the voice of the *imám*.

The *imám* says, 'Allah hears whoever declares His praise', as he raises his head from the Bowing, and so does the follower. The *imám* does not make more than three repetitions of the Praises of the Bowing and the Prostration, and adds nothing more in the First Witnessing after his saying, 'O Lord, have mercy on Muḥammad and on the family of Muḥammad'

He confines himself in the last two *rak'as* to the Fátiḥa, and is not lengthy for the people. He does not make his Supplication in the Last Witnessing exceed the extent of the Witnessing itself and the Supplication for the Messenger of Allah.

He has in mind, in the Salutation, salutation upon the people and the angels. The people have in mind, in their Salutation, a reply to him.

The *imám* remains still a while, until the people finish the Salutation, and he turns his face towards the people. It is preferable that he remain still, if there are women behind the men, so that the women may depart before him. Not one of the people stands up until the *imám* stands up and departs whither he will, to the right or left. I prefer the right.

The *imám* does not particularize himself in the Supplication in the *qunút* of the Morning Worship, but says, 'O Allah, guide us!' He says it audibly, and the people say, '*Ámín*', raising their hands opposite their chests. He wipes his face at the close of the Supplications, according to a tradition related about it. Otherwise, an analogy would indicate that the hand should not be raised, as at the end of the Witnessing.

Prohibited Things

The Messenger of Allah has forbidden: (*a*) the raising of the foot in the Worship; (*b*) the fettering (these we have already mentioned);[1] (*c*) sitting on the shanks; (*d*) enveloping; (*e*) turning up; (*f*) placing the hands on the sides; (*g*) placing the hands akimbo; (*h*) merging; (*i*) the Worship of one suffering with retention; (*j*) of the costive; (*k*) of the pinched; (*l*) of the hungry; (*m*) of the angry; and (*n*) of the muffler, which means one who covers his face.

(*c*) Sitting, among lexicographers, means sitting on the shanks, lifting the knees and placing the hands on the ground like a dog. Among traditionists it is sitting on the shanks, kneeling, with no part of him on the ground but the tips of the toes and the knees.

(*d*) Enveloping. The belief of the traditionists about it is that it means that he wraps himself in his garment and puts his hands inside and so bows and prostrates. This was the practice of the Jews in their Worship, and the Muslims were forbidden to imitate them. The shirt is also meant, for it is not fitting that he should bow and prostrate with his hands in the body of his tunic. But it is said to mean placing the middle of the cloak on the head and letting its two sides fall on his right and left, without placing them on his shoulders. The first is nearer right.

(*e*) Turning up. This is raising his garment before him or behind him when he wishes to prostrate. Sometimes *kaff*, 'turning up', is used of the hair of the head, so let no one perform the Worship with his hair twisted. This prohibition applies to men.

(114) In Tradition we read, 'I was commanded to prostrate on seven members, and not to twist up the hair or the garment'.

[1] They are on pp. 63, 64.

(115) Aḥmad bin Ḥanbal[1] disliked to put on the *izár*, 'inner cloth', over the shirt in the Worship, considering it was a case of turning up.

(*f*) *Al-ikhtiṣár* is the placing of the hands on the sides.

(*g*) *Al-ṣalb*[2] is placing the hands on the sides during the Standing Posture and leaving a space between the upper arms and the sides [i.e. standing akimbo].

(*h*) Merging is of five kinds, two applying to the *imám*, not to merge his Recital with the Opening *takbír*, nor his Bowing with his Recital; two applying to the follower, not to merge his Opening *takbír* with the *imám's takbír*, nor his Salutation with the latter's Salutation; one applying to both of them, not to merge the prescribed Salutation with the Second Salutation, but to separate them.

(*i*) Retention applies to urination.

(*j*) The costive means the constipated.

(*k*) A pinched person is one with a tight boot. All of these things hinder humbleness. The same applies to the hungry and the perplexed.

(*l*) The prohibition of [the Worship of] the
(116) hungry is inferred from the words of Muḥammad, 'Whenever your supper is ready and the Worship has begun, have supper first, unless time presses or you are quiet of heart', i.e. can wait until the Worship is finished.

(117) (*m*) In Tradition we read, 'Let not any one of you enter upon the Worship while he is frowning, and let not anyone of you enter upon the Worship while he is angry'.

(118) Al-Ḥasan said, 'Every Worship in which the

[1] Aḥmad bin Muḥammad bin Ḥanbal, celebrated theologian, for whom one of the four schools of canon law is named (d. 241). *Ency. of Islam*, i. p. 188; SM i. p. 214 f.

[2] *Ṣalb* is forbidden because it resembles the position of a man when he is crucified; Lane, *Lexicon*, p. 1711C, quoting *Táj al-'Arús*, i. p. 338D. The *Fá'iq*, ii. p. 18, also says, 'That resembled the action of the crucified in his extending his hand upon the timber'.

heart is not present is swifter to punishment [than to reward[1]]'.

(119) In Tradition we read, 'Seven things in the Worship are due to Satan: nose-bleed, drowsiness, evil suggestions,[2] yawning, scratching, turning round, and playing with anything'. Some add, 'Unmindfulness and uncertainty'.

(120) One of the Fathers said, 'Four things in the Worship are coarse: turning round, wiping the face, clearing away pebbles, and worshipping in the path of one who will pass in front of you'.[3]

(*n*) It is also prohibited to interlace the fingers, or to crack the fingers, or to cover the face, or to place
(121) one palm against the other and push them between the thighs during the Bowing. Some of the Companions said, 'We used to do that and were forbidden it'. It is also disliked to blow on the earth
(122) during the Prostration, to clean it, and to level the pebbles with the hand, for these are actions that may be dispensed with. He does not raise one of his feet and put it on his thigh, and does not lean in the

[1] This tradition is repeated on p. 90 (SM 115) and there the SM adds this additional phrase from the *Qút al-Qulúb* of Abú Ṭálib al-Makkí. See note 2, p. 90.

[2] The special influences that effect the heart are *al-khawáṭir* fancies and memories, new or remembered thoughts.

The *khawáṭir* stir up desire; desire stirs up determination; intention stirs up the members.

The *khawáṭir* divide into two classes: (1) Those that call to evil, i.e. what is ultimately harmful; these *khawáṭir* are the distractions and evil suggestions (noun of action, *waswasa*). (2) Those that call to good. This is called *ilhám*, 'revelation'.

Both *waswasa* and *ilhám* have *asbáb*, 'causes': The cause of the former, as al-Ghazzálí says here also, is named *Shaiṭán*, 'Satan'. The cause of the *ilhám* is named *malak*, 'angel messenger'.

The kindness by which the heart is disposed to receive the *ilhám* is called *tawfíq*, 'help', and that through which it is disposed to receive the *waswás* of Sátan is called *ighwá'*, 'seduction', (cf. Qur'án vii. 15), and also *khidhlan*, 'desertion', i.e. Allah's failing to preserve a man from an evil action (cf. Qur'án iii. 154). (The above is taken from SM vii. pp. 264 ff.; on *ilhám*, see the article by Macdonald, *Ency. of Islam*, ii. p. 467 f.).

[3] See further on this, Tradition No. 262.

Standing Posture against a wall, for, if he leans so that he would fall if that wall were drawn away, the most obvious result would be the invalidating of his Worship, and Allah knows better!

The Distinction Between the Prescribed Elements and the Usage Portions

All that we have mentioned applies equally to the *farḍ*, Prescribed Elements, the *sunna*, Usage Portions, the *ádáb*, Proprieties, and the *hai'át*, Forms,[1] of all the things that it is fitting for the devotee[2] of the way of the next abode to observe.

The Prescribed Elements are twelve in number: (1) The statement of the Intention; (2) the *takbír*; (3) the Standing Posture; (4) the Fátiḥa; (5) bending down in the Bowing until the palms reach the knees, with coming to rest in it; (6) Straightening from this position, standing; (7) the Prostration, with coming to rest in it, but the placing of the hands [on the ground[3]] is not obligatory; (8) Straightening from this, sitting; (9) the Sitting for the Last Witnessing; (10) the Last Witnessing; (11) the Blessing upon the Prophet; (12) the First Salutation.

The statement of the Intention to withdraw from the Worship is not obligatory. Whatever is additional to this is not obligatory, but rather is *sunna*, Usage, and *hai'át*, Forms, connected with the actions in them, i.e. the *sunna* and the *farḍ*.

The Usages connected with the actions are four [in number]: (1) Raising the Hands in the Opening *takbír*, and (2) when bending for the Bowing, and (3) when rising for the Standing Posture, and (4) the Sitting for the First Witnessing.

[1] For these terms see the Introduction, pp. 13-15. The analytical chart will help to make this chapter clear.

[2] The *muríd*, 'devotee', is one who has stood the test and entered among those who are separated to Allah. *Ta'ríf al-Aḥyá' bi Faḍá'il al-Iḥyá'*, on the margin of the 1334 Cairo edition of the *Iḥyá'*, i. p. 67.

[3] This is added in the SM.

What we have mentioned about the manner of spreading the fingers and the limit of raising them, is part of the Forms following this Usage. The sitting on one foot and the laying down of the foot are Forms connected with the Sitting. The lowering of the head and the refraining from turning are Forms connected with the Standing Posture. The beautifying of the external manner of the Standing Posture and the Sitting for Rest,[1] we do not reckon among the fundamental Usages connected with the actions, as they are like the beautifying of the Form of the rising from the Prostration to the Standing Posture. Since they are not purposed in themselves they were not singled out for mention.

The Usages connected with the Invocations are: (1) the Introductory Supplication; (2) the Seeking Refuge;[2] (3) saying '*āmīn*',[3] for it is indeed a Confirmed Usage; (4) the Recital of the *sūra*;[3] (5) the *takbīrs* of the transitions;[4] (6) the Invocation in the Bowing and (7) in the Prostration; (8) the Straightening from them; (9) the First Witnessing, and (10) the Blessing in it upon the Prophet; (11) the Supplication at the end of the Last Witnessing, and (12) the Second Salutation.

These, although we have gathered them all together under the name of *sunna*, Usage, yet have degrees of gradation, since four of them are made up for by the Oversight Prostration.[5] Of the actions there is one such: it is the First Sitting for the First Witnessing, for it produces an effect, in the carrying-out of the order of the Worship, in the eyes of beholders to the extent that there is known by it

[1] After the Second Prostration in each *rak'a*, adds the SM.

[2] Before the Recital in each *rak'a* (SM).

[3] After the *Fātiḥa* (SM).

[4] The word adopted to translate *intiqālāt* is 'transitions', to indicate the changes of position between the Standing, Bowing, Prostration and Sitting postures.

[5] For the *sajdat al-sahū*, 'Oversight Prostration', see the Introduction, p. 29.

whether it is a four-fold Worship or not. as opposed to the raising of the hands, for it [the raising of the hands] does not produce an effect in changing the
(123) order. So it is termed a *ba'ḍ*, Part, of the Worship, and it is said, 'The Parts are made good by the Oversight Prostration'.

As for the Invocations, only three of them require the Oversight Prostration: (1) the *qunût*; (2) the First Witnessing, and (3) the Blessing upon the Prophet in it, whereas it is just the contrary with the *takbîrs* of the transitions and the Invocations in the Bowing and the Prostration and the Straightening from them, because the Bowing and the Prostration, in their external manner, are different from ordinary habit, so the sense of an act of a service of worship is conveyed by them even though there should be omission of the saying of the Invocations and the *takbîrs* of the transitions. The absence of these Invocations does not change the external manner of a service of Worship.

The Sitting for the First Witnessing is a customary action, and was added only for the sake of the Witnessing, so the omitting of it produces a distinct effect.

As for the Opening Supplication and the *sûra*, omitting them does not produce an effect, although the Standing Posture has become occupied by the Fátiḥa and is distinguished from ordinary habit by it.

Likewise the Supplication in the Last Witnessing and in the *qunût* is farthest from what is made good by the Oversight Prostration. But the prolongation of the Straightening in the Morning Worship was enjoined on [the *qunût's*] account, so it is like the prolongation of the Sitting for Rest, since that Sitting became, by prolongation, along with the Witnessing, the Sitting for the First Witnessing. So this remains a Standing Posture,[1] prolonged, customary, in which

[1] The SM adds here an important note (p. 100C): 'The Standing Posture, or, whatever has its meaning. And we say that only because the Standing Posture itself is not an Element,

there is no obligatory Invocation. And in this description of this Standing Posture as 'prolonged', there is a guarding against any other Worship but the Morning, and in its description as 'free from any obligatory invocation', there is a guarding against the fundamental character of the Standing Posture in the Worship.

If you say that the distinction between the *sunna*, Usage, and the *farḍ*, Prescribed Element, is intelligible, since validity departs with the departure of the Prescribed and not of the Usages, and punishment is faced on account of them, but not on account of the Usages, but, as for the distinction[1] between one *sunna*, Usage, and another, seeing that all are commanded as being liked, and there is no punishment for omitting all of them, and merit pertains to all of them, what is the meaning of that latter distinction?—then know that their participation in reward and punishment and desirability does not do away with their gradation. Let us reveal that to you by a similitude. This is that a man is not an existent, perfect man except by means of an inner reality, *ma'na*, together with external members. The inner reality is the life and the spirit. The external are his material members. Further, some

rukn, absolutely, in the Worship, in distinction from the *takbîr* and the recital, since Sitting in the Supererogatory Worship is allowable, even though one is able to stand. So then, the Element is "the Standing Posture or whatever takes its place". Were one unable to stand in the Prescribed, *farḍ*, Worship, he might sit, and if he is unable to sit, he may perform the Worship on his side, and if he is unable to do that, then lying on his back, with the soles of his feet toward the *qibla*, and he must be placed over against a pillow so that his face will be towards the *qibla*, for, if he is without ability he has the acts of the Worship pass over his heart, and there will be no *i'âda* 'repetition', of it due from him, and the Worship is not lost to him, while his mind remains fixed that the task is far removed (from his ability).'

[1] The SM says, 'The Shâfi'ites need to differentiate the *sunan*, Usages, as *ab'aḍ*, Parts, and *hai'ât*, Forms, because they do not differentiate between the *farḍ* and *wâjib*. There is a class requiring the Oversight Prostration, whether they are called *wâjib* or *ab'aḍ*.'

of these members are those through whose non-existence the man becomes non-existent, such as the heart, liver and brain, and every other member with the departure of which life departs. Life does not depart on account of some other members, but the purposes of life depart, such as the eye, the hand, the leg, and the tongue. Some of them do not entail departure of life or of the purposes of life, but on their account beauty departs, such as the eyebrows, the beard, the eyelashes and a good complexion. Some of them do not entail the departure of the elements of beauty but its perfection, such as the arching of the eyebrows, the blackness of the hair of the beard and the eyelashes, the symmetry of the shape of the members and the commingling of red and white in the complexion. These are degrees of gradation.

So, similarly, worship is a form that the law has made and our devotion is given reality by acquiring it. Its spirit and inner life are humbleness, intention, presence of the heart and singleness of devotion,[1] as shall appear, seeing we are now considering the external parts. So the Bowing, Prostration, Standing Posture and the rest of the Elements act like the heart, head and liver, since the existence of the Worship departs with their departure.

The *sunan*, Usages, we have mentioned, such as the Raising of the hands, the Opening Supplication and the First Witnessing, act like the hands, eyes and legs. The validity of the Worship does not depart with their departure, as life does not depart with the departure of these members, but the person becomes,

[1] *Al-ikhlāṣ*, 'singleness of devotion', with the *sālik*, 'wayfarer', is the exclusion of *al-khalq*, 'the world', from his dealing with Allah, i.e. he does not act at all except for Allah. It is that all his movements, works and words are for Allah. *Dict. of Tech. Terms*, p. 431. Its opposite is *shirk*, 'associating' something with Allah. This forms with the Intention and Truthfulness the subject of Book vii of the Fourth Quarter of the *Iḥyā'*. SM x. pp. 42 ff.; German translation by Hans Bauer, *Über Intention*, p. 45; *Ency. of Islam*, ii. p. 458.

on account of their departure, deformed in shape, blamed[1] and undesirable. Just so, whoever contents himself with the least of what suffices of the Worship is like one who gives to some king a slave that is alive but with his extremities cut off.

The Forms, being those that come after the Usages, act like the causes of beauty, such as the eyebrows, beard, eyelashes and a good complexion.

As for the duties of the Invocations in those Usages, they are the perfectors of beauty, such as the arching of the eyebrows, the roundness of the beard, and so on.

The Worship, for you, is an offering and a valuable present with which you draw near to the presence of the King of kings, such as a young slave-girl, that one seeking proximity to a sultan,[2] presents to him. This present is offered to Allah, and then is returned to you on the greatest Presentation Day. So yours is the choice either to make its form beautiful or to make it ugly. If you do well it is for yourself. If you do wrong you wrong yourself.

It is not fitting that your pleasure, O lawyer,[3] in the practice of canon law, should be that 'Usage is differentiated from Prescribed Element', and then none of the qualities of the Usages are fixed in your understanding but this, that 'abandoning them is allowable and there is no punishment in that', and then you abandon them. For that resembles the saying of the physician, 'Putting out the eye does not nullify the existence of a man, but it excludes him [from being a factor] in the realization of the hope of one seeking to make himself acceptable to the sultan, whenever he brings the one-eyed man as a gift'.

Similarly, it is fitting that you should understand

[1] Possibly the reference here, is to the maiming of the criminal by the cutting off of the hand, so that his maimed condition is a blameworthy matter.

[2] The other texts have the plural.

[3] This is added by the SM in his commentary.

the grades of the Usages, Forms and Proprieties, for every Worship whose Bowings and Prostrations a man does not complete will be the first adversary
(30) against its owner, saying, 'May Allah neglect you as you have neglected me!' So, study the traditions[1] which we have set forth on perfecting the elements of the Worship, in order that their important position may be apparent to you.

[1] They are Traditions Nos. 25-32, pp. 47, 48.

CHAPTER III

INWARD STIPULATIONS FOR THE ACTS OF THE HEART

Let us mention, in this chapter, the close connection of the Worship with humbleness[1] and the presence of the heart.[2] Next let us mention the inner realities, their bounds, causes and treatment. Next let us mention in detail what it is fitting should be present in the heart in every one of the elements of the Worship, that the Worship may be beneficial as provision for the next abode.

Elucidation of the Stipulation[3] for Humbleness and the Presence of the Heart

Know that there are many proofs for this requirement. Among them is the saying of Allah, 'Institute

[1] The SM remarks here, 'Most of the learned, e.g. al-Ráfi'í and al-Nawawí, make *khushú'* a *sunna*, Usage, part of the Worship, while Abú Ṭálib al-Makkí and others make it a *sharṭ*, Stipulation, in the Worship; the author, i.e. al-Ghazzálí, agreeing with them. Some of the Fathers said it was quietness in the Worship, while al-Baghawí said it is submissiveness. Others say it is guidance to the truth, and others say it is the fear that persists in the heart. Abú al-Baqá' said it is humility and demeaning oneself and humbleness toward Allah in the heart and the members. There is difference of opinion as to whether it is one of the works of the heart, or a work of the members, as quietness, or an expression for both. Al-Rází preferred the third alternative.'

[2] The 'heart' is not the seat of the emotions with al-Ghazzálí, but rather the seat of his experiential apprehension of the world. It is a transcendant spiritual refinement or subtlety. Its connection with the physical heart has been the despair of the minds of men. For al-Ghazzálí's use of the word see SM i. p. 331; vii. pp. 201 ff.; it is fully discussed in Macdonald, *Religious Attitude*, chap. viii, on 'The Nature, Working and Use of the Heart'.

[3] The *sharṭ*, 'stipulation', of a thing is something upon which the soundness of the thing depends, but which is not a *juz'*, 'part', of the thing. By this definition the *rukn*, 'essential element', is excluded from the term *sharṭ*, for it is a *juz'*, 'part', of the Worship (Al-Bájúrí, op. cit., i. p. 142B).

the Worship for remembrance of me' (Qur'án xvii. 80). The evident meaning of a command is its obligation. Now, unmindfulness is the opposite of remembering, and so, how can one who is unmindful in all his Worship, be an institutor of the Worship for remembrance of Him?

Likewise, the saying of Allah, 'And do not be of the unmindful!' (Qur'án vii. 204), is a prohibition, and the evident meaning of it is to make unlawful.

The saying of Allah, 'So that you may know what you are saying' (Qur'án iv. 46), is an assignment of a motive for the prohibition of inebriety, and it is also of general application to the unmindful, anxiously engrossed in evil suggestions and thoughts of this life.

(68) The saying of Muḥammad, 'The Worship is verily humbling and abasing oneself', is restrictive on account of the definite article. The word 'verily' is for confirmation and emphasis. The canon lawyers have understood the saying of Muḥammad, 'The right of pre-emption[1] verily[2] applies to what has
(124) not been divided', as meaning restriction, affirmation and negation.

(72) The saying of Muḥammad, 'Whosoever Worship does not prohibit him from the excessive and the disapproved has no increase from Allah except of distance', applies, seeing that the Worship of the unmindful does not prohibit from the excessive and the disapproved.

(125) Muḥammad said, 'How many standing up will have as their portion from their Worship only

[1] The right of pre-emption is obtaining possession of neighbouring property by purchase through a compelled sale. Lane, *Lexicon*, p. 1572 (voce *shuf'a*), gives several instances of its application.

[2] The discussion here is on the meaning of the word *innamá*, which usually means 'only', implying negation. Al-Ghazzálí uses it in his proof-tradition in the meaning of 'verily', and instances another tradition in which the word can have only that meaning. Lane, *Lexicon*, p. 110B, gives the tradition usually quoted as evidence of the word's meaning 'verily'.

fatigue and misfortune!' and he meant by that none other than the unmindful.

(126) He said, 'A creature gets from his Worship only what he comprehends of it'. The verification of this is in the fact that the worshipper is in communion
(73) with his Lord, as the tradition about it has declared, and speech with inattention is not communion at all. The demonstration of that is in the fact that the quarter-tithe, if a man is unmindful of it, for instance, is still, in itself, opposed to his natural craving and oppressive to the lower self. Likewise fasting overcomes the physical powers, breaking the dominion of the fleshly inclination, which is an instrument of Satan's, the enemy of Allah. So it is not strange that that which is intended should be secured from them [the quarter-tithe and fasting], in spite of unmindfulness. Likewise the activities of the Pilgrimage are a great hardship, and entail from the exertion something from which suffering results, whether the heart is present with its activities or not.

Now, the Worship comprises only Invocation and Recital, Bowing and Prostration, Standing and Sitting. The Invocation is conversation and communion with Allah. Then, either the object of it is its being an address and a conversation, or the object of it is the letters and the sounds for the sake of testing the tongue by the exercise, just as the stomach is tested by restraint in the fast, and as the body is tested by the hardships of the pilgrimage, and the heart is tested by the hardship of giving out the quarter-tithe and parting with property that is exceedingly dear. There is no doubt that this character of the Worship is invalid, for the moving of the tongue in nonsense is easy for the unmindful! For there is no testing in it in so far as it is an exercise. The object is not utterance by means of the letters because it is simply utterance, but because it is beneficial utterance, and it becomes beneficial utterance only whenever it expresses what is in the mind, and it becomes such an expression only by the presence of the heart. Thus, what request is there in the saying, 'Guide us into the Straight Road!' (Qur'án i. 5), when the heart is unmindful and when one does not intend that it should be an intercession and a supplication? For what hardship is there in moving the tongue with it, along with unmindfulness, especially after it has become customary?

This is the rule for the Invocations. Nay more, I say, were a man to take an oath, saying, 'I will indeed thank such a one, and praise him, and ask him for some need', and then have the expressions indicating these meanings pass over his tongue in his sleep, he would not have fulfilled his oath. Were they to pass over his tongue in the darkness, with that man present, but without the first knowing of his presence or seeing him, he would not have fulfilled his oath, since his speech would not be an address, and talking with him, as long as he [the second] was not present in his [the first's] heart. Even were these words to pass over his tongue while he is present, with himself, though it is daylight, nevertheless unmindful of him because he is submerged in some anxious thought or other, having no purpose of presenting the address to him as he spoke, he would not have fulfilled his oath.

Now there is no doubt that the object of the Recital and the Invocations is praise and lauding, intercession and supplication, and the One addressed is Allah, even though the heart, by the veil of unmindfulness, is hidden from Him. He does not see Allah or observe Him, so is unmindful of the One addressed, but his tongue moves in accordance with habit. How far this is from the object of the Worship, which was enjoined in order to give lustre to the heart, and to renew the remembrance of Allah, and in order that the bond of faith in Him may be established!

This is the rule of the Recital and the Invocation. In brief, there is no way to deny this property [of mindfulness in the Worship] to the speech part of it, or to differentiate it from the act.

As for the Bowing and Prostration, their object is to magnify, absolutely. If it were possible for one to be a magnifier of Allah by his action, while he is unmindful of Him, then it would be possible for him to be a magnifier of an idol placed in front of him, while he is unmindful of it, or for him to be a magnifier of a wall in front of him, while he is unmindful of it.

Whenever the act ceases to be magnifying, nothing remains but the movement of the back and head. There is no hardship in that, the purpose of which could be testing, and which would make it 'the support
(2) of the religion', so that it decides between unbelief and Islam, and takes precedence over the pilgrimage and other religious services, and is something on whose account killing[1] is obligatory when it is abandoned intentionally. I do not think that all this importance belongs to the Worship because of its external acts, unless there is connected with them the object of communion, for that takes precedence over fasting, quarter-tithes, pilgrimage and anything else, nay, even sacrifices and offerings, which are a warring against the flesh because they decrease wealth. Allah said, 'Assuredly their flesh and their blood will not reach Allah, but wary fear on your part reaches Him' (Qur'án xxii. 38), that is, the quality that rules over the heart to the extent that it induces the heart to obey the commands, is what is desired. For of what sort is a command to perform the Worship if there is no need to perform its component actions. So then, as regards the inner reality of the Worship, this is what points to the requirement of the presence of the heart.

Were you to say, 'If you pronounce the Worship to be invalid, seeing that you make the presence of the heart a stipulation for its validity, then you go against the agreement of the canon lawyers, since they have stipulated for the presence of the heart

[1] On this point see Introduction, p. 19.

only at the *takbír*', then know that I have already said in the Book of Knowledge (Book I of the *Iḥyá'*), that canon lawyers do not concern themselves with what is within, and are not troubled about hearts or the way of the next abode. Rather, they build up the external side of the laws of the religion upon the external side of the acts of the members, since the external side of the acts are a sufficient guard against being killed or chastised by the sultan.

As to whether the external side of these acts benefits in the next abode, this is not within the bounds of canon law, because it is not possible to claim agreement on this point.

(127) It has been handed down from Bishr bin al-Ḥárith,[1] in what Abú Ṭálib[2] related from him by oral tradition from Sufyán al-Thawrí,[3] that he said, 'The Worship of anyone who is not humble, is invalid'.

(118) It is related from al-Ḥasan that he said, 'Every Worship in which the heart is not present is swifter to punishment [than to reward]'.

(128) From Ma'ádh bin Jabal[4] it is related, 'Whoever acquaints himself with the one who is on his right or his left, purposely, while he is at Worship, has no Worship'.

(129) There is related also this tradition with a complete *isnád*,[5] or chain of authorities, 'Truly, a creature

[1] Abú Naṣr Bishr al-Ḥáfí bin al-Ḥárith al-Marwazí (d. 226-27), De Slane, op. cit., i. p. 257; *Ency. of Islam*, i. p. 732.

[2] Abú Ṭálib Muḥammad bin 'Alí b. 'Aṭiya al-Ḥárithí al-Wá'iẓ al-Makkí (d. 386), author of the *Qút al-Qulúb*, Ṣúfí reference book, upon which al-Ghazzálí based the *Iḥyá'* (SM i. p. 134; Nicholson, *Literary History of the Arabs*, p. 338; Brockelmann, op. cit., i. p. 200).

[3] Abú 'Abdalláh Sufyán bin Sa'íd al-Thawrí (d. 161). De Slane, op. cit., i. p. 576.

[4] Ma'ádh bin Jabal, al-Khazrají, Helper, foremost *imám* in the knowledge of allowed and prohibited things (d. 17) (SM i. p. 107; *Ibn Hajar's Biographical Dictionary*, iii. p. 872; Schwally, *Ibn Saad, Biographien*, b. ii. th. ii. p. 107).

[5] The SM adds, 'He means that it is traced back to the Prophet'. On the varieties of the *musnad*, 'supported', traditions, see Juynboll's article in the *Ency. of Islam*, ii. p. 191B.

may offer Worship of which not a sixth or a tenth is
(126) written down for his credit', and 'There is written down for a creature's credit only what he comprehends of his Worship'. This, were it related from any one else, would have been made a tenet, so why is it not held to?

(130) 'Abd al-Wáḥid bin Zaid[1] said, 'The learned agree that there is nothing of the Worship reckoned to a creature except what he comprehends'. So he made it a matter of Agreement.[2] What is related along these lines from the scrupulous canon lawyers and from the learned of the next world is more than can be reckoned.

The right thing is to return to the legal proofs, seeing that the Traditions and the Records[3] are clear as to this Stipulation, with this proviso, that the standing of a *fatwá*, 'legal opinion', in regard to an external duty is restricted by the measure of the deficiency of mankind. For it is not possible to place Stipulations upon men for the presence of the heart in the entire Worship, for only the fewest of mankind are capable of doing that. Since the Stipulation of total comprehension is, of necessity, not possible, it is unavoidable for him that he should require as little of it as the name would apply to, were it only of the duration of a glance, the most preferable moment for it [the presence] being the moment of the *takbír*.

So we limited ourselves to laying down that as a duty, hoping, along with that, that the state of the unmindful in all his Worship may not be like the state of one abandoning it altogether, for he, on the whole, is more eager to perform the Worship

[1] 'Abdalwâḥid bin Zaid al-Baṣrî (Abû 'Ubaida) (d. 128), *Fihrist*, p. 183; *Ibn Ṭagri Bardii*, i. p. 342.

[2] *Al-ijmá'* is the agreement of the *mujtahids*, 'those who by reason of religious learning have the right to pronounce an opinion, of the people of Muḥammad in any age upon any religious matter'. *Ta'rífát*, p. 9; *Ency. of Islam*, ii. p. 448.

[3] The SM reads here 'verses' but he mentions the other reading in his comment.

outwardly, and has his heart present more than the other for a moment. And why should it not be so, seeing that the Worship of one who worships while ceremonially unclean, through forgetfulness, is invalid with Allah, nevertheless he gets a certain amount of reward, according to his act and the measure of his deficiency and his excuse.

But, in spite of this hope, we[1] fear that his state may be worse than the state of one abandoning it altogether; and why not, since the one who presents service, but treats the Divine Majesty with contempt, and speaks the speech of the unmindful and the disdainful, is in a worse state than the one who turns away from the service? Whenever the causes of fear and hope oppose each other, and the matter becomes dangerous in itself, then you must make your choice afterwards between taking it seriously and taking it lightly.

For all that, it is not desired to oppose the canon lawyers in their rulings concerning the validity of the Worship along with unmindfulness, for that is the necessary character of the *fatwá*, 'judicial opinion', as has been noted. Whoever knows the inner reality of the Worship knows that unmindfulness contradicts it. But we have mentioned in the chapter on 'The Difference between Superficial and Mystic Knowledge',[2] in the 'Book of the Foundations of the Articles of the Faith',[3] that the deficiency of mankind

[1] The other texts have 'he'.

[2] There are three knowledges: *záhir*, 'surface, superficial', for the populace; *bátin*, 'inner, mystic', reserved for those who are worthy, and private, which is between Allah and himself and which he discloses to no one. The mysteries which those brought near apprehend, but which they may not disclose, have five classes: (1) abstruse in themselves, e.g. *rúḥ*, spirit; (2) understandable, but not expedient, as the Decree; (3) what is alluded to metaphorically, as in Traditions Nos. 29 and 339; (4) the inner experience and realization of knowledge, apart from its outward shell, as when he sees a man near after he has been distant; (5) the actual state expressed by words when these are not taken literally (SM ii. pp. 67 ff.).

[3] This is Book ii, of the First Quarter of the *Iḥyá'* (SM ii. pp. 17-287).

is one of the causes hindering the clear exposition of all that may be revealed of the mysteries of the law. So let us content ourselves with this measure of discussion, for in it is sufficient for the devotee seeking the way of the next abode, but the factious disputer we do not intend to argue with now.

The result of the discussion is that the presence of the heart is the spirit of the Worship, and that the least of that by which the last gasp of the spirit remains is the presence at the *takbîr*, and less than it is ruin. According to the measure of the increase over it, the spirit extends into the other parts of the Worship. How many living there are, without movement, nearly dead! For the Worship of the unmindful in all except the *takbîr* is like one alive, but without movement. We ask Allah for His excellent help!

Exposition of the Inner Realities by which the Life of the Worship is Distinguished[1]

Know that for these inner realities there are many modes of expression, but six phrases will comprehend them. These are: (*a*) the presence of the heart; (*b*) apprehension; (*c*) magnifying; (*d*) awe; (*e*) hope, and (*f*) shamefacedness. So let us give detailed statements of them; next of their causes, and then of the treatment for acquiring them.

Now for the details; (*a*) First, the presence of the heart. By this we mean that the heart is free from everything but what the worshipper is engaged in and what he utters, so that the work[2] may be associated with both the acts and the words, and that the thought may not be wandering to other things. Whenever the thought turns away from what it is not engaged in, and there is in one's heart remembrance of what he is about, and he is not unmindful of anything, the presence of the heart results.

[1] The other texts have 'perfected'.
[2] The other texts have 'the knowledge'.

(*b*) But the apprehension of the signficance of the words is a matter that comes after the presence of the heart. For it may be that the heart is present with the utterance, but not present with the significance of the utterance. So the heart's comprehension of the significance of the utterance is what we meant by 'apprehension'. This is a place where men differ, since men do not share in the apprehension of the significations of the Recital and Praisings. How many subtle significations the worshipper understands during the Worship which did not occur to his heart before! From this point of view the Worship becomes a 'restrainer from the excessive and the disapproved',[1] for it gives understanding of matters, and these matters forbid the excessive and the disapproved inevitably.

(*c*) The magnifying is a matter which comes after the presence of the heart and the understanding, since a man addresses to his slave words in which his heart is present and of which he apprehends the meaning, but he does not magnify him. So magnifying is additional to them.

(*d*) The awe is something additional to magnifying; rather, it is an expression for fear whose source is magnifying, for whoever does not fear is not called full of awe, seeing that fear of the scorpion, and of the evil nature of mankind, and of similar low causes of fear, is not called awe, but, fear of a magnified sultan is called awe, for awe is fear whose source is majesty.

(*e*) As for hope, there is no doubt that it is additional. How many there are who magnify some king, are in awe of him, and fear his might, but they do not hope to be rewarded by him! So it is fitting that the creature should be hopeful, on account of his Worship, of the reward of Allah, as he is fearful, on account of his deficiency, of the punishment of Allah.

[1] This is an allusion to Qur'ān xxix. 44.

(*f*) Shamefacedness is additional to the whole, for its basis is the feeling of deficiency and the supposition of guilt. Exaltation, magnifying, fear and hope may be conceived of, without shame, where there is no supposition of deficiency and committing of sin.

Now for the causes of these six inner realities. Know that the cause of the presence of the heart is your solicitude about it, for your heart follows your solicitude. For your heart is present only in what you are solicitous about. Whenever a matter is one of solicitude to you, your heart is there present, willingly or unwillingly, for it is constituted that way, and is under compulsion in it. The heart, whenever it is not present in the Worship, is not without employment, but rather is roaming about in whatever matters of this life one's solicitude is turned to. So there is no expedient and no treatment for the presence of the heart except through turning one's solicitude to the Worship, for solicitude is not directed to the Worship, as long as it is not clear that the object desired depends on the Worship. That includes faith and assurance that the next abode is better and more lasting, and that the Worship is a means of reaching it. So, whenever this faith is joined to real knowledge of the insignificance of this life and its chief concerns, there results from their association the presence of the heart in the Worship. By means similar to this your heart is present whenever you come before some great people who are not able to harm or benefit you. So, whenever it happens that it is not present during communion with the King of kings, in whose hand are the Seen and the Unseen Worlds,[1] and benefit and bane, do not suppose that there is any other reason than

[1] The *'alam al-malakût* is the World of the Unseen, applying especially to the spirits of the selves (SM i. 63D). In *Al-Insân al-Kâmil* every existing thing is divided among three classes, the outward class, which is termed *al-mulk*, the inner class, which is called *al-malakût*, and the third class, which is exclusive of the first two, and it is *al-jabarût al-ilâhî*. *Dict. of Tech. Terms*, p. 1339. See also SM i. p. 173 ; Macdonald, *Religious Attitude*, p. 243.

weakness of faith. So be zealous now to strengthen faith. The way to it will be gone into elsewhere.[1]

As for the apprehension, the cause of it, after the presence of the heart, is persevering in thinking and turning the mind to the comprehension of the significance [of the purpose[2]]. The treatment for it is whatever is a treatment for the presence of the heart, together with turning towards thinking and exerting oneself in repelling idle fancies. The treatment for repelling engrossing fancies is to cut off the materials out of which they spring. I mean, abstaining from those causes to which one's thoughts are attracted. As long as those materials are not cut off, idle fancies will not turn away from them. For, whoever loves a thing increases his remembrance of it, and remembrance of what is beloved rushes upon the heart inevitably, and therefore you see that whoever loves another than Allah does not have a single act of Worship free from idle fancies.

The magnifying is a state of the heart born of two cognitions, one of which is the knowledge of the majesty and greatness of Allah. This is one of the fundamentals of the faith, for whoever does not believe in His greatness has a self which does not submit to magnifying Him. The second is the knowledge of the insignificance of the self, and of its vileness, of its being a creature, under compulsion, lorded over, to the point that there is born of these two knowledges submission, brokenness and humbleness towards Allah, and that is what is meant by magnifying. As long as knowledge of the insignificance of the self is not commingled with knowledge of the majesty of Allah, the state of magnifying and humbleness is not attained. For, the one who needs no other, and trusts to himself, may recognize qualities of majesty in some one else, without his state being one of humbleness and magnifying,

[1] This is on p. 100.
[2] This is added by the SM.

because the other counterpart, which is the knowledge of the insignificance of the self and its need, was not joined to it.

As for awe and fear, that is a state of the self born of one's knowledge of the power and might of Allah, and of the execution of His will in him, with small regard for him, and of the knowledge that, were He to destroy the first and the last,[1] He would not diminish His dominion a particle. This holds along with observation of the misfortunes and various trials that happen to prophets and saints, in spite of the power [of Allah] to repel them, as opposed to what is seen among earthly kings. In brief, whenever the knowledge of Allah increases, fear and awe increase. The causes of that will follow in the Book of Fear, of the Quarter of the *Iḥyā'* on Saving Matters.[2]

As for hope, its cause is knowledge of the graciousness of Allah, His generosity, the universality of His bestowing of kindnesses, the favours of His work, and also the knowledge of His truthfulness in His promise of the Garden in exchange for Worship. So, whenever certain assurance of His promise and knowledge of His graciousness result, hope issues from their association, inevitably.

As for shamefacedness, its cause is in one's sense of deficiency in religious service, and one's knowledge of his inability to perform the great right of Allah. It grows strong through knowledge of the blemishes and faults of the self, the littleness of its sincere devotion, the vileness of its inner nature, and its inclination to what is fleeting in all its actions, in spite of the knowledge of the great things that the majesty of Allah requires, along with the knowledge that He is an observer of the secret thoughts and the idle fancies of the heart, although they are subtle

[1] The reference is to Qur'ān lxxvii. 16, 17.

[2] This is Book iii, of the Fourth Quarter of the *Iḥyā'*, SM ix. pp. 163, 196.

and hidden. Whenever these cognitions assuredly result, there is sent forth from them a state called shamefacedness.

So these are causes of these qualities. If the securing of anything is desired, the treatment is to make its cause to be present, for the knowledge of its cause is the knowledge of the treatment for securing it. The bond of connection in all these causes is faith and assurance; by faith, I mean these cognitions which we have mentioned, and the meaning of their being assured is the denial of doubt, and their taking complete rule over the heart, as has preceded in the exposition of Assurance in the Book of Knowledge. According to the measure of assurance the heart is humble.

(75) For that reason 'Ā'isha said, 'The Messenger of Allah used to talk to us and we to him, and, when Worship-time came, it was as if he did not recognize us and we did not recognize him'.

(131) It is related that Allah revealed to Moses, 'O Moses, whenever you make mention of Me, mention Me while you are shaking in your members, and while mentioning Me, be humble and composed, and whenever you mention Me, keep your tongue behind your heart, and whenever you stand before Me, stand as a humble slave, and commune with Me with a timorous heart and a truthful tongue'.

(132) It is related that Allah revealed to him, 'Say to the rebellious of the people, "They shall not mention Me, for I have taken an oath upon Myself, that I will mention whoever mentions Me, so whenever they mention Me, I will mention them with a curse"' This applies to one disobedient but not unmindful in his mentioning, and how will it be when unmindfulness and disobedience are joined together?

In accordance with the diversities of the inner realities in the hearts which we have mentioned, men are divided into the unmindful who completes his Worship, but whose heart is not present in a single moment of it, and the one who completes it with his

heart not absent a single moment, nay, rather, he may perhaps be so completely solicitous about it that he does not perceive what happens in front of
(83) him. On that account Muslim bin Yasár did not perceive the falling of a column in the mosque about which men gathered. One of them used to
(133) attend the Congregational Worship for a long time and never recognized at all who was on his
(77) right and on his left. The palpitation of the heart of Ibráhím (the mercies and peace of Allah be
(84) upon him), used to be heard two miles. A
(85) company used to turn yellow of face and to tremble in their shoulder muscles. All that is not improbable, for double of it is seen in the concern of the people of the world and in fear of the kings of the earth, for all their impotence, their weakness and the vileness of the bits of fortune that may be secured from them, so that one may come before a king or a minister and address him concerning his matter of importance and then go out, and, were he asked about those around him, or about the king's raiment, he customarily would not be able to give information about it, because of the pre-occupation of his concern with the king himself, rather than his raiment, or those present around him.

(126) So for all degrees of what men do, the portion of every one from his Worship is according to the measure of his fear, his humbleness and his magnifying. For, the place where the gaze of Allah falls, is the hearts, not the outward movements. For
(134) that reason one of the Companions said, 'On Resurrection Day mankind will be assembled in accordance with the pattern of their forms in the Worship, consisting of composure, quietness and the existence of delight and pleasure in it'. He surely spoke the truth, for every one will be assembled according as he died, and die according as he lived, and in that the state of his heart will be considered, not the state of his person. So, from the qualities of the heart will the forms be fashioned in the next abode. No one

will escape except him who brings to Allah a sound heart.

We ask Allah for His excellent success,[1] by His kindness and generosity.

Exposition of the Remedy Beneficial for the Presence of the Heart

Know that the believer must be a magnifier of Allah, be in fear of Him, hopeful towards Him and ashamed of his shortcoming: one must consequently not become free of these states after becoming a believer in Islam. And if the strength [of the states[2]] is in proportion to the strength of his assurance, his departure from them in the Worship can have no cause except (*a*) scattering of thought, (*b*) division of interest, (*c*) the absence of the heart from the communion, or (*d*) unmindfulness towards the Worship. Nothing disturbs from the Worship except invading, engrossing fancies.

The remedy for the presence of the heart is the repelling of those fancies. The thing itself is not repelled except by the repelling of its cause, so, learn its cause. The cause for the coming together of engrossing fancies is either some external matter, or a matter that is itself inward.

The external thing may be what strikes the hearing or appears to the sight, for that sometimes snatches away the attention, so that it follows the thing and busies itself with it. Then the thought is drawn away to something else and it goes linking on. Likewise the sight of things becomes a cause of thought about them, and then some of those thoughts give rise to others. But for him whose intention is strong and whose solicitude is lofty, what occurs to his senses does not occupy him. But for one who is weak it is a matter of course that his thought

[1] For *tawfīq*, see note 2, p. 77, last paragraph.
[2] This is added by the SM.

branches off on it. The remedy for that is cutting off these causes, by lowering the gaze, or worshipping in a dark house, or by not leaving before one what will engage his sense, or by drawing near to a wall in his Worship, so that the range of his vision may not be extended, and guarding against Worship in the streets and in places decorated and worked, and on dyed carpet.[1] For that reason the devotees[2] used to worship in a small, dark house, just large enough for prostration, that their attention might be more concentrated. The strongest ones among them used to be present in the mosques and to lower their gaze and not to let it pass the place of prostration, and to consider that the perfection of Worship consisted in not recognizing those who were on their right or left.
(135) Ibn 'Umar[3] would not leave in the place of Worship either a book or a sword without removing them, nor any writing without erasing it.

The inward causes are more difficult, for he whose concerns carry him off into the vales of the earth is one whose thinking is not confined in one department—rather he does not cease to fly from one side to another. The lowering of the gaze is of no use

[1] The SM adds this unhappy note: 'Dyed with pleasing colours, for they divert the worshipper from being present (attentive), and he turns to the beauty of its colour and its workmanship, and He has tried us by the Worship upon these Byzantine rugs and ornamental carpets in our mosques and houses, so that the one who worships on anything else is near to being counted coarse, of little politeness, deficient in manliness. And there is no might and no strength but in Allah! I do not think that that is anything but one of the number of the evil suggestions of the Franks (Europeans), may Allah, who is exalted in and of Himself, curse them! which they have introduced to the Muslims while they were unmindful of it and not knowing that. And stranger than that! I saw a carpet in one of the mosques on which was pictured work, and in the centre of the pictured work was the figure of a cross, and my wonder increased at that, and I became certain that it was one of the artifices of the Naṣárá (Oriental Christians) and Allah knows better (than any one else)!'

[2] These are the *ṣúfí* masters, says the SM.

[3] 'Abdalláh bin 'Umar b. al-Khaṭṭáb, Companion, son of the second khalífa (d. 73; the SM says 74). SM i. p. 188; *Ency. of Islam*, i. p. 28 f.

to him, for what took place in the heart previously is sufficient for the pre-occupation. So this is the way for him: let him restore the self forcibly to an understanding of what he is reciting in the Worship, and employ himself in this rather than anything else. It will help him to do that if he prepares for it before the Opening *takbír* by renewing to himself the remembrance of the next abode, the place of communion where he is, and the peril of his position before Allah, which is a place of perception [of things of the next abode[1]]. He empties his heart, before entering upon the Worship, of whatever he is solicitous about, and does not leave to his lower self any business to which his interest may turn.

(136) The Messenger of Allah said to 'Uthmán bin Abú Shaiba,[2] 'I forgot to tell you to cover the two horns[3] which are in the House of Allah, for it is not fitting that there should be in the House anything that disturbs men from their Worship.'

This is the way to quiet the thoughts. Then, if the thing that excites one's thoughts does not quiet down by this quieting remedy, nothing will save him except the purge that drains the matter of the disease from the deepest veins. This is to look into the matters turning him away and pre-occupying him from the presenting of the heart. There is no doubt that they have reference to his chief concerns, and they have become the things of importance only on account of his desires. So he chastises his lower self by breaking away from those desires and cutting off those bonds. For, whatever pre-occupies him from his Worship is an opponent of his religion, and is of the army of Satan, his enemy. Holding on

[1] This is added by the SM.

[2] The SM omits the Abú before Shaiba. Al-I'ráqí (d. 806), the author who worked on the sources of al-Ghazzálí's traditions, says this tradition is not from 'Uthmán bin Shaiba, but from 'Uthmán bin Ṭalḥa al-Ḥajabí, the keeper of the Ka'ba, who is reported in *Ibn Hajar's Biographical Dictionary*, ii. p. 1097 f. (d. 42).

[3] The other texts read 'cooking pot'.

to it is more harmful for him than casting it out, for he saves himself from it by casting it out, just as it
(137) is related that Muḥammad put on the black robe which Abú Jahm[1] brought him, and which had a border on it, and worshipped in it and then took it off after his Worship and said, 'Take it to Abú Jahm, for it distracted me a while ago from my Worship, and bring me Abú Jahm's coarse woollen garment'.

(138) The Messenger of Allah ordered a renewal of the strap of his sandal, and then looked at it during his Worship, since it was new, and then ordered it to be taken off of it and the worn out strap to be restored.

(139) He had put on some sandals and their excellence pleased him. So he performed a Prostration. Then he said, 'I humbled myself before my Lord, that He might not detest me'. Then he went out with them and delivered them to the first beggar he met. Then he ordered 'Alí to buy him two smooth raw-hide sandals, and he wore them.

(140) He had a gold ring on his hand before it was made unlawful while he was in the pulpit, and he threw it away, saying, 'This occupied me with one look at it and one look at you'.

(141) It is related that Abú Ṭalha[2] worshipped in an enclosure he had, in which were trees. Then a wood-pigeon[3] flew among the trees, looking for an exit,[4] and his sight followed it awhile. Then he did not know how many *ra'kas* he had performed. So he mentioned

[1] Abú Jahm 'Ámir bin Hudaifa al-'Adarí al-Qarashí al-Madaní (d. 60). Wüstenfeld, *Ibn Doreid's genealogisch-etymologisches Handbuch*, p. 87.

[2] Abú Ṭalḥa Zaid bin Sahl b. Aswad b. Kharám al-Madaní, Helper (d. 51). Muir and Weir, op. cit., p. 194 f.

[3] The *dubsí* or *dabsí* (a relative noun from the syrup of ripe dates) is a small bird, a wild pigeon found in Egypt, al-Ḥijáz and al-'Iráq, of blackish colour, or it is a male dove, or a collared turtle-dove (Ad-Damírí, *Ḥayát al-Ḥayawán*, i. p. 586 ; Lane, *Lexicon*, p. 848C).

[4] Perhaps it is to be understood that the tree was covered with a net, 'the net of the fowler', and it was looking for a way of escape.

to the Messenger of Allah what had occurred to him and then said, 'It is an alms, so put it wherever you wish'.

(142) It is related of another man that he worshipped in an enclosure belonging to him, while the date-palms were encircled by their fruit, and he looked at them and they pleased him. So he mentioned that to 'Uthmán and said, 'It is alms, so make use of it in the path of Allah'. So 'Uthmán sold it for fifty thousand. They were accustomed to do that, cutting off the matter they thought about, and it was an atonement for whatever deficiency of the worship had occurred.

This is the remedy that overcomes the disease, when nothing else suffices. For, what we have mentioned concerning what is favourable for giving quietness and causing a return to an understanding of the remembrance, is beneficial with weak desires and cares which do not occupy more than the margin of the heart. But quieting does not benefit the strong, overcoming desires. Rather, they continue to attract you, and you to attract them. Then they overcome you, and all your worship comes to an end in the occupation of pulling this way and that. It is like a man under a tree who wants to do some clear thinking for himself. Then the voices of the sparrows[1] disturb him, and he continually drives them away with a stick in his hand and returns to his thinking. Then the sparrows return and he repeats striking at them with his stick. Then it is said to him, 'This is the proceeding of a water wheel, and does not end. If you wish salvation, cut down the tree'. So likewise the tree of the desires, whenever it spreads out and its branches extend themselves, has thoughts attracted to it as sparrows are attracted to trees and as flies are attracted to filth, and the business of getting rid of them is a long one. For,

[1] For the *'aṣfúr*, a sparrow or any passerine bird, see Jayakar, *ad-Damírí's Ḥayát al-Ḥayawán*, ii. pp. 296 ff.

a fly, as often as it is repelled, returns, and for that reason it is called *dhubáb*,[1] something that is repelled and returns.

So likewise the stray thoughts and desires are numerous, and rarely is a creature free from them. There is one root that includes them all, and that is
(143) love of this life. 'That is the head of all sin', the foundation of all deficiency and the source of all wickedness. Let not the man, whose heart harbours love of this life so that he inclines to it for its own sake, and not in order to provide for his journey, nor to seek aid, by means of it, for the next abode, hope that the pleasure of communion in the Worship will be clear to him. For, whoever rejoices in this life will not rejoice in Allah and in communion with Him. The solicitude of a man is for that by which his eye is refreshed. If that by which his eye is refreshed is in this life, inevitably his concern goes out to it. Yet, for all that, it is not fitting that he should leave off the struggle to turn the heart to the Worship to reduce the disturbing causes, for this is the bitter remedy. On account of its bitterness the natural disposition abhors it. The illness remains chronic, and the disease becomes difficult to cure, so that the elders were zealous to Worship two *rak'as* without letting any thing worldly occur to themselves in them, but were unable to do that. So it is not for people like us to have desire for that, but, would that half or a third of the Worship were preserved for us from distractions, that we may be of those who mingle a good work with another thing that is bad! In brief, the solicitude of this life and solicitude for the next abode are in the heart like water which is poured into a vessel full of sesame oil.[2] According to the amount

[1] *Dhabb* means 'he repelled' and *áb* means 'he returned', but the Murtada refuses to accept this bit of etymology and refers to his dictionary, the *Táj al-'Arús*. See also Lane, *Lexicon*, p. 952A.

[2] The other texts read *khall*, 'vinegar', instead of *ḥall*.

of water that enters into it the oil goes out, inevitably, for they do not mix.

Detailed Exposition of What it is Fitting Should be Present in the Heart at Every Element and Stipulation of the Acts of the Worship

We say, it is your duty, if you are among the seekers of the next abode, not to be unmindful, first, of the admonitions which are in the Stipulations and the Elements of the Worship.

The Preliminary Stipulations[1] are: the Call to Worship, the Purification, the Covering of the person, Facing the *qibla*, Standing erect and the Intention. So, whenever you hear the Call of the *mu'adhdhin*, present to your heart the dread of the Call on Resurrection Day, and prepare yourself outwardly and inwardly for replying and hastening, for, those who hasten to this Call are those who are called in favour on the greatest Presentation Day. So, apply your heart to this Call, and, if you find it full of joy and rejoicing, laden with desire to hasten, know that the Call brings you glad tidings and deliverance on the Day of
(144) Judgement. For that reason Muḥammad said, 'Rest us, O Bilál!'[2] that is, 'Rest us by it, and by the Call to it', since the refreshing[3] of his eye was in it.

As for the Purification, whenever you purify your place, which is your outermost container, and then your clothing, which is your nearest covering, and then your skin, which is your closest shell, do not be unmindful of your kernel, which is your essence, and that is your heart. So, exert yourself on its behalf, cleansing it by repentance and remorse for previous acts, renewing the resolve to abandon such things

[1] These Preliminary Stipulations, says the SM, are *sunna*, thus excluding them from the *faráʼiḍ* class of the parts of the Worship.

[2] Bilál bin Rabáḥ al-Ḥabashí (Abyssinian), the first *mu'adhdhin* (d. 20). *Ency. of Islam*, i. p. 718 f.

[3] This is a Qur'ánic expression, xxviii. 8; also xxv. 74, xxxii. 17.

in the future. So cleanse by repentance your inward parts, for that is the place the One you worship observes.

As for the Covering of the person, know that it means to cover the shameful things of the body from the gaze of people, for the outward part of your body is the place people observe. And what is your opinion about the disgraceful things of your inner self, and the dishonourable things of your secret thoughts, which no one gazes upon but your Lord? So present these disgraceful things to your mind, and ask yourself to cover them, but be assured that no covering covers them from the eye of Allah, and only remorse, shamefacedness and fear cover them. For you acquire, by their presence in your heart, the sending forth of the armies of fear and shame from their places of hiding, and your self is humbled by them, and your heart becomes lowly under the shame, and you stand before Allah in the posture of a creature who is guilty and wicked, and a fugitive who has repented and returned to his Lord, bowing his head from shame and fear.

The Turning towards the *qibla* is a turning of the outward face from other directions to the direction of the House of Allah. Do you suppose that turning the heart from other things to the matter of Allah is not desired of you? Away with you! for there is nothing else desired but it! These external activities are only settings in motion of the inward activities, a restraining of the members, and a quieting of them by the holding on to one direction, so that they may not wrong the heart. For, whenever they do wrong, and act oppressively in their movements and their turnings to their directions, they desire the heart to follow, and they turn away with it from the Face of Allah. So, let the face of your heart be with the face of your body, and know that as a face does not turn toward the direction of the House except by turning away from everything else, so the heart does not turn towards Allah except by being free of all

(145) else besides. Muḥammad has said, 'Whenever a creature stands up for the Worship, with his inclination, his face and his heart towards Allah, he departs [from his sins[1]] innocent as he was the day his mother bore him'.

The Standing erect is only standing in person and heart before Allah. So let your head, which is your highest member, be bent, lowered and inclined, and let the placing of your head out of its erect position be an indication of the heart's grasp of humility, abasement and freedom from headship and pride. Let there be on your mind at this point the peril of standing before Allah, in dread of the place of observation, upon the presentation of your request. Know at once that you are standing before Allah, He being your Examiner. So, stand before Him as you stand before some earthly king, if you are unable to perceive the extent of His majesty. Nay more, consider, during the continuance of your standing in your Worship, that you are regarded and watched by the watchful eye of a righteous man of your family, one whom you desire to recognize you as righteous. For, upon that, your members calm down, and become subdued, and all parts of you quiet down, fearful lest that miserable weak king will ascribe to you but little humility. So, whenever you feel in yourself the restraint there is under the observation of some miserable creature, chide yourself, and say to it, 'You claim knowledge and love of Allah! Then are you not ashamed of your boldness toward Him, you esteem one of His creatures and fear men, without fearing Him, who has more right that you
(146) should fear Him?' For that reason when Abú Huraira asked, 'Of what sort is shamefacedness toward Allah?' Muḥammad said, 'Be ashamed before Him as you are ashamed before a righteous man of your family'.[2]

[1] This is an addition of the SM's from other versions of the tradition.

[2] The other texts read 'of your people'.

As for the Intention, resolve to respond to Allah by obeying His command to perform[1] the Worship, completing it and abstaining from what[2] it prohibits and what corrupts it, and by sincerely doing all that for the Face of Allah, hoping for His reward, fearing His punishment, seeking nearness to Him, taking upon yourself His favour in His permitting you to have communion, in spite of your evil manners and your numerous disobediences. Magnify to yourself the dignity of communion with Him, and consider whom you are communing with, and how you are communing, and with what you are communing. At that it is fitting that your brow should perspire from shame and your muscles should quiver from awe, and your face turn yellow from fear.

As for the *takbîr*, the exclamation, 'Allah is greater!' whenever your tongue pronounces it, it is fitting that your heart should not give it the lie. For, if there is in your heart anything greater than Allah, Allah testifies that you are a liar, even though the words be truthful, as was testified against the Hypocrites, in their saying, 'Muḥammad is the Messenger of Allah'. For, if your inclination is more powerful than the command of Allah, you are more obedient to it than you are to Allah. Then you have adopted it as your god, and have magnified it, for it is about to happen that your saying, 'Allah is greater!' is speech on your tongue alone, while your heart hangs back from assisting it. How great would be the peril in that, were it not for repentance and asking forgiveness, and thinking well of the kindness and pardon of Allah!

As for the Opening Supplication, its first words are, 'I have turned my face to Him who divided the heavens and the earth'. The meaning of 'face' is not the external face, for you turned it only to the direction of the *qibla*, while Allah is far removed

[1] This follows the marginal reading, *bi* instead of *fî*.
[2] The other texts read 'defects in it'.

from the circumstance that directions should limit Him, so that you might turn towards Him by the face of your body. The face of the heart is the only thing by which you may turn to the Divider[1] of the heavens and the earth. So look to it, as to whether it is turned to its wishes, and its concerns in the house and the bazar, following its desires, or whether it is turned to the Divider of the heavens: look out for yourself, lest the first broaching of the communion be by a lie and a fabrication. The face will surely not turn toward Allah except by its turning away from all else. So strive at once to turn it to Him, and if you are unable to do it continually, let your speech, at the time, be truthful.

When you say, 'Ḥaníf,[2] Muslim',[3] it is fitting that there should occur to your mind that the Muslim is one from whose tongue and hand Muslims are secure. If it is not so, then you are a liar. So strive to resolve upon it in the future and have repentance for previous conditions.

When you say, 'I am not one of the associators',

[1] The SM's note adds that the one who has knowledge of Allah says, 'I turn my face (and the face of a thing is its essence and its real existence), that is, I set myself standing, as Thou has commanded me, before the One who divided the heavens and the earth. The thought is directed to the saying of Allah, "Then We severed them both", (Qur'án xxi. 31); that is, the One who differentiated my outward and my inward (being), and my unseen and my seen, and set limits between the spiritual powers in my essence, as He differentiated the heavens one from another.'

Baiḍáwí explains the Qur'án reference by saying that the heavens were one, and were divided by the different movements into the firmaments, and the earths were one, and were made, by the variation of their modes of entity and their circumstances, into layers or sections.

[2] The SM's definition of the term is 'one inclining from the false faith to the real'. See the article by Buhl, *Ency. of Islam*, ii. pp. 258 ff.

[3] The Muslim is 'one who keeps Muslims safe from his tongue and hand'. The tradition referred to is 'The Muslim is a brother of the Muslim, who does not oppress him and does not calumniate him'. There is a discussion of the meanings of both terms Ḥaníf and Muslim in the *Journal of the Royal Asiatic Society*, 1903, pp. 467-93 and 781-84.

let there occur to your mind the hidden association. For, the saying of Allah, 'So, let him who hopes to meet his Lord, do good and not associate any one else in the religious service of his Lord! (Qur'án xviii. 110), came down concerning anyone who seeks, by his religious service, both the Face of Allah and the praise of men. So beware, guarding against this association, and have the feeling of shame in your heart, since you have described yourself as not being among the associators without being innocent of this kind of association, for the name of 'association' applies to little or much of it.

When you say, 'My Worship and my devotion, my living and my dying belong to Allah', know that this is the state of one lost to himself, found to his Lord, and that if it proceed from one whose pleasure and anger, whose rising and sitting, whose desire in life and dread of death are on account of things of this life, such a one is not adapted to the state.

When you say, 'I take refuge in Allah[1] from Satan the Stoned', know that he is your enemy and is lying in wait to turn your heart away from Allah, envious of you on account of your communion with Allah, and your prostration before Him, although he was accursed on account of one prostration [to Adam[2]] which he abandoned and was not disposed[3] tc by Allah. And know that your seeking refuge in Allah from him is by abandoning whatever he loves and exchanging it for what Allah loves, and is not only by your saying, 'I take refuge in Allah', for, when a wild beast or an enemy purposes to tear to pieces or to kill anyone, and the latter says, 'I take refuge from you in this strong fortress', while remaining in his place, that does not benefit him. Rather, nothing rescues him but the changing of place. Likewise,

[1] The SM interprets the phrase 'in Allah', as 'in the strength and greatness and power of Allah, and in His strong fortress, which the spears of the evil of Satan do not pierce' (SM p. 146).

[2] This is added by the SM.

[3] See note 2, p. 77, last paragraph.

the words only will not do any good to him who follows the desires, which are the things liked of Satan, and disliked of the Compassionate One. So let him unite the words with the resolve of taking refuge in the fortress of Allah from the evil of Satan. His fortress is, 'There is no god but Allah!' since Allah[1]
(147) said, in something which our Prophet related, '"There is no god but Allah" is My fortress, and whoever enters My fortress is safe from My punishment'. The one guarded in it is the one who has no object of worship but Allah. But the one who adopts his inclination as his god is in the open field of Satan, not in the fortress of Allah.

Know that his device is to engage you in your Worship with thinking of the next abode and the method of carrying out benevolences, in order to prevent you from understanding what you are reciting. So, know that all that diverts you from understanding the meaning of your Recital is evil suggestion [from Satan[2]], for the movement of your tongue is not what is intended, but rather, what is intended is the meaning.

As regards the Recital, there are three kinds of people: (*a*) the man who moves his tongue while his heart is unmindful; (*b*) the man who moves his tongue with his heart following his tongue, so that he hears and understands from it, as if he heard it from some one else, this being the degree of those who will be on the right hand; and (*c*) the man whose heart goes ahead to the meanings first, and then the tongue serves the heart and interprets it, for there is a difference between having the tongue as the interpreter of the heart and the teacher of it, while 'those who are drawn near'[3] are those whose tongues interpret their hearts, and whose hearts are not followers of their tongues.

[1] The SM supplies this subject.
[2] This is added from the SM.
[3] The allusion is to Qur'án lvi. 11, 12.

Further, the detailed interpretation of the inner realities is that, when you say, 'In the name of Allah the Merciful and Compassionate', you intend by it the seeking of the blessing for the beginning of the Recital of the speech of Allah. Understand that its meaning is that all matters are by [the act of] Allah, and that what is meant by 'the name' here is 'the One named', and, if the affairs are by Allah, assuredly the praise is Allah's. The meaning of 'the praise' is that thanks belong to Allah, since favours are all from Allah. Whoever thinks any favour is from any other than Allah, or has in mind, by his thinking, some one else besides Allah, not realising that any other is a benefactor because he is made subservient by Allah, is defective in his saying the *basmala* and the Praise according to the measure of his turning to anyone besides Allah.

So, when you say, 'the Merciful and Compassionate', let there be present in your heart the kinds of His favours, that His mercy may be evident to you, and your hope may be raised by it. Next, stir up from your heart, magnifying and fear, by saying, 'Possessor of the Day of Judgement'—magnifying, because there is no right of possession that is not His, and fear, because of the dread of the Day of Recompense and Accounting, of which He is Possessor. Then renew the singleness of your devotion by saying 'To Thee do we render the service of slaves', and renew the sense of inability, of need and of being devoid of power and strength, by saying, 'Of Thee we ask aid'. Be assured that your obedience was made easy only by His aid, that His was the gift, since He helped you to obey Him, and employed you for His religious service, and made you worthy for communion with Him, for, if He had forbidden you His assistance, you would be one of the outcasts, along with Satan the Cursed.

Next, when you finish the Seeking Refuge and saying the *basmala* and the Praise, and [expressing[1]]

[1] This is in the other texts.

that you need help absolutely, specify your request, but do not request anything but your most important needs, and say, 'Guide us into the Straight Road, which leads to Thy vicinity, and brings us to Thy pleasure'. Add to this explanation and detail, with emphasis, calling to witness those of the prophets, saints, martyrs and righteous, upon whom He poured out the favour of guidance, rather than of the unbelievers and those of the Jews and Christians and Sabeans who turned aside, with whom He was angry.

Next, beg for an affirmative answer, and say, '*ámín!*' for, when you recite the Fátiḥa so, you are like one of those of whom Allah said, in that about
(148) which the Prophet told us, 'The Worship is divided between Me and My Creature into two halves, one half to Me and one half to My creature. [My creature has what he asked.[1]] The creature says, "Praise belongs to Allah, the Lord of the worlds", and Allah says, "Allah hears whoever says His praise. My creature has said My praise and My eulogy."' That is the meaning of His saying, 'Allah hears whoever says His praise', and so on.

Did you not have from your Worship any good fortune except Allah's remembrance of you, in His majesty and greatness, that would suffice you as a prize. Do you ask, 'How so?' Because of what you may hope for of reward and kindness from Him.

Likewise it is fitting that you should understand what you recite from the *súras*, as shall appear in the Book of the Recital of the Qur'án, so that you may not be unmindful of His command, of His prohibition, promise, threat, or warning, and of the stories of His prophets in the Qur'án, and mention of His gifts and His goodness. To everyone there is a right. Hope is the right of a promise. Fear is the right of a threat. Determination is the right of a command and a prohibition. Taking warning is the right of admonition. Thankfulness is the right of the mention

[1] The SM omits this from his text, but quotes it in his comment.

of a favour. Taking a lesson is the right of the stories of the prophets.

(149) It is related that when Zurára bin Ūfí[1] reached the saying of Allah, 'So, when the trumpet is blown' (Qur'án lxxiv. 8) he fell down dead.

(150) Whenever Ibráhím al-Nakha'í[2] heard the words of Allah, 'When the heavens split asunder' (Qur'án lxxxiv. 81), he was so troubled that his limbs knocked together.

(151) 'Abdalláh bin Wáqid[3] said, 'I saw Ibn 'Umar worship with the appearance of one fried'.[4] He had a right to have his heart burn at the promise and threatening of his Lord, since he was a guilty and humble creature before an overpowering Tyrant.[5]

These inner realities exist according to the degrees of understanding. The understanding is according to the greatness of the knowledge and the purity of the heart, and the degrees of that are not limited. The Worship is the key of the hearts, in which the secrets of the words are revealed.

So this is the right belonging to the Recital, and it is the right of the Invocations and of the Praises also.

Next he observes awe in his Recital, for he recites with distinctness, without haste, for that makes meditation easier. He also makes a distinction between the tones in verses of mercy and of punishment, of promise and threat of praise, magnifying

[1] Zurára bin Ūfí al-'Ámirí al-Ḥarathí al-Baṣrí (Abú Ḥájib) Successor, judge in al-Baṣrá (d. 93). *Ibn Ṭagri Bardii*, i. p. 216; De Slane, op. cit., p. 528.

[2] The SM says that others say it was not Ibráhím al-Nakha'í (see note 4, p. 50), but Ibráhím bin Adham b. Manṣúr b. Yazíd b. Jábir (Abú Isḥáq) al-Tamíní al-'Ijlí, famous ascetic of Balkh (d. 160-68), (*Ency. of Islam*, ii. pp. 432 ff.).

[3] 'Abdalláh bin Wáqid bin 'Abdalláh b. 'Umar b. al-Khaṭṭáb, al-Qarashí al-'Adawí al-Madaní (d. 119). *Ibn Coteiba*, p. 93.

[4] The 1334 text has 'overcome'.

[5] This is one of the names of Allah, Qur'án lix. 23.

(152) and glorifying. Al-Nakha'í,[1] whenever he passed over anything like the saying of Allah, 'Allah has not adopted any son' (Qur'án xxiii. 93), and, 'There is no deity along with Him' (cf. Qur'án xxvii. 61-65), used to lower the voice, as one ashamed to make mention of Him by means of anything [not befitting Him[2]].
(153) It is related that it used to be said to a reciter of the Qur'án, 'Recite, pronounce elegantly and read distinctly, as you were accustomed to recite distinctly in the world'.

The continuance of the Standing Posture is a reminder of the setting up of the heart with Allah,
(154) according to one description of presence. Muḥammad said, 'Allah receives the worshipper kindly as long as he does not turn away'. As it is obligatory to guard the head and the eye from turning to different directions, so likewise it is obligatory to guard the heart from turning to anything else than the Worship. So, whenever it turns to anything else than Him, remind it of the gazing of Allah upon you, and of the unseemliness of treating lightly the One who is communed with, when the one who is communing is unmindful, so that it should return to it [the Worship[3]]. Impose humbleness upon the heart, for freedom from turning away, inwardly and outwardly, is the fruit of humbleness. Whenever the inward is humble, the outward is humble. Muhammad, seeing a man at Worship playing with
(79) his beard, said, 'As for this one, were his heart humble, his members would be'. For the flock is under the rule of the shepherd, and for this reason it
(155) is set forth in the supplication, 'O Allah, restore the shepherd and the flock!' that is, the heart and the other members.

(156) Abú Bakr al-Ṣiddíq, in his Worship, used to be as

[1] The SM says this is probably Ibráhím al-Nakha'í, but may be his maternal uncle, note 4, p. 50.

[2] This is omitted from the SM's text.

[3] This is the SM's interpretation. Some texts read *hu*, which would refer to Allah.

(157) if he were a tent-stake, and Ibn al-Zubair[1] used to be
(158) as if he were wood. A certain one of them used to be quiet in his prostration to such an extent that sparrows alighted on him as if he were inanimate. All that is what the natural disposition requires before one of the sons of the earth who is to be magnified, so how shall it not demand it before the King of kings in the case of anyone who has experiential knowledge of the King of kings? Every one who is composed submissively before any other than Allah, while, as a trifler, his extremities are restless before Allah, does that because of deficiency of knowledge of the majesty of Allah, and of His gazing upon his heart and his conscience.

(159) 'Ikrima[2] said about the saying of Allah, 'Who sees you when you stand up, and your turning over among those prostrating' (Qur'án xxvi. 18, 19), that this meant his [i.e. Muḥammad's[3]] standing up, his bowing, prostrating and sitting.

At the Bowing and Prostration it is fitting that you renew the remembrance of the mightiness of Allah, and that you raise your hands, seeking protection in the pardon of Allah from His punishment, by the renewal of intention, following the usage of His Prophet. Next, make a fresh beginning for Him, as to lowliness and humbleness, in your Bowing, and strive to move your heart, and renew your humbleness, and you should feel that, as well as the might of your Lord, together with your own lowliness, and the highness of your Lord. You seek aid in establishing that in your heart by means of your tongue. Then you say the praise of your Lord and bear witness to Him of His greatness, and say, 'O the

[1] 'Abdalláh bin al-Zubair, Quraishite general, cousin of the Prophet (d. 72). *Ency. of Islam*, i. p. 33.

[2] Abú 'Abdalláh 'Ikrima, manumitted slave of Ibn 'Abbás, Successor (d. 105; and it is said, 106 and 107). Margoliouth, *Dictionary of Learned Men of Yáqút*, vol. v. pp. 62 ff.; *Haji Khalfae Lexicon*, ii. p. 335, as Akrama).

[3] This is the SM's addition.

praise of my great Lord!' and, 'He is greater than every great one!' Reiterate that in your heart, that you may confirm it by your reiteration.

Next, you rise from your Bowing, hoping that He may be a Merciful One to you, and confirming the hope in yourself by saying, 'Allah hears whoever says His praise', that is, answers whoever thanks Him.

Next, you follow that with thanksgiving which is demanded as additional, and you say, 'O our Lord, Thine is the praise', and you increase the praise by saying, 'To the fulness of the heavens and the fulness of the earth'.

Next you bend down for the Prostration, which is the highest degree of submission, for the dearest of your members, which is your face, gets hold of the humblest thing, which is the dust. If it is possible for you not to put any obstruction between them, so that you prostrate on the ground, do so, for it produces greater humbleness and is more conducive to lowliness. Whenever you place yourself in the place of lowliness, know that you have placed it in its proper place, and have returned the branch to the trunk, for of the dust were you formed and to it you return.[1]

So, at this, renew to your heart the remembrance of the greatness of Allah, and say, 'Oh the praise of my Lord, Most High!' and confirm it by many repetitions, for one repetition is of weak effect. Then, when your heart is moved, and that is evident, let your hope find assurance in the mercy of Allah, for His mercy makes haste towards weakness and lowliness, and not towards pride and conceit.

Then raise your head, say the *takbîr* and request what you need, saying, 'O Lord, forgive and have mercy, and pass over what Thou knowest', or whatever supplication you wish. Then strengthen your humility by repetition and then return to the Prostration a second time.

[1] The reference is to Qur'án xx. 57.

As for the Witnessing, when you sit down for it, sit down in a proper manner, and state that all the performances of the Worship and good things, i.e. pure dispositions by which you seek access, are Allah's, and likewise the dominion is Allah's, this being the meaning of the *taḥiyât*, Greetings. Then cause the Prophet to be present to your heart, and also his noble personality and say, 'Peace be upon you, O Prophet, and the mercy and blessing of Allah!' Let your expectation be firm that it will reach him, and that he will return to you one more perfect than it.

Next, salute yourself and the righteous creatures of Allah. Then consider that Allah will return to you a perfect Salutation, according to the number of His righteous creatures.

Next, bear witness to Allah of His oneness, and to Muḥammad, His Prophet, of his mission, renewing the covenant of Allah, by repeating the two words of the witness,[1] beginning anew to seek protection in it.

Then make your Supplication at the end of your Worship in the words of the traditional supplication, with humbleness, submissiveness, imploration and true hope of an answer. Associate in your supplication your parents and the rest of the Muslims.

In the Salutation have in mind a salutation upon the angels and those present, and have the Intention of closing the Worship by it. Then have the sense of thankfulness to Allah for His assistance in the completion of this obedience, and imagine to yourself that you are taking leave of this Worship of yours, and that you perhaps may not live for another like it.
(160) Muḥammad said to the one he commanded, 'Make your Worship a leave-taking Worship'.

Then make your heart feel caution and shame on account of your deficiency in the Worship. Fear that your Worship may not be accepted, and that you are hated on account of some guilt, outward and

[1] These are the two parts of the Muslim testimony.

inward, and your Worship will be returned to your face. Yet, for all that, hope that He will accept it,
(161) through His generosity and favour. Yaḥyá bin Waththáb,[1] whenever he worshipped, used to wait as long a while as it pleased Allah, with the pain of the
(162) Worship evident upon him. Ibráhím al-Nakha'í used to remain after the Worship for a while, as if he were ill.

This is the detailed description of the Worship of the humble, 'Those who in their Worship are humble' (Qur'án vi. 92; lxx. 34) and 'Those who in their Worship are persistent' (Qur'án lxx. 23), and who commune with Allah as much as they are able in their relationship as slaves.[2]

So, let a man apply himself to these performances of the Worship. It is fitting for him to rejoice in proportion to the amount of them which was made easy for him by Allah, and, in proportion to the amount that escapes him, it is fitting for him to grieve. In his attending to this he should be energetic.

As for the Worship of the unmindful, it is perilous, unless Allah cover the failing with His mercy, but His mercy is wide and His generosity overflowing. So we ask Allah to cover us over with His mercy, and submerge us in His forgiveness, since we have no means of gaining access except confession of inability[3] to perform obedience to Him. Know that keeping the Worship free from faults, and

[1] Yaḥyá bin Waththáb al-Asadí, Kúfí, a most excellent reciter (d. 103), Wüstenfeld, *el-Nawawi, Tahdhíb al-Asmá'*, p. 631 f.

[2] The term here is *'ubúdiya*; see note 4, p. 49.

[3] The doctrine of 'inability' is here plainly stated by al-Ghazzálí, but this statement of inability must be supplemented by the other doctrine of the ultimate salvation of every true believer in the unity of Allah for a correct picture of the Muslim's prospects hereafter. Islam also developed early the doctrine of intercession by Muḥammad, the prophets and believers in general (see Macdonald, *Development*, p. 307, and Tradition No. 303 in the present text). In addition mention should be made of the doctrine of the intercession for parents by children who die in infancy (SM v. p. 299).

devoting it solely to the Face of Allah, and the payment of it in accordance with the inward Stipulations which we have mentioned of humbleness, magnifying and shame, are the cause of securing illuminations in the heart. These illuminations become keys of the unveiled knowledges. The intimates of Allah are those to whom is revealed the unseen world of the heavens and the earth. The divine secrets are unveiled only in the Worship, and particularly in the Prostration, since a creature comes near to his Lord in the Prostration. For that reason Allah said, 'And prostrate yourselves and draw near' (Qur'án xcvi. 19).

The unveiling every worshipper receives is only according to the measure of his freedom from the troublings of this life. That varies in strength and weakness, in littleness and greatness, in clearness and obscurity, so that there is disclosed to some the thing itself, and the thing is disclosed to others in a likeness of it, just as this life[1] is disclosed to some as a carcass with Satan, in the form of a dog, crouched upon it, calling upon it [and calling men to it[2]].

There is a difference also as to what the unveiling consists in, for to some are revealed certain of the qualities and majesty of Allah, and to another, some of His deeds, and to another, particulars of the sciences[3] of practical religion. There are, to distinguish these inner realities, at all times, hidden means, without number. Of these the strongest is suitable solicitude, for, whenever it is turned to some

[1] 'Life' here is one of the metaphysical qualities, explains the SM.

[2] This clause is an addition of the SM's.

[3] Knowledge pertaining to the next abode is of two kinds, *'ilm al-mu'ámala* and *'ilm al-mukáshafa*. The former is the science of practical religion, including questions of faith, ethics and canon law, including such duties as are incumbent on him on recurring occasions, such as the duties of the Worship, Fasting, etc. The knowledge of the Unveiled is an expression for the light that appears in the heart after its purification and reveals the inner and spiritual meanings and realities. The definitions of them are in the *Book of Knowledge*, the first of the *Iḥyá'* (SM i. pp. 162 ff.; cf. *Religious Attitude*, p. 237 f.).

specified thing, that is the first to be unveiled. Since these are not reflected except in a polished mirror, when the mirror is altogether rust coloured, guidance is veiled from it, not on account of stinginess on the part of the One who bestows guidance, but rather on account of the evil of the rust accumulated upon the place where the guidance is given.

Tongues are hasty in denying anything like that, since the natural disposition is so constituted that it denies what is not present. Had the unborn child intelligence, it would deny the possibility of the existence of man in the expanse of the air. Had a child any power of differentiation at all, it would perhaps deny what the intelligent claim to apprehend of the unseen world of the heavens and the earth. In like manner, man in every state is on the point of denying what is beyond him. Whoever denies saintship[1] must necessarily deny prophetship. Mankind was formed to be of all sorts, so no one should deny what is beyond his degree. Yea, some, since they sought this state on account of a disputatious and confusing discussion, and did not seek it on account of a clearing of the heart of all things other than Allah, missed it, and so they denied its existence. Now, whoever does not belong to the people of unveiling, must at least believe in the Unseen, and acknowledge belief in it until he sees by experi-
(163) ence. For, in Tradition it is said, 'Whenever a creature stands up for the Worship, Allah raises the veil between Himself and His creature, and meets him face to face, and angels from before his shoulders to the firmament stand worshipping with his Worship and say, "*ámín*" to his supplication, while righteous-

[1] *Ṭawr al-waláya*, says the SM here (p. 164), is an expression for a creature's standing in *al-Ḥaqq* (Allah) when he passes away from his own *nafs*, 'self', and this happens through *al-Ḥaqq's* taking him as a friend, *walí*, until He causes him to reach the utmost place of nearness and enabling. This is the special *waláya*, Saintship, while the general *waláya* is an expression for uninterrupted acts of obedience, without interruptions of disobedience.

ness from the clouds of the sky is rained upon the worshipper into the parting of his hair, and a crier calls out, "Did this communing one know the One he is communing with, he would not turn!" and the doors of heaven are open to those who worship—and Allah makes His creature who worships Him excel His angels in beauty'.

Now, the opening of the doors of heaven and the meeting of Allah with him face to face are a metaphor for the unveiling which we have mentioned.
(164) In the *Tawrá*[1] it is written, 'O son of Adam, do not lack strength for standing before Me as a worshipper, weeping, for I am Allah, who drew near to you, and in the unseen world you saw
(165) My light!' Someone said, 'We used to think that that weakness and weeping and the unexpected attainment[2] of unveiling which the worshipper finds in his heart are from the nearness of the Lord to his heart'. If this nearness is not nearness in location,[3] it has no other meaning than nearness of guidance and mercy and uncovering of the veil.

(166) It is said, 'When the worshipper performs two *rak'as*, ten rows of angels marvel at him, each row having ten thousand, and Allah makes him excel a hundred thousand angels. That is because the creature has brought together in the Worship the Standing Posture, the Sitting, Bowing and Prostration, while Allah has distributed that upon forty thousand angels, for, those who stand do not bow until Resurrection Day, and those who prostrate do not stand until Resurrection Day, and likewise those who bow and those who sit.' For, whatever nearness and rank Allah has apportioned to the angels is

[1] The *Tawrá* is the Law of Moses.

[2] *Al-futúḥ* is the attainment of something from that from which that thing was not expected. It is of three kinds: (*a*) an unexpected attainment of the service of worship outwardly; (*b*) of sweetness, inwardly; and (*c*) of unveiling. *Ta'rîfât*, pp. 171, 292.

[3] On account of the impossibility of such a thing, because Allah is free from all that pertains to bodies. So comments the SM

inseparably connected with them, continuing in one state which does not increase or decrease. For that reason Allah has stated about them, that they said, 'And there is no one of us but hás a certain position' (Qur'án xxxvii. 164).

A man is distinguished from the angels in his
(167) ascent from one degree to another, for 'He does not cease to draw near to Allah'. He has the advantage of nearness and increase of it, since the door of increase is closed to the angels. Each one has only the rank which is his endowment, and the religious service in which he is engaged. He does not change over to anything else and is not remiss in it. So they do not esteem themselves too great for His Worship, and do not tire uttering praises: by night and by day they are not remiss.[1]

The key of increase of the degrees is the performances of the Worship. Allah said, 'Those believers have prospered who in their Worship are humble!' (Qur'án xxiii. 1, 2). So He praised them, after referring to their faith by mentioning Worship which is united with humbleness. Then He sealed the qualities of those who prosper by the Worship, also saying, 'And those who in their Worship are persevering'. (Qur'án xxiii. 9). Then He said, regarding the fruit of these qualities, 'Those are the inheritors, who inherit Paradise, in which they remain eternally' (Qur'án xxiii. 10, 11). So He ascribed to them, prosperity at first, and then the inheritance of Paradise at the last.

I do not hold that the gabbling of the tongue, together with unmindfulness of the heart, end at this goal. For that reason Allah said, about those in the opposite condition, 'What caused you to enter into the Saqar [Plane of Hell]?'[2] They said, 'We were not of those who worship' (Qur'án lxxiv. 43, 44). So the worshippers are the inheritors of Paradise. They are those who see the light of Allah, and who have

[1] The allusions are to Qur'án xxi. 19, 20.
[2] This is the SM's explanation.

enjoyment in His nearness and His approach to their hearts.

We ask Allah to make us to be of them, and to rescue us from the punishment of him whose words seem good and whose deeds are evil. He is the Gracious Giver, and the Ancient Doer of good. May Allah bless every elect creature of His!

Stories and Traditions About the Worship of the Humble

Know that humbleness is a fruit of faith and a result of the certainty consequent upon [observing] the majesty of Allah. Whoever is apportioned that, is humble in the Worship and at other times, even in solitude of any kind. For the cause of humbleness is the knowledge of the gaze of Allah upon His creature, and the knowledge of His majesty and the knowledge of the creature's short-coming. So, from the recognition of these things humbleness
(168) is born, and it is not confined to the Worship. On that account it is related about a certain one that he did not raise his head to the sky for forty years, out of shamefacedness towards Allah, and lowliness before Him.

(169) Al-Rabí' bin Khuthaim,[1] because of his strictness in lowering his gaze and bending down his head, was thought by some to be blind. He used to go frequently to the residence of Ibn Mas'úd during twenty years, and whenever his maid-servant would see him she would say to Ibn Mas'úd, 'Your blind friend has come', and Ibn Mas'úd used to laugh at her remark. And whenever he would knock on the door, the slave girl would go out to him and then see him bending down and lowering his gaze, and Ibn Mas'úd, whenever he would look at him, used to say, '"And bear glad tidings to those who humble themselves!" (Qur'án xxii. 35). Is it not so, by Allah,

[1] Al-Rabí' bin Khuthaim (d. 60-64). *Ibn Saad, Biographien*, vol. vi. p. 134; Wüstenfeld, *Ibn Doreid's Handbuch*, p. 112.

that were Muḥammad to see you, he would rejoice in you!' and in another variation it says, 'He would glorify you', and in another variation[1] it says, 'He
(170) would love you!' He walked one day with Ibn Mas'úd among the blacksmiths, and when he looked upon the forge blowing and the fires blazing he fainted and fell unconscious. Ibn Mas'úd sat at his head until Worship time and he did not revive, so he carried him on his back to his residence. Thus he remained, unconscious, until the same hour [next day] in which he fainted, so that five Worship times escaped him, with Ibn Mas'úd at his head, saying, 'This, by Allah, is fear!'

(171) Rabí' used to say, 'I have never entered upon the Worship at all, except what concerned me in it was only what I was saying and what was being said to me'.

(172) 'Âmir bin 'Abdalláh[2] was one of the most lowly of worshippers, and when he would worship his daughter would perhaps beat the tambourine and the women would speak of whatever they would want in the house, and he would hear that but would not understand it.

(173) He was asked one day, 'Does your self speak to you in the Worship about anything?' He replied, 'Yes, about my standing before Allah, and my departure to one of the two places of abode'. He was asked, 'Then do you experience anything of what we experience of matters of this life?' He replied, 'Indeed, that lanceheads should repeatedly pierce me is more desirable to me than that I should experience in my Worship what you experience'.
(174) He used to say, 'Were the veil removed I would not become more certain'.

(83) Muslim bin Yasár was also one of that kind, and we have already reported that he did not become aware of the falling of a column in the mosque while he was at the Worship.

[1] This is added by the other texts.

[2] 'Ámir bin 'Abdalláh b. al-Zubair (see note 1, p. 117). Wüstenfeld, *Ibn Coteiba*, p. 116.

(175) One of the extremities of one of them was consumed by a wasting disease and required amputation, but it was not possible. So it was said, 'In the Worship he does not feel anything happening', and so it was cut off while he was at the Worship.

(176) A certain one said, 'The Worship belongs to the next abode, so, when you enter upon it you pass out of this life'.

(177) It was said to another, 'Does your self speak about anything of this life in the Worship?' He replied, 'Neither in the Worship nor at other times'.

(178) A certain one was asked, 'Do you recall anything in the Worship?' Then he replied, 'And is anything more dear to me than the Worship, so that I should recall it in it?'

(179) Abú al-Dardá'[1] used to say, 'It is an indication of a man's understanding of canon law that he attends to his need first, before his entering upon the Worship, that he may enter upon the Worship with his heart empty of care'.

(180) One of them used to do the Worship quickly, out of fear of evil suggestions.

(181) It is related that 'Ammár bin Yasír[2] performed a Worship and did it quickly. So it was said to him, 'You did it quickly, O Abú al-Yaqẓán!' So he asked, 'Did you see me diminish its limits any?' They replied, 'No'. He said, 'I strove to outstrip the oversight caused by Satan'.

(129) The Messenger of Allah said, 'A creature performs the Worship with not half of it, or a third or a fourth or a fifth or a sixth or a tenth, of it credited to him'.

(126) He [i.e. 'Ammár[3]] used to say, 'There is credited to a creature only what he comprehends of his Worship'.

[1] Abú al-Dardá' al-Khazrají al-Anṣárí (d. 31). *Ency. of Islam*, i. p. 82.

[2] 'Ammár bin Yasír b. 'Ámir b. Málik (Abú al-Yaqẓán), partisan of 'Alí (d. 37). *Ency. of Islam*, i. p. 333 f.

[3] The SM adds this.

(182) It is said, 'Ṭalḥa[1] and Zubair[2] and a group of the Companions with them were the quickest of men at the Worship, and they said, "We outstrip by it the suggestions of Satan"'.

(183) It is related that 'Umar bin al-Khaṭṭáb[3] declared from the pulpit, 'A man may grow white of the two sides of his beard, in Islam, without having performed for Allah a single Worship'. He was asked, 'And how is that?' So he replied, 'He does not complete its humbleness and its lowliness and his approach to Allah in it'.

(184) Abú al-'Áliya[4] was asked about the saying of Allah, 'Those who were forgetful of their Worship' (Qur'án cvii. 5). He replied, 'It is he who is forgetful of his Worship, for he does not know how many *rak'as* he goes out from, whether an even number or an odd'. Al-Ḥasan said, 'It is he who forgets the time of the Worship until it departs'. One of them said, 'It is he, who, if he performs the Worship early in its time, does not rejoice, and, if he delays it after its early time, does not grieve, for he does not consider hastening it as a benefit, or deferring it as a sin'.

Know about the Worship that a part of it is reckoned and part of it is recorded without the rest, as the traditions have shown, although canon lawyers used to say, 'The Worship, as regards its validity, is not divided into parts'. But that has another meaning which we have mentioned.[5] This meaning the
(185) traditions have indicated, since it is related, 'The deficiency of the prescribed Worship is made up by

[1] Ṭalḥa b. 'Ubaidallah, Companion (d. 36). Wüstenfeld, *al-Nawawi*, pp. 323 ff.; *Ibn Hajar*, ii. pp. 584 ff.

[2] Abú 'Abdalláh al-Zubair bin al-'Awwám al-Qarashí al-Asadí al-Madaní (see note 1, p. 177), Companion. Wüstenfeld, *al-Nawawi*, pp. 250 ff.; *Ibn Hajar*, ii. pp. 7 ff.; *Ibn Saad*, iii. pp. 70 ff.

[3] 'Umar bin al-Khaṭṭáb, the second khalífa (d. 23). Muir and Weir, op cit., pp. 82 ff.; Hughes, *Dict. of Islam*, pp. 650 ff.

[4] Abú al-'Áliya, Rafí' bin Mihrán al-Baṣrí (d. 90), *Ibn Coteiba*, p. 231.

[5] The reference is to Traditions Nos. 129 and 126, pp. 90, 91 of Translation.

(186) the Supererogatory ones'. In Tradition, it is said, 'Īsá[1] said, 'Allah says, "By the Prescribed Worships 'My creature is saved from Me, and by the Supererogatory ones My creature draws nigh to Me'"'

(187) The Prophet said, 'Allah said, "My creature is not saved from Me except by the payment of what I prescribed upon him"'

(188) It is related that the Prophet performed a Worship, and omitted a verse from its recital. So, when he turned away he said, 'What have I recited?' The people kept quiet, so he asked Ubai bin Ka'b,[2] and he replied, 'You recited such a *súra*, and omitted such a verse, and we do not know whether you exchanged or removed'.[3] Upon which he remarked,

[1] 'Īsá, the proper name of Jesus in Islam. *Ency. of Islam*, ii. pp. 524 ff.

[2] Ubai bin Ka'b, Helper (d. 22, or 30), *Ibn Hajar*, i. pp. 30 ff.

[3] The terms *nasakhta* and *rafa'ta* have been translated 'exchanged' and 'removed' respectively, in accordance with the kinds of abrogation possible.

In law *nasakha* means that a later legal proof enjoins what is contrary to a previous divine judgement. The later proof is called *násikh* and the former *mansúkh*. The real *násikh*, however, is Allah. The proof may be a Scripture or a *sunna*, Usage, whether of statement or act. Among Sháfi'ites Scripture abrogates Scripture, and Usage abrogates Usage, but the Ḥanafites add that Scripture can abrogate Usage, and Usage can abrogate Scripture. Abrogation applies only to commands and prohibitions, although these may be in declarative form.

There are three kinds of abrogation: (1) The abrogation of both the recital and the force of a revelation; (2) the abrogation of its force only; and (3) of its recital only. Another classification is: (1) The abrogation of a command before it is obeyed; (2) the abrogation of something enjoined upon predecessors; (3) what is commanded for cause falls into abeyance for cause.

Abrogation is not really the changing, *tabdīl*, of a rule, although it may seem so to men, but it is the manifestation of the ending of that rule. It is also described as the 'removal', *raf'*, of a legal proof by a later legal proof, but this is explained as, not the annulling, *buṭlán*, of the former rule, but the ceasing, passing away, of what men would still consider to be connected with the future, were it not for the abrogating verse of tradition. But the word *raf'*, 'removal', is disliked, and *baián*, 'explanation', is preferred. *Dict. of Tech. Terms*, pp. 1377 ff.

For the summary of the doctrine of abrogation, and bibliography of Arabic sources, see the article by Macdonald in *The Moslem World*, Oct., 1917, vol. vii. pp. 420-23.

'You are the man, O Ubai!' Then he advanced to the others and said, 'What can people be thinking of who are present at their Worship and who complete their ranks with their Prophet before them, and do not know what he recites to them from the Book of their Lord! Did not Baní Isrá'íl do so, so that Allah revealed to their Prophet, "Say to your people, 'You present Me your bodies and you give Me your tongues, but you are absent from Me your hearts! Vain is what you proceed upon!'"' This proves that hearing and understanding what the *imám* recites is a substitute for the recital of the *súra* by oneself.

(189) One of them said, 'There is a man who performs a Prostration: according to his own thought, he has come near to Allah by means of it, but, were his sins in his Prostration distributed upon the inhabitants of a city, they would perish'. He was asked, 'And how is that?' He replied, 'He is prostrating before Allah while his heart is attentive to some desire or observing some vanity that has taken possession of him'.

This, then, is the description of the humble, and so these narratives and traditions, together with what has preceded, prove that the root of the Worship is humbleness and the presence of the heart, and that the movements alone, with unmindfulness, are of little profit in the Place of Return.[1] And Allah knows better. We ask of Allah the beauty of His assistance.

[1] That is, the next abode.

CHAPTER IV

LEADERSHIP AND EXAMPLE

UPON the *imâm* there are duties before the Worship, during the Recital, in the Elements of the Worship and after the Salutation.

The duties which precede the Worship are six in number:

The first of them is that one should not go forward to the leadership for a people who dislike him. If they disagree, regard is to be shown to the majority. Yet, if the minority are people of benevolence and
(190) piety, regard to them is preferable. In Tradition it says, 'Three there are whose Worship does not pass beyond their heads: the runaway slave, a woman whose husband is displeased with her, and an *imâm* who leads a people who dislike him'.

As he is prohibited from going forward by their dislike, so likewise he is prohibited from going forward if there should be behind him one who is more learned than he [or a better reciter[1]], except whenever he who would be preferable to him declines. But, if it is not his duty to refrain for reasons like these, let him go forward whenever he is first and knows that the conditions of the leadership exist in
(191) him. In that case any refusal is disliked, for it is said, 'A people one after the other refused the leadership after the Worship had begun, and the ground swallowed them up'.

As for what is related of the refusal of the leadership on the part of the Companions, the reason for that was their choosing one whom they thought to be preferable for that, or, their fear, for themselves, of forgetfulness and the peril of the responsibility of

[1] This phrase is additional in the SM's text.

(192) their Worship, for, 'The *imáms* are the guarantors'. It might be that the heart of one who was not accustomed to that position would perhaps feel anxious and that would disturb the singleness of heart desired in his Worship, because of his diffidence towards those imitating him, especially in the audible part of the Recital. So, the cautiousness of some who guarded themselves against that was on account of reasons of this sort.

The second is that, whenever a man is given the choice between giving the Call to the Worship, and the leadership, he should choose the leadership. For, each one of them has some excellence, but uniting them is disliked. Nay, rather, it is fitting that the *imám* should be other than the one who gives the Call, and, if the joining of the two offices is objectionable, the leadership is preferable. Those who say, 'The Call to Worship is preferable,' say so on account of what we have reported concerning the excellence of the Call to Worship, and on account of the saying of Muḥammad, 'The *imám* is a guarantor
(192) and the *mu'adhdhin* is a trustee'. So they said, 'In the leadership there is the guarantor's risk'.

(193) Muḥammad said, 'The *imám* is *amír*,[1] so, whenever he bows, bow, and whenever he prostrates, prostrate'.

(194) In Tradition it is said, 'If he completes the Worship it is credited to him and to them, and if he comes short, it is against him and not against them'.

(195) A further reason for their opinion is because Muḥammad said, 'O Allah, guide the *imáms* and forgive the *mu'adhdhins*', for forgiveness is preferable in an intercession, for, a request for forgiveness includes guidance.

(196) In the Record it is said, 'Whoever acts as *imám*[2] in a mosque seven years has the Garden due him with-

[1] The other texts have '*amín*', 'trustworthy'.

[2] The SM reads, 'acts as *mu'adhdhin*', here and in the second part of the record. The first is then evidently a misprint, as the other texts have 'acts as *imám*'.

out any reckoning, and one who has been a *mu'adhdhin* for forty years will enter the Garden without a reckoning'. For that reason it is reported about the Companions that they used to decline the leadership, one after another, for the truth is that the leadership is more excellent, since the Messenger of Allah continued at it, as well as Abú Bakr, 'Umar and the *imáms* after them. True, there is in it the peril of the responsibility, but, excellence goes with peril, just as the rank of the amirate and the khalifate is more honourable, on account of the saying of Muḥammad,
(197) 'A day of a just sultan is more honourable than the religious service of seventy years'. Nevertheless, in it there is peril, and for that reason it is obligatory to put forward the most honourable and most learned.
(198) Muḥammad has said, 'Your *imáms* are your intercessors', or he said, 'Your envoy to Allah', so, if you wish your Worship to thrive, put forward the most excellent among you.

(199) Someone of the Fathers said, 'After the prophets there are none more honourable than the learned, and after the learned there are none more honourable than the *imáms* performing the Worship. For, all these stand before Allah and His creation, one with prophesy, and another with learning, and the other
(2) with "the support of the religion, which is the Worship".' This argument the Companions adduced in putting forward Abú Bakr al-Ṣiddíq for the khalifate, since they said, 'We considered, and lo! "the Worship is the support of the religion", and so we chose for this life of ours the one whom the Messenger of Allah preferred for our religious affairs'. They did not put forward Bilál, arguing that Muḥammad had preferred him for the office of *mu'adhdhin*.

(200) As for the matter that is related, that a man said to him, 'O Messenger of Allah! lead me to a work by which I may enter the Garden', he said, 'Become a *mu'adhdhin*!' He replied, 'I am not able'. He said, 'Become an *imám*!' He replied, 'I am not

able'. Then he said, 'Worship beside the *imám*!' perhaps he thought that he would not be acceptable in his leadership, since the calling to Worship was his own affair, while the leadership and their putting him forward was the affair of the congregation. Then afterwards he supposed that he had ability to achieve the leadership.

The third is that the *imám* shows regard for the times of the worshippings, for he performs the Worship at the beginnings of them—in order to please
(201) Allah. For, 'The superiority of the beginning of the time over the end of it is like the superiority of the next abode over this life'. Thus it is related from the Messenger of Allah. In Tradition it is said, 'A creature may perform the Worship [at the end of its time[1]], and so it does not escape him, but truly, that of the beginning[2] of its time which escaped him had more benefit for him than this life and what is in it'.

It is not fitting that he should delay the Worship out of expectation of a large congregation. Nay rather, it is for him to lose no time to obtain the excellence of the first of its time, for that is more excellent than the large size of the congregation and than the lengthening of the *súra*.

(202) It has been said, 'They were accustomed, whenever two were present in the Congregational Worship, not to wait for the third, and, whenever four were present at a funeral, they would not await a fifth'.

(203) The Messenger of Allah had been delayed from the Dawn Worship, while they were on a journey (he was delayed only for the sake of the purification), and he was not waited for, and 'Abd al-Raḥmán[3] came forward and conducted the Worship with them, so that one *rak'a* escaped the Messenger of Allah.

[1] The SM's text omits this clause.
[2] See note 2, p. 165 f.
[3] 'Abd al-Raḥmán bin 'Awf, Quraishite (d. 31). *Ency. of Islam*, i. p. 54.

Then Muḥammad stood up and performed the *qaḍá'*, Substitution, Worship. Then we were anxious about that, so Muḥammad said, 'You did well in doing that and keep on doing so'.

(204) He had been delayed at the Noon Worship, so they put forward Abú Bakr until the Messenger of Allah came, while they were still at Worship, so he stood at his side.

It is not for the *imám* to wait for the *mu'adhdhin*, and it is necessary for the *mu'adhdhin*, to wait only for the *imám*, for the Institution of the Worship. So, when he comes, he should not await anyone else.

The fourth requirement is that he should act as *imám* as one sincerely seeking Allah's Face [and that which He has to give[1]], and as one paying back the 'trust' of Allah, in respect of his purification and all the stipulations of his Worship.

As for singleness of devotion, it means that he does not accept any reward for the Worship, for the
(205) Messenger of Allah gave an order to 'Uthmán bin Abú al-'Aṣ al-Thaqafí[2] and said to him, 'Select as *mu'adhdhin* one who does not take any reward for giving the Call to Worship!' For the Call to the Worship is a way to the Worship, and the Worship is better when a reward is not accepted for it. But, if he takes some sustenance from a mosque which has been entailed upon the one who has the position of *imám* of it, or from the sultan, or from individuals of the people, there should be no ruling to make it unlawful, but it is disliked, and dislike with regard to prescribed things is stronger than it is with regard to supererogatory acts. He may have a reward for persevering attendance upon the place, and for his watchfulness over the interests of the mosque, in establishing the Congregational Worship in that place, but not for the Worship itself.

[1] This is according to the SM's interpretation.

[2] Abú 'Abdalláh 'Uthmán bin Abú al-'Áṣ al-Thaqafí, al-Ṭá'ifí (d. 51). *Ibn Hajar*, ii. p. 1098 f.

As for the 'trust', it is cleanness within from transgression and the great sins, and from persistence in minor sins. For, it is fitting that he who would be prepared for the office of *imám* should guard against that with his best energy, for he is as the envoy and intercessor for the people, so it is fitting that he should be the best of the people. Similarly as to cleanness outwardly, he should guard himself from uncleanness and impurity, for no one perceives that, so far as he is concerned, except himself. So, if he should recall, during the Worship, any uncleanness . . . he should not be ashamed, but rather, let him take the hand of the one who is near to him
(206) and appoint him to succeed him. For the Messenger of Allah recalled a *janába*, 'greater uncleanness', during the Worship, so he appointed a successor, and bathed. Then he returned and entered into the Worship.

(207) Sufyán[1] said, 'Worship behind everyone, just and unjust, except one addicted to wine, one notorious for transgression, one disobedient to parents, one with an innovation or a runaway slave'.

The fifth duty is that he should not recite the *takbír* until the rows are arranged. So, let him turn to the right and the left, and, if he sees any defect, he should order it to be arranged. It is said, 'They
(208) were accustomed to place themselves beside one another, shoulder to shoulder, and to place their ankles together'. He does not recite the *takbír* until the *mu'adhdhin* finishes the Institution. The *mu'adhdhin* delays instituting the Worship after the Call by as long as it takes for the men to get ready
(209) for the Worship. In the Record it says, 'Let the *mu'adhdhin* grant between the Call to Worship and the Institution a respite as long as an eater takes to finish his food. . . . The reason for is that that . . . it

[1] This is either Sufyán al-Thawrí, note 3, p. 90, or Abú Muḥammad, Sufyán bin 'Uyaina b. Abú 'Imrán Maimún al-Hilálí (d. 198), De Slane, op. cit., i. pp. 578 ff.

is commanded that the evening meal should precede the Evening Worship, out of desire that the heart should be disengaged.

The sixth is that he should raise his voice in the single *takbîrat al-iḥrâm* and the rest of the *takbîrs*, and the follower should not raise his voice except enough for himself to hear. He states the Intention to lead, in order to obtain the reward. But if he should not state the Intention, his Worship would be valid as well as the Worship of the people, if they stated the Intention of the imitation, and they obtain the reward of the imitation, while he does not obtain the reward of the leadership. Let them delay their *takbîr* after the *takbîr* of the *imâm*, and begin after he has finished. And Allah knows better.

The duties of the Recital are three in number:

The first of them is that he should recite the Opening Supplication inaudibly, and likewise the Seeking Refuge, as does one worshipping alone. He utters audibly the Fátiḥa and the *súra* after it in both *rak'as* of the Morning Worship, and in the first two *rak'as* of both the Evening and the Sunset Worships. So also the one who worships alone. He utters audibly the '*ámín*' in the audible Worship, as does the follower. The follower says his *ámín* in unison with the *ámín* of the *imâm*, not afterwards. He utters audibly the words, 'In the name of Allah the Merciful and Compassionate One'. The Records about it are contradictory, and the preference of al-Sháfi'í[1] is for saying it audibly.

The second is that the *imâm* should make three pauses in the Standing Posture, and so Samura bin Jundub[2] and 'Imrán bin al-Ḥaṣín[3] record, from the

[1] Muḥammad bin Idrís al-Sháfi'í al-Hijází, Wüstenfeld, *Schafi-'iten*, pp. 29 ff.; *el-Nawawi*, pp. 56 ff. For SM's *manâqib*, 'merits', of al-Sháfi'í, see SM i. pp. 191 ff.

[2] Abú Sa'íd Samura bin Jundab (d. 58). Companion. *Ibn Coteiba*, p. 155; *Ibn Doreid*, p. 172.

[3] 'Imrân bin Ḥaṣín bin 'Ubaid bin Khalaf, Companion, *qâḍí* in al-Baṣra (d. 52). Ibn Hajar, iii. p. 50 f.

Messenger of Allah. The first of them is when he says the *takbir*, and it is the longest of them, long enough for one who is behind him to recite the Fátiḥa of the Book. That is the time for his reciting the Opening Supplication of the Worship. For, if he should not pause, they would not be able to hear his recital, and then whatever is short in their Worship would be recorded against him. But if he should pause and they should not recite the Fátiḥa during his pause, or should be occupied with something else, that would be against them and not against him. The second pause is when he finishes the Fátiḥa, in order that the one who did not recite the Fátiḥa in the first pause may finish his Fátiḥa. This is half the time of the first pause. The third pause is when he finishes the *súra*, before he bows. It is the briefest of them, and that is as long a time as separates the Recital from the *takbír*, for there is a prohibition against bringing them together.

The follower does not recite after the *imám* anything but the Fátiḥa. But if the *imám* does not pause, he recites the Fátiḥa of the Book with him, and the one who is remiss is the *imám*. If the follower should not hear the Recital of the *imám* in the audible Worship on account of his distance, or if he should be engaged in the inaudible Worship, there is no objection to the recital of the *súra* along with the Fátiḥa.

The third duty is that he should recite in the Morning Worship two *súras* from the *mathání* which are less than a hundred verses. For, to be lengthy in the Recital of the Dawn Worship and to perform it before daybreak are *sunan*, Usages, but to finish it in the clear dawn does not harm one.

There is no objection if he recite in the second of the two *rak'as* of the Morning the latter parts of the *súras* from the thirtieth or the twentieth verses until he finish them, for they are not repeated upon the hearing often, and so
(210) are more effective in admonition, and summon better

to meditation. Some of the *'ulamá'*, 'learned', have expressed dislike for the recital of only some of the
(211) first part of the *súra* and then breaking it off. But it has been related that Muḥammad recited part of the *súra* of *Yúnus* (x), and after he had completed it to the mention of Moses and Pharaoh (verses 76 to 84), he broke off and did the Bowing.

(212) It is related that Muḥammad recited in the Dawn Worship a verse from 'The Cow' (ii) which was His saying, 'Say, We believe in Allah and what He sent down to us' (verse 130), and in the second *rak'a*, 'Oh our Lord! We have believed in what Thou didst send down' (iii. 46).

(213) He heard Bilál recite from here and there. So he asked him about that, and he replied, 'I mingle the pleasant with the pleasant'. So he remarked, 'You have done well'.

The *imám* recites at the Noon Worship the long *súras* of the *mufaṣṣal*, up to thirty verses, and in the Afternoon Worship half of that, and in the Sunset
(214) Worship the latter parts of the *mufaṣṣal*. The last Worship of the Messenger of Allah was the Sunset Worship. In it he recited the *súra*, 'The Sent ones' (lxxvii). He did not perform a Worship after that before he was taken.

On the whole, to do it quickly is preferable,
(215) especially when the congregation is large. Muḥammad said concerning this concession, 'When one of you leads the Worship with the people, let him do it quickly, for among them are the weak and the aged and those who have a need. When he worships by
(216) himself, let him be as long as he likes.' It happened that Ma'ádh bin Jabal was worshipping with some people at the evening time, and he recited 'The Cow' (ii), and a man went out from the Worship and finished by himself. So they said, 'The man has become a hypocrite'. Then they both brought counter-charges before the Messenger of Allah. So the Messenger of Allah chided Ma'ádh and said, 'Are you a disturber, O Ma'ádh? Recite the *súra* of "Praise" (lxxxvii), and

"The Skies and the Night-traveller" (lxxxvi), and "The Sun and its Morning Brightness" (xci)'.

The duties respecting the Prescribed Elements are three in number:

The first is that he does the Bowing quickly and also the Prostration, and does not increase the number
(217) of the Praises over three. For it is related from Anas that he said, 'I have not seen anyone more quick as regards the Worship than the Messenger of
(218) Allah, and, at the same time, complete'. It is true that it is related also that Anas bin Málik, when he worshipped behind 'Umar bin 'Abdal'azíz, when he was Amir in al-Madina, said, 'Indeed, I have not worshipped behind anyone whose Worship is more like the Worship of the Messenger of Allah than that of this young man'. He said, 'We used to say the
(219) Praise behind him by tens'. It is related inclusively that they said, 'We used to recite the Praise behind the Messenger of Allah in the Bowing and the Prostration by tens'. And that is excellent. But three, when the congregation is large, is better. But when there are none present but those devoted to religion there is no harm in the ten repetitions. This is the way to combine the narratives. It is fitting that the *imám* should say, at the raising of his head from the Prostration, 'Allah hears whoever says His praise'.

The second duty concerns the follower. It is fitting that he should not bow and prostrate along with the *imám*. Rather, he should delay. So he does not bend for the Prostration until the forehead of the *imám* reaches the place of prostration. Such was the practice of the Companions with the Messenger of Allah. He does not bend for the
(220) Bowing until the *imám* completes his Bowing. It is said, 'Men leave the Worship in three divisions: One party have twenty-five Worships, and they are those who say the *takbír* and bow after the *imám*. Another party has one Worship, and they are those who keep up with him. Another party

has no Worship, and they are those who go ahead of the *imám*.'

There is disagreement as to whether the *imám*, in the Bowing, should wait until one coming in joins in and overtakes that *rak'a*, in order that he may obtain the reward of worshipping with the congregation. Perhaps the preferable opinion is that that is without harm, if singleness of devotion is preserved, whenever no noticeable interval becomes apparent to those present, for their right is to be regarded, in desisting from the lengthening of the service for them.

The third duty is that he does not increase in the Supplication of the Witnessing beyond the amount given to the Witnessing itself, guarding against being too long, and he does not include only himself in the Supplication, but rather uses the form of the plural, and says, 'O Allah, forgive us!' and does not say, 'Forgive me'. For it is disliked in an *imám* to include only himself. There is no harm in his use of the Invocation of the protection of Allah in the Witnessing, using the five phrases transmitted from
(221) the Messenger of Allah. So he says, 'We take refuge in Thee from the punishment of Hell and the punishment of the grave, and we take refuge in Thee from the testing[1] of life and death, and from the testing of the Anti-Christ[2] and, whenever Thou willest testing a people, take us to Thyself without
(222) our being tested'. It is said, 'He is called *masíḥ* "rubber", because he rubs upon the earth in all its length', and it is said, 'He is called *masíḥ*, "one-eyed", because he is smooth of one eye, i.e. blind in it'.

The duties of the finishing of the Worship are three in number:

The first is that he have the Intention, in the two Salutations,[3] of salutation upon the people and the angels.

[1] On the word *fitna*, cf. Baid, on Qur'án ii. 96.

[2] For the Muslim account of the al-Masíḥ al-Dajjál and bibliography, see *Ency. of Islam*, i. p. 886 (Dadjdjál) and ii. 524 ('Ísá).

[3] That is, upon the right and the left, says the SM.

The second is that he remain stationary after the
(223) Salutation. So did the Messenger of Allah, Abú Bakr and 'Umar. He performs the *náfl*, Supererogatory, Worship in another place. But if there are women behind him he does not rise until they depart.
(224) In the *mashúr*,[1] 'well-known', record it is stated that Muḥammad was not accustomed to remain sitting more than long enough for him to say, 'O Allah! thou art the Peace,[2] and from Thee comes peace! Thou art blessed in and of Thyself, O Possessor of majesty and honour!'

The third is that when he springs up it is fitting that he should turn his face toward the people. It is disliked for the follower to get up before the turning
(225) of the *imám*. For it is related about Ṭalḥa and Zubair that they worshipped behind an *imám*, and, after they had said the Salutation, they said to the *imám*, 'How excellent was your performance of the Worship, and how complete it was, except for one thing!—after you said the Salutations you did not turn your face to the congregation'. Then they said to the people, 'How excellent was your Worship, only, you withdrew from it before your *imám* turned'.

Then the *imám* departs, whither he will, to his right or left, the right being more liked.

This is the duty of the performances of the Worship.

With regard to the Morning Worship, the *imám* adds to it the *qunút*, Supplication, and says, 'O Allah, guide us!' and d es not say, 'Guide me'. The follower says, '*ámín*!' When he reaches the words, 'Thou dost judge, and art not judged!' the saying of the '*ámín*!' is not fitting, since it is praise, so he recites it with him. He says what the *imám* says, or he says, 'Yes indeed! and to that I am one of the

[1] The SM says, the word *mashhúr*, 'well-known', is not used here in its technical sense; see note 1, p. 151.

[2] *Al-Salám*, 'The Peace' (but see article on Allah by Macdonald in *Ency. of Islam*, i. p. 303A). This is one of the 'most beautiful names' of Allah, and occurs in the Qur'án only at lix. 23.

witnessers', or, 'You have spoken truly and done right', or some similar expression.

(226) There is related a tradition for the raising of the two hands in the *qunút*, Supplication, and, if the tradition is valid, that is preferable, although it is different from the Supplications at the end of the Witnessing, since the hands[1] are not raised on account of them on that occasion, but, reliance is to be placed on explicit statement.[2] Between the two there is also a great difference, that being that the hands have a duty in the Witnessing, and have to be placed on the thighs in a special form. They have no duty here, so it is not strange that the raising of the hands should be a duty in the *qunút*, Supplication, for it is fitting in supplication. And Allah knows better.

This is the whole duty of the proper manner of performing the example and the leadership. And Allah is the Helper!

[1] The other texts read, 'he does not raise his hand'.

[2] The use of the technical term *al-tawqífiya* is explained in *Tuḥfat al-Muríd 'alá Jawharat al-Tawḥíd*, by al-Bájúrí (Cairo, 1324, p. 48C), where he says, '*al-tawqífiya*, that is, the possibility of the application of names to Allah depends upon their appearance in a book, or in a "sound" or "beautiful" *sunna*, "tradition", or in an "agreement"'. In the *Qámús* (iii. p. 199) *tawqíf* in Tradition means 'explanation', and in law means 'a definite statement' (*naṣṣ*) (Lane, *Lexicon*, pp. 3058C; 2797C).

CHAPTER V

THE EXCELLENCE OF THE FRIDAY OBSERVANCE; ITS PROPRIETIES, USAGES AND STIPULATIONS

KNOW that this is a great day, by which Allah has magnified Islam and by which He has given distinction to the Muslims. Allah said, 'When there is a call to Worship on Friday, hasten to the remembrance of Allah, and cease selling' (Qur'án lxii. 9). So, being busy in affairs of this life and in all that hinders from hastening to the Friday Observance was made unlawful.

(227) Muḥammad said, 'Allah prescribed the Friday Observance upon you in this my day and in this
(228) my position'. He said, 'Whoever abandons the Friday Observance thrice without excuse has Allah
(229) put a seal upon his heart',[1] and, in another version, 'has thrown Islam behind his back'.

(230) A man kept returning to Ibn 'Abbás, asking him about a man who died without being accustomed to being present at the Friday Observance or a Congregational Worship. So he said, 'He is in the Fire'. But he did not cease returning to him monthly about that, and he would say, 'He is in the Fire'.

(231) In Tradition it is said, 'The People of the Two Books[2] were given Friday, and they disagreed about it and departed from it, and Allah guided us to it, and kept it back for this people and made it a feast-day for them, they being the people worthiest of it, in the

[1] The SM explains, 'Puts a veil upon it, so that he does not understand, and prevents him from obedience'. The allusion is to Qur'án iv. 154, and similar passages.

[2] They are the Jews and Christians.

matter of precedence, while the People of the Two Books follow after them'.

(232) In the tradition of Anas from the Prophet it is related that he said, 'Gabriel[1] brought me in his palm a white mirror and said, "This is the Friday Observance: your Lord prescribes it upon you to be a feast day to you and to your people after you". I said, "And what is there for us in it?" He said, "There is for you 'the best hour', in which, whoever makes a supplication for a good that has been apportioned to him, has it given to him by Allah, or, if it be not apportioned to him, has stored up for him something greater than it; or else, he escapes from an evil decreed upon him, unless Allah protects him from a greater evil. It is the 'lord of the days' among us, and we call it, in the next abode, 'the day of increase'." I asked, "Why?" He said, "Your Lord chose in the Garden a valley more odourous than white musk, so, when Friday comes, He descends from the highest heaven upon His throne, and reveals Himself to them so that they look upon His Generous Face".'

(233) Muḥammad said, 'The best day the sun shines upon is Friday. On it Adam was formed; on it he was introduced into the Garden and on it he was cast down to the earth; on it he was forgiven and on it he died; on it the Resurrection Hour will come, and it is, with Allah, the "day of increase". So the angels name it in heaven, and it is the day for seeing Allah, in the Garden.'

(234) It is said in Tradition, 'Allah has on every Friday six hundred thousand freed from the Fire'.

(235) In the tradition of Anas it is recorded that Muḥammad said, 'Whenever Friday is safe,[2] all the days are safe'.

(236) Muḥammad said, 'Hell-fire is kindled every day

[1] For the eight different spellings of this name see Baiḍ, on Qur'án ii. 191.

[2] The SM adds, 'from the occurrence of sins in it'.

before the passing of the meridian, at the sun's standing balanced in the heart of the sky, so do not perform the Worship at that hour, except on Friday, for it is a Worship itself, all of it, and Hell is not kindled on that day'.

(237) Ka'b[1] said, 'Allah gave preference, among cities, to Mecca, and, among the months, to Ramaḍán, and among the days, to Friday, and, among the nights, to the Night of Decree'.[2]

(238) It is said, 'The birds and the serpents[3] meet each other on Friday and say, 'Peace, peace, a goodly day!'

(239) Muhammad said, 'Whoever dies on Friday, or on the eve of Friday, has Allah decree for him the reward of a martyr and preservation from the testing of the grave'.

Exposition of the Stipulations of the Friday Observance

Know that it shares the Stipulations of all the performances of the Worship, and is differentiated from them by six additional Stipulations.

The first is the time. If the Salutation of the *imám* occurs within the time of '*aṣr*, 'mid-afternoon', the Friday Observance has escaped, and it is incumbent upon him to complete it as an ordinary Noon Worship of four *rak'as*. There is disagreement about the man[4] who is late, when his last *rak'a* falls after the time.

[1] Abú Isḥáq Ka'b bin Máni' al-Ḥimyarí al-Aḥbár (al-Ḥabr), (d. 32). *Ibn Coteiba*, p. 219.

[2] For the Night of Decree see Macdonald, *Development of Muslim Theology*, etc., p. 335 ; Lane, *Modern Egyptians*, p. 484, (Everyman edition).

[3] These are reptiles that are deadly poisonous, but the word is applied also to creeping things that do not kill (Lane, *Lexicon*, p. 105 f.).

[4] The *masbúq* is the man who has not arrived in time for the beginning of a Worship performed in a congregation. Redhouse, *Muntakhabáti Lugháti 'Osmániya*.

The second is the locality. It is not valid to celebrate the Friday Observance in the deserts, or on the plains, or among the tents, but it must be in a space containing buildings that are not moveable and that can contain forty of those upon whom the Friday Observance is incumbent. In this matter a village is like a town. The presence of the sultan at it is not stipulated, but it is preferable to ask his permission.

The third is the number. It is not confirmed as a valid Friday Observance with less than forty males, responsible, free, and domiciled, i.e. who do not move away from it winter or summer. Then, if they disperse, so that the number comes short, either in the time of the address or the Worship, that Friday Observance in not valid. Rather there is need of them from the first to the last.

The fourth is the congregation. Were forty in a village or a town to worship in different parties, their Friday Observance would not be valid. But a late-comer, whenever he is in time for the second *rak'a* [with the *imám*[1]] overtakes the Friday Observance, and it is allowable for him to perform the second *rak'a* by himself. But, if he does not overtake the Bowing of the *imám* in the second *rak'a*, he does not overtake the Friday Observance, so he follows the *imám*, but he states the Intention to perform the Noon Worship and when the *imám* says the Salutation, he stands and completes it as a Noon Worship.

The fifth is that the Friday Observance should not be preceded by any other in that town. If their meeting together in one congregational mosque should be impossible, it is allowable to meet in two or three or four, according to the need. If there should be no need, the valid one is the Friday Observance in which the Opening *takbír* occurred first. When the need is a proved one, the more

[1] This is added by the SM.

excellent is the Worship behind the more excellent of the two *imáms*. If they are on a parity, then in the older mosque, and if they are on a parity, then in the nearer one. The largeness of the number of the men has an excellence that should be considered.

The sixth is the two addresses, which are both Prescribed. Standing up during them is a Prescribed act, and sitting down between them is a Prescribed act. In the first there are four Prescribed parts: the Praising, the minimum of it being, 'Praise belongs to Allah'. The second is the Blessing upon the Prophet. The third is the Command of fear towards Allah. The fourth is the Recital of a verse from the Qur'án. Likewise, the Prescribed parts of the second address are four in number, except that in it the Supplication is obligatory instead of the Recital. The hearing of the two addresses is obligatory upon the forty.

The Usages

When the sun passes the meridian and the *mu'adhdhin* gives the Call and the *imám* sits on the pulpit, the individual Worship stops, except for the Worship of Greeting upon entering the mosque. Talking need not stop until the opening of the address. The speaker, *khaṭíb*, salutes the people when he turns his face toward them and they return the salutation. Then, when the *mu'adhdhin* finishes the Call, he rises, facing the people. He does not turn to the right or left, but occupies his hands with the hilt of the sword or staff,[1] and with the pulpit, in order that he may not play with his

[1] The SM notes here (p. 229) that the author mentions both the sword and the staff, because the sword indicates that the city was taken forcibly by the sword, like e.g. Damascus, and if you turn back from Islam it is still in the hands of the Muslims to fight against you with it until you return to Islam. In every city that was taken peaceably, e.g. Cairo and its districts, the wooden staff is used. But the learned differ and say that half was taken forceably and half peaceably, and the present practice is to adopt a sword of wood to combine both statements.

hands, or place one of them on the other. He delivers two addresses, with a brief sitting between them. He does not use strange language, and does not drawl, and is not indistinct.[1] The address should be brief, elegant, and comprehensive. It is liked that he recite a verse in the second also. Whoever enters while the speaker is making the address should not give the salutation. But if he gives a salutation, he has no right to have it returned, but a gesture in return is excellent. Also, he does not say, 'Allah bless you', to those who sneeze.

These are the Stipulations for validity.

As for the Stipulations regarding the obligation to perform this Worship, it may be said, 'The Friday Observance is not obligatory except upon the male who is mature, sane, Muslim, free, resident in a village that includes forty possessing these qualities, or in a village which is a suburb which is reached by the Call from the town on the side near it when the sounds have ceased and the *mu'adhdhin* has a high voice, in accordance with the saying of Allah, 'When there is a Call to the Worship on Friday, hasten to the remembrance of Allah, and cease selling' (Qur'án lxxii. 9). It is permitted to those to omit the Friday Observance on the excuse of rain, mud, fright, illness and attending to the sick when the sick one has no other attendant. Then it is desirable for them, I mean those who have excuses, to delay the Noon Worship until the people finish the Friday Observance. If there should be present at the Friday Observance one who is ill, or one on a journey, or a slave, or a woman, their Friday Observance is valid,[2] and it serves as a substitute for the Noon Worship. And Allah knows better.

[1] The other texts have, 'does not chant'.

[2] On these four the Friday Observance is not prescribed, but it is to their advantage to be present.

Exposition of the Proprieties of the Friday Observance, in Accordance with the Usual Order, including Ten Particulars

The first is that he prepares for the Friday Observance on Thursday, resolving upon performing it and anticipating its excellence. So he engages in Supplication and Seeking Forgiveness and in saying the Praise after *'aṣr*, mid-afternoon, on Thursday, for the time of it, i.e. the hour after *'aṣr*, is equivalent[1] in
(240) excellence to 'the hour'[2] of Friday. Some one of the Fathers said, 'Allah has a favour apart from the apportioned sustenance of mankind: none is given of that favour except one who asks for it on Thursday afternoon and on Friday'.

He washes his clothes on that day and whitens them, prepares perfume, if he has none, and empties his heart of the pre-occupations which hinder it from early attendance at the Friday Observance. He states the Intention, on this night, of fasting on Friday, for that has excellence. Let the fasting be connected with Thursday or Saturday, not be by itself, for that is disliked. He engages in enlivening[3] this night by the performance of Worship and the complete recital of the Qur'án, for it has great excellence, and the
(241) excellence of Friday is drawn to it. . . . Some relate the saying of Muḥammad, 'Allah is merciful to one who hastens and goes to the mosque early and causes his family to bathe and bathes himself'. It is

[1] The other texts read, 'It is an hour that is compared to the "undefined" hour'.

[2] On this hour see Traditions, Nos. 288-93.

[3] 'To cause the night to live' is to perform in it acts of devotion, such as 'the Worship, supplication and intercession' (SM i. pp. 209, 210, 1.3), or, 'the Worship, invocations, praises, the formulæ for requesting forgiveness, blessing upon the Prophet and the completion of the recital of the Qur'án' (SM iii. p. 241A). *Iḥyā'* in legal terminology is turning to use uncultivated land by building upon it, or planting, sowing or watering it, or the like (*Dict. of Tech. Terms*, p. 401). It is probable from this use the meaning was extended to apply to spending the night in religious service (cf. Lane, *Lexicon*, p. 680).

said, 'Its meaning is, "He washed his clothes", for the word is handed down as "*ghasala*", "washed", [the other form was *ghassala*, "caused to wash"]'.

With this the proprieties of the anticipation of Friday are made complete, and he separates himself from the party of the unmindful, who, when they get
(242) up, say, 'What is this day?' One of the Fathers said, 'The man with the most perfect portion of the Friday Observance is the one who awaits it and observes it from the previous day. The one with the least portion is the one who says, when he gets up on Friday morning, "What's to-day?"' One of them used to spend the night before Friday in the mosque on its account.

Second. When he rises he begins with bathing after the appearance of dawn. If he does not go out in the early morning, the nearer his bathing is to his going out to the mosque the more liked it is, in order that it may be more close in time to the cleanness necessary for the Observance, for, bathing is one of the assuredly liked acts. Some of the learned have
(243) held it to be an obligation. Muḥammad said, 'The bathing of the Friday Observance is obligatory upon
(244) every one who has attained puberty'. There is the *mashhúr*,[1] 'well-known', tradition, handed down by Náfi'[2] from Ibn 'Umar, 'Let whoever comes to the Friday Observance bathe!'

(245) Muḥammad said, 'Let whoever is present at the Friday Observance, whether man or woman, bathe!'

(246) When two of the people of al-Madina reviled one another, they used to say, one to the other, 'Indeed you are worse than the one who does not bathe on Friday!'

(247) 'Umar said to 'Uthmán, when he entered while

[1] *Mashhúr*, 'well-known', is a statement which is handed down by at least three different reliable authorities, or a statement, which although widely disseminated later, was originally only transmitted by one person in the first generation (*Ency. of Islam*, ii. p. 192A).

[2] Abú 'Abdalláh Náfi' bin Hurmuz al-Madaní, *mawlá* of Ibn 'Umar, a most reliable traditionist (d. 116, or 120). *El-Nawawi*, p. 589.

he [i.e. 'Umar] was delivering the Friday address, 'Is this the hour?' so expressing disapproval of him for omitting to come early. He replied, 'I did nothing more, after I heard the Call to Worship, than perform the ablution and come out'. So he said, 'And the ablution too, when you know that the Messenger of Allah used to command us to bathe!' The allowability of omitting the complete bathing is known by the ablution of 'Uthmán, and by what is
(248) related to the effect that Muḥammad said, 'If anyone performs the ablution on Friday, good and well, and whoever bathes—bathing is more excellent!'

Let whoever bathes for the legal impurity pour water over his body a second time with the Intention of its being for the bathing of the Friday Observance. If he must be content with one bathing it will suffice him and he will secure the excellence if he states the Intention of them both, for the bathing of the Friday Observance will enter into and become part of the
(249) bathing of the legal impurity. One of the Companions came upon his son who had just bathed, so he asked him, 'Is it for the Friday observance?' He replied, 'Rather for legal impurity'. So he said, 'Do a second bathing', and he related the tradition of the washing of the Friday Observance as obligatory upon every person who has attained puberty. He gave him the command only because he had not stated the Intention of doing it as a Friday bathing. It was not strange that it should be said, 'The purpose is uncleanness', seeing that it is attained without the statement of the Intention. However, this position is impugnable in the case of the ablution also seeing it was made in the law a means of access, and its excellence must be sought. Whoever bathes and then becomes ceremonially unclean, does the ablution without invalidating his bathing, but it is more liked to guard against that.

The third is adornment. This is liked on this day. It is in three respects: clothing, cleanliness, and perfuming with scent.

(*a*) The cleanliness is attained by the use of the tooth stick, shaving the hair, paring the nails, cutting the moustache, and the rest of what has preceded in
(250) the Book of the Purification.[1] Ibn Mas'úd has said, 'Whoever pares his nails on Friday has Allah expel from him disease and introduce into him healing'. If he has entered the bathing place on Thursday or Wednesday he has attained the object.

(*b*) Let him perfume himself on this day with the best scent he has, to overcome disagreeable odours by it, and extend by it the essence and the scent to the noses of his neighbours who are present. The most liked perfume for men is the kind whose odour is apparent and whose colour is indistinguishable, and the perfume for women, whose colour is apparent and whose odour is indistinguishable. That is
(251) related in the Records of the Fathers. Al-Sháfi'í said, 'Whoever cleans his garment decreases his anxiety, and whoever chooses a good scent increases his sense'.

(*c*) As for the clothing, the best liked is white garments, since the best liked to Allah are white ones. One should not wear that which has something striking in it, and the wearing of black is not *sunna*, Usage, and does not have excellence. Rather a company disliked to look at it, for it is an innovation[2] that has taken place after the Messenger of Allah. The '*imáma*, 'turban', is liked on this day.

(252) Wáthila bin al-Asqa'[3] related that the Messenger of Allah said, 'Allah and his angels bless the wearers of the turban on Friday'. However, if the heat distresses one, there is no harm in his removing it before the Worship and after it, but he should not remove it

1 This is Book iii, of the First Quarter of the *Iḥyá'* (SM v. pp 302 ff.).

2 *Bid'a*, 'innovation', is something novel in practice or doctrine, and is the opposite of *sunna*, 'the (old) way'. *Ency. of Islam*, p. 712 f. (Macdonald); *Development of Muslim Theology*, p. 74.

3 Wáthila bin al-Asqa' al-Laithí, Companion (d. 83, or 85 or 86); *el-Nawawi*, p. 612.

during the time of his hastening from his residence to the Friday Observance, nor at the time of the Worship, nor when the *imâm* ascends the pulpit nor during the address.

The fourth is going early to the congregational mosque. It is liked that he set out for the mosque from a distance of two or three parasangs [of three miles]. Let him go early. The time of going early begins with the appearance of the dawn. The excellence of going early is great. It is fitting that during his hastening to the Friday Observance he should be humble, lowly, stating the Intention of the *i'tikâf*,[1] 'the Retreat into the mosque for religious occupation' until [the end of[2]] the Worship, purposing to lose no time in answering the call of Allah to him to the Friday Observance, and to hasten to obtain His forgiveness and the pleasing of Him.

(253) Muḥammad said, 'Whoever goes to the Friday Observance in the first hour, it is as if he offered a camel. Whoever goes in the second hour, it is as if he offered a head of cattle. Whoever goes in the third hour, it is as if he offered a ram. Whoever goes in the fourth hour, it is as if he offered a chicken. Whoever goes in the fifth hour, it is as if he gave an egg. Then when the *imâm* comes out, the leaves are rolled up, and the pens are raised, and the angels meet at the pulpit to hear the Invocation. So, whoever comes after that, comes only for the duty of the Worship, and has nothing at all of the excellence.' The first hour is until the appearance of the sun. The second is until its rising above the horizon. The third is to its broadening out, when the feet are burned,[3] and the fourth and fifth are after the middle of the morning until it passes the meridian. The excellence of these two is small—and the time of the passing of the meridian is the Worship's right and has no excellence attached to it.

[1] For the *i'tikâf*, Retreat, see Introduction, p. 34.
[2] This is added by the SM. [3] By the heat of the sun.

(254) Muḥammad said, 'Three things there are, that men, if they knew what was in them, would [ride their camels[1]] for. They are the Call, the first row, and the very early arrival at the Friday Observance.'

(255) Aḥmad bin Ḥandal said, 'The most excellent of them is the early arrival at the Friday Observance'.

(256) In Tradition it is said, 'When it is Friday the angels sit on the doors of the mosque with leaves in their hands and pens of gold, writing the first as the first, accord-
(257) ing to their orders'. It appears in the Records that 'The angels miss a creature when he delays after his time on Friday, and they ask one another about him, "What has such a one done, and what is it that delays him after his usual time?" So they say, "O Allah! If poverty delays him, make him rich! If illness delays him, make him well! If work engages him, free him for Thy divine service! If amusement delays him, turn toward him, that he may turn with his heart to Thine obedience!"'

In the first century, early at dawn and after the dawn, on Friday, the roads were seen full of men walking with lanterns, pressing together in the roads to the congregational mosques as in the Feast days, until that practice disappeared. It is said that the first innovation that occurred in Islam was the abandonment of going early to the mosque. And how should the Muslims not be ashamed before the Jews and Christians, seeing that they go early to the synagogues and churches on Saturday and Sunday, and the pursuers of this life go early to the open spaces around the congregational mosque, sell and seek profits, and why do those seeking the next abode not get ahead of them?

(258) It it said, 'Men will be near, when they look upon the Face of Allah, in proportion to the earliness of their going to the Friday Observance'.

(259) Ibn Mas'úd entered the mosque early and saw three persons who had preceded him in earliness, and was grieved at that and began to say to himself,

[1] The other text has 'they would run like camels'.

blaming himself, 'The fourth of four!' And yet the fourth of four is early.

The fifth is the manner of entry. One should not pass over the necks of the people, nor pass before them, earliness making that easy for him, for a very great threat has been issued regarding stepping over the necks, which is that he is made a bridge on Resurrection Day that men will step over. Ibn
(260) Juraij[1] has related a *mursal*[2] tradition, 'lacking the authority of a Companion', that the Messenger of Allah, while he was giving the Friday address, saw a man stepping over the necks of the people until he got in front, and then he sat down. So after the Prophet had finished his Worship he went towards the man until he caught up with him and said, 'O such a one! what hindered you from celebrating the Friday Observance with us to-day?' He said, 'O Prophet of Allah! I have celebrated the Friday Observance with you'. So the Prophet said, 'Did I not see you stepping over the necks of the people?' He indicated by it that he had rendered his work useless.

(261) In a *musnad*, 'supported', tradition it is related that he said, 'What hindered you from worshipping with us?' He replied, 'And did you not see me?' So Muhammad said, 'I saw you; you procrastinated, and you did harm!' That is, 'You were late from the early attendance, and you harmed the attendance'.

Whenever the first row is left empty one may step over the necks of the people, for they have lost their right and have left the place of excellence. Al-Ḥasan said, 'Step over the necks of the people who sit upon the doorways of the mosques on Friday, for they do not deserve any respect'.[3]

[1] 'Abdalmalik bin 'Abdal'azíz bin Juraij al-Makkí, *mawlá* Baní Umaiya (d. 149-51, 155). *Haji Khalfae Lexicon*, i. p. 80; iii. 28; *Ibn Coteiba*, p. 246.

[2] The SM states that it lacks also the Successor's authority, and therefore is what is technically called *mu'ḍal*.

[3] Strictly, 'they have no inviolability'.

When there are not in the mosque any but those who are at the Worship, it is fitting that he should not give the greeting,[1] for it imposes the responsibility of an answer that would be out of place.

The sixth is that one does not pass before the people. He sits by himself, near a column or a wall, so that they may not pass before him, I mean, before the worshipper, for, although that does not stop the
(262) Worship, it is something prohibited. Muhammad said. 'Indeed, that he should stand forty years were better for him than to pass before a worshipper'.

(263) Muḥammad said, 'Indeed, that a man should be ashes, fine and copious, which the winds blow away, were better for him than that he should pass before one who is worshipping'.

(264) It has been related in another tradition, regarding the passer and the worshipper, when the latter worships in the road and comes short in repelling the passer, that Muḥammad said, 'If the one passing in front of a worshipper and the worshipper himself could know their responsibility in that regard, they would know that to stand forty years would be better for him than to pass before him'.

The column and the wall and the worship-mat as spread out are a bound for the worshipper, so he should repel whoever passes by it.

(265) Muḥammad said, 'Let him repel him, and, if he objects [still let him repel him, and, if he objects[2]] let him contend with him, for he is a devil'.

(266) Abú Sa'íd al-Khudrí[3] used to repel whoever passed before him to the extent that he threw him down, for perhaps the men hung on to him. Then the man implored the protection of Mirwán[4] against him, and

[1] That is, should not say, 'Peace be upon you!'

[2] The SM omits this repetition.

[3] Abú Sa'íd Sa'd bin Málik al-Khudrí al-Anṣárí (d. 74). *Ibn Hajar*, ii. p. 333; *Ibn Doreid*, p. 269; *Annales at-Ṭabari*, i. pp. 1492, 1682; ii. p. 418; iii. p. 2338.

[4] Mirwán bin al-Ḥakím b. Abú al-'Áṣ al-Umawí (d. 65), the fourth Umaiyad khalífa. Muir and Weir, op. cit., p. 318.

then he would inform him that the Prophet ordered him to do that.

If any should not find a column let him set up before him something about a cubit long, in order that that may be an indication of his boundary.

The seventh is that he seeks the first row, for its excellence is great, as we have related in the tradition.[1]
(267) In Tradition it is related, 'Whoever causes his family to bath and bathes himself and hastens and arrives early at the mosque and gets near the *imám* and hearkens, has that as an atonement for what he committed between the two Friday Observances, along with three days extra'. And in another
(268) version, it says, 'Allah forgives him until the next Friday Observance'. It is stipulated in one of the versions that he should not step over the necks of the people.

In seeking the first row, one should not be unmindful of three things: (*a*) The first of them is that, when he is used to seeing, near the one giving the address, a thing disapproved by Allah, which he is unable to change, such as the wearing of silk on the part of the *imám* or someone else, or worship with a heavy weapon, which engages the attention, or a golden weapon, or something else which ought to be disapproved, then to be in back is more safe, and more concentrating for careful thought. So did a company of the learned, seeking safety.

(269) It was said to Bishr bin al-Ḥárith,[2] 'We notice that you go early but worship in the last of the rows'. So he said, 'Nearness of hearts only is desired, not nearness of bodies'. He indicated by it that the rear gave him greater safety of heart.
(270) Sufyán al-Thawrí looked at Shu'aib bin Ḥarb[3] near

[1] This is Tradition No. 254.

[2] Abú Muḥammad Bishr bin Manṣúr al-Sulamí (d. 209). De Slane, op. cit., i. p. 517; *Fihrist*, p. 184. This is the one to whom the SM applies the tradition, rather than Bishr bin Ḥárith, note 1, p. 90.

[3] Shu'aib bin Ḥarb (Abú Ṣáliḥ) al-Madá'iní (d. 197). *Ibn Ṭagri Bardii*, i. p. 562.

the pulpit, listening to an address from Abú Ja'far al-Manṣúr.[1] So after he finished the Worship he said, 'Your nearness to this man disturbed my heart. Were you safe in hearing a speech, the disapproval of which is incumbent upon you, and you do not do so?' Then Sufyán mentioned what the tradition said about wearing black. So he replied, 'O Abú
(271) 'Abdalláh! is it not related in Tradition, 'Draw near and hear?' Then he answered, 'Woe to you! That refers to the khalífas,[2] the orthodox, the rightly guided, but as for these, the more you keep your distance from them and do not consider them, the nearer you are to Allah!'

(272) Sa'íd bin 'Ámir[3] said, 'I performed a Worship at the side of Abú al-Dardá', and then he began to go back in the rows until we were in the last row. So after we had done the Worship I said to him, "Is it not said, 'The best of the rows is the first of them?'" He replied, "Yes, only, this people is one that has obtained mercy, and is given regard from among the peoples, and Allah, when he gives regard to a people in the Worship, forgives him and whoever of mankind is behind him. So I went back only hoping that He would forgive me on account of one whom Allah regards."'

(273) One of the traditionists relates that he said, 'I heard the Messenger of Allah say that'. So, whoever stays back for this purpose, preferring and manifesting excellence of disposition, does no harm, and of
(274) this it is said, 'Works are to be judged by intentions'.

[1] Abú Ja'far al-Manṣúr (d. 158), second 'Abbásid khalífa. Muir and Weir, *Caliphate*, index; Nöldeke, *Sketches from Eastern History*, pp. 107 ff.

[2] The SM says these are the first four and also 'Umar bin 'Abdal-'azíz. They are in notes 1, p. 47; 3, p. 128; 2, p. 49; 1, p. 58; and 4, p. 53.

[3] Sa'íd bin 'Ámir, Successor, unknown; Ibn Khalfún was sure he was Sa'íd b. 'Ámir b. Khudhaim (Judhaim in the SM is a misprint), but Ibn Hajar objected that the latter died in the khiláfate of 'Umar I. Bin Khudhaim, according to the *Tajríd Asmá' al-Ṣaḥába*, governed Ḥamṣ for 'Umar I (p. 240).

(*b*) The second is that, if there is no enclosure[1] near the one giving the address, separated from the mosque for the use of the sultans, then the first row is liked. [Otherwise the enclosure is to be preferred.[2]] But some of the learned have expressed dislike of enter-
(275) ing the enclosure. Al-Ḥasan and Bakr[3] al-Muzaní were wont not to worship in the enclosure, considering that it was restricted to the use of the sultans, as it is an innovation in the mosques that occurred after the time of the Messenger of Allah. A mosque is free for all men, and that enclosure was cut off in contradiction to this principle.

(276) Anas bin Málik and 'Imrán bin Ḥaṣín worshipped in the enclosure, and did not express dislike of that, out of desire for nearness. Perhaps the dislike is especially for its exclusiveness and the prohibition [against others worshipping in it[4]], but as for the single matter of the enclosure, if there is no prohibition, dislike of it is not obligatory.

(*c*) The third is that the pulpit cuts some of the rows. The first row is only the one continuous row which is in the space in the front of the pulpit, and what is on its two sides is cut off. Al-Thawrí used to say,
(277) 'The first row is the outside one in front of the pulpit', and it is reasonable, because it is continuous and because the one sitting in it faces the one giving the address and hears him. It might be said, 'The one nearest to the *qibla* is the first row, and no regard is paid here to [the pulpit]'.[5]

Worship in the 'azars and the open spaces outside the mosque is disliked. Some of the Companions used to beat the men and make them get up from the open spaces.

[1] The SM adds that these were first built in the times of al-Umaiya out of fear of enemies; cf. also Lane, *Lexicon*, p. 2536A, and *Modern Egyptians*, App. F.

[2] This is omitted by the SM.

[3] The SM objects to the reference of the traditions to Bakr.

[4] This is added by the SM.

[5] The other texts read, 'to this meaning'.

The eighth is that one cuts off his preliminary Worship when the *imám* comes out [to ascend the pulpit[1]], and he stops talking also. Rather, he occupies himself with the reply to the *mu'adhdhin*, and then with hearing the address. It was the custom of some of the common people to make a Prostration at the standing up of the *mu'adhdhins* [for the Call to Worship], but there is no basis established for it in any record or tradition. But if it fits in with a Prostration of Recital there is no harm in it, for it is an excellent time to make a supplication, and there is no judgement of unlawfulness against this Prostration, for there is no cause to
(278) make it unlawful. It is related from 'Alí and 'Uthmán that they said, 'Whoever listens and is silent has two rewards; whoever does not listen and is silent has one reward; whoever hears and lets a word[2] slip has two sins against him, and whoever does not hear and lets a word slip has one'.

(279) Muḥammad said, 'Whoever says to his companion, while the *imám* is making the address, "Be silent", or "Hush", has himself let a word slip, and whoever lets a word slip while the *imám* is making the address has no Friday Observance to his credit'. This indicates that causing others to be silent should be by gesture, or by throwing a pebble, not by utterance.

(280) In the tradition of Abú Dharr[3] it is stated, 'When he questioned Ubai while the Prophet was making an address and said, "When was this *súra* sent down?" Ubai gestured to him to keep silent. So when the Messenger of Allah came down from the pulpit Ubai said to him, "Go, and you have no Friday observance". So Abú Dharr complained to the Prophet, and he replied, "Ubai spoke the truth".'

[1] This is the SM's explanation.
[2] This is the SM's definition.
[3] Abú Dharr al-Ghifárí, Companion (d. 32 or 33). *Ency. of Islam*, i. p. 83; *el-Nawawi*, p. 108; Muir and Weir, op. cit., pp. 211 ff.

If anyone is far from the *imám* it is not fitting that he should talk, about learning or anything else, but rather keep silent, since all that has its chain of consequences, and results in murmuring, so that it reaches the listeners. He does not sit in a circle with anyone who is speaking. So, let whoever is unable to listen on account of his distance keep quiet, for that is liked. Since the Worship is disliked in the time of the address of the *imám*, much more is
(281) talking disliked. 'Alí said, 'The Worship is disliked at four times: after the dawn, after *'aṣr*, "mid-afternoon", at mid-day and while the *imám* is making the address'.

The ninth is that he observe, in following out the *imám's* pattern in the Friday Observance, that which we have mentioned in regard to the other Worships. So, when he hears the Recital of the *imám*, he does not recite anything but the Fátiḥa. When he finishes the Friday Observance he recites the *súra* of 'The Praise[1] belongs to Allah' (i), and, 'Say, It [the fact[2]] is, Allah is One!' (cxii), and the two *súras* of Seeking
(282) Refuge (cxiii, cxiv), each seven times. One of the Fathers related that whoever does that is preserved from sin from one Friday Observance to the next Friday Observance, for it is a guard for him against Satan.

It is liked that he say, after the Friday Observance, 'O Allah! O Rich One! O One of Praise! O Beginner! O Returner! O Merciful! O Loving One! make me, by Thy lawful things, do without Thine unlawful
(283) things, and, by Thy favour, any other besides Thyself!' It is said, 'Whoever perseveres in this supplication has Allah make him do without His creatures, "and apportions him a sustenance from a source he does not expect"' (Qur'án lxv. 2).

Then, after the Friday Observance, he performs a

[1] This is one of the names of the Fátiḥa; the list of them is given in SM v. 132C and the *Dict. of Tech. Terms*, p. 660.

[2] This is one of the possible translations of the verse. Zamakhsharí, *Mufaṣṣal* (ed. Broch, 1840), pp. 50, 112; Baiḍ, *ad loc.*

(284) Worship of six *rak'as*. Ibn 'Umar has related that Muḥammad used, after the Friday Observance, to perform a Worship of two *rak'as*, and Abú Huraira states four, and 'Alí and 'Abdalláh bin 'Abbás six and all are valid, in different circumstances, and the most complete the most excellent.

The tenth is that he remains at the congregational mosque until he performs the '*aṣr* Worship, and if he should remain until the Sunset one, that would be
(285) most excellent. It is said, 'Whoever performs the '*aṣr*, "mid-afternoon", Worship in the mosque has the reward of a Pilgrimage, and whoever performs the Sunset one has the reward of a Pilgrimage and a minor visit to the Ka'ba'.

If he is not safe against merely affecting a goodly way and against the coming of evil [e.g. pride] upon him from men's looking upon him in his Worship in retreat, or, if he fears wading into something that does not concern[1] him, it is more excellent that he should return to his house, invoking the remembrance of Allah, considering His benefits, thanking Allah for His giving of help, fearful of his coming short, watching over his heart and his tongue until the setting of the sun, so that the 'hour of honour' may not escape him. He does not engage, in the congregational mosque or the other mosques, in talk of
(286) this life. Muḥammad said, 'There will come upon men a time when their talk in the mosques will be of this life's concern. Allah is not in need of them, so do not sit with them.'

Exposition of the Proprieties and Usages Not Included in the Preceding Arrangements

This applies to the whole day and is in seven particulars:

[1] This advice is related to the very important doctrine of 'Utilitarianism in Islam', that only things of immediate benefit for this life and the next are to be undertaken, based on the tradition that part of the elegance of a man's *islám*, 'resignation to Allah', is leaving alone what does not concern him, for which see Lane, *Lexicon*, p. 2180A; Macdonald, *Religious Attitude*, pp. 119 ff.

The first is that he is present at the assemblies of learning in the early morning and after mid-afternoon, and does not attend the gatherings of the story-tellers, for there is no benefit in their talk. It is fitting that the devotee should not be unoccupied during the whole of Friday with good deeds and supplications, so that the 'hour of honour' may meet him while he is at some good. It is not fitting that he should be present at the circles of men before the Worship.
(287) 'Abdalláh bin 'Umar related that the Prophet forbade sitting in a circle on Friday before the Worship, unless there is one knowing about Allah, who reminds of the days of Allah, and gives understanding in the religion of Allah, speaking in the congregational mosque in the early morning. Then he may sit before him and so will be uniting early attendance and hearing. The hearing of learning beneficial in the next abode is more excellent than his occupying himself with supererogatory performances of the
(288) Worship. For Abú Dharr has related that presence at an assembly of learning is more excellent than a Worship of a thousand *rak'as*.

(289) Anas bin Málik said, about the saying of Allah, 'And when the Worship is finished, scatter abroad in the earth, and desire some of the favour of Allah' (Qur'án lxii. 10), 'Is it not that it is not seeking this life, but visiting some sick one, and being present at a funeral, and acquiring learning, and calling on a brother in Allah?' Allah has called learning excellent in a number of places. He said, 'And he taught you what you did not know, and the favour of Allah to you was great' (Qur'án iv. 113). He said, 'And We indeed brought David favour' (Qur'án xxxiv. 10), meaning learning. So acquire learning on this day. Teaching is one of the most excellent of good works. Worship is more excellent than sitting with the story-tellers, since they were used to consider it an innovation, and to exclude story-tellers from the congregational mosque.

(290) Ibn 'Umar was present[1] at his place of sitting in the congregational mosque, and behold, a story-teller was telling a story in his place. So he said, 'Get up from my sitting place!' Then he replied, 'I'll not get up, for I have sat down and got to it before you!' So Ibn 'Umar went to the master of the guard and he got him up. But if that [i.e. story-telling] were a part of the *sunna*, Usage, to get him up would not have
(291) been lawful, for, indeed, Muḥammad has said, 'Do not, by any means, any of you, get his brother up from his sitting-place and then sit there, but make room and
(292) be comfortable'. Ibn 'Umar, whenever a man got up for him from his sitting place, used not to sit in it
(293) until the man should return to it. It is related that a story-teller sat in the space before the room of 'Â'isha, so she sent to Ibn 'Umar, 'This one has harmed me by his stories and distracted me from my Supererogatory Worship'. So Ibn 'Umar beat him until he broke his stick over him, and then cast him out.

The second is that he watch well for the 'hour of
(294) honour', for, in the *mashhûr*, 'well-known', tradition, it is related that on Friday there is an hour that no Muslim creature meets while asking something of
(295) Allah without His giving it to him. In another tradition it is said, 'Does not come upon it while worshipping'. There is disagreement for it is said, 'It is the hour of the appearing of the sun', and it is said, 'It is at the passing of the meridian', and it is said, 'With the Call to Worship', and it is said, 'When the *imám* mounts the pulpit and begins the address', and it is said, 'When the people stand up for the Worship', and it is said, 'The last part of the time of '*aṣr*, "mid-afternoon", I mean, in the "hour of preference"',[2] and it is said, 'Before the setting of the

[1] The other texts read, 'went early to'.

[2] The '*aṣr* is divided by al-Bájúrí into five periods, as regards the acceptability of the Worship, termed the times of (1) excellence; (2) preference; (3) allowability; (4) allowable but disliked; and (5) prohibition. Others add (6) the time of necessity, which is the last

(296) sun'.[1] Fáṭima[2] used to observe that time, and order her servant to look at the sun, and inform her of its going down. Then she would begin with Supplication and Seeking Forgiveness, until the sun set, and she used to relate that that hour was the one waited
(297) for, and that she handed it on from her father. Some of the learned said, 'It is undefined during the whole day, like the Night of Decree, so that those who supplicate may do much watching for it'. It is said,
(298) 'It moves about among the hours of Friday, like the moving about of the Night of Decree'. And this is the more likely. It has a mystery which it is not fitting to mention in the Science of Practical Religion. Notwithstanding, it is fitting that he should believe
(299) that Muḥammad said, 'Your Lord has in the days of your age gifts. Is it not so? Therefore address yourselves to them.'

Friday is one of that whole number of days, so it is fitting that the creature should be, during the whole day, attentive to it, by presenting his heart and continuing in the remembering, and discarding the evil suggestions of this life. Then perhaps he will have the good fortune to obtain some of
(300) those gifts. Ka'b al-Aḥbár has said, 'It is in the last hour of Friday, and that is at the setting of the sun'. Then Abú Huraira said, 'And how is it the last hour, when I heard the Messenger of Allah say, "No creature who is worshipping meets it", but the setting of the sun is not a time for Worship?' Then Ka'b replied 'Did not the Messenger of Allah

when it may be done; (7) excusable, at noon; (8) the time of overtaking; and finally (9) the time when the Substitution payment is made.

The sunset has one period; the evening has two, of preference and of allowability; the morning has five, and noon has one extended period. Al-Bájúrí, *Commentary on Abu Shujá'*, i. p. 128 f.; *Kitáb al-Ṣalá, faṣl*, i.

[1] The SM says there are more than twenty statements about it, and al-Ghazzálí mentions only as many as Abú Ṭálib has in the *Qút al-Qulúb*

[2] Fáṭima, the daughter of Muḥammad (d. 11). *Ency. of Islam*, ii. pp. 85 ff.

say, "Whoever sits down waiting the Worship is himself at Worship"?' He replied, 'Yes indeed!' He rejoined, 'So then, that is Worship!' And Abú Huraira kept silent. Ka'b was inclined to the idea that it was a mercy of Allah to those who performed the rightful duties of this day, and the time of sending it was at the finishing of the work.

In short, this time is honourable, along with the time of the *imám's* mounting of the pulpit, so let him increase supplication at those two times.

The third is that it is liked to increase the intercession for the Messenger of Allah on this day.
(301) For Muḥammad said, 'Whoever performs the intercession, *ṣalá*, for me on Friday eighty times, has Allah forgive him the sins of eighty years'.
(302) It was said, 'O Messenger of Allah, what is the manner of the intercession for you?' He replied, 'You say, "O Allah, bless (*ṣallí 'alá*), Muḥammad, Thy creature, Thy Prophet, Thy Messenger, the unlettered[1] Prophet", and count one. It is also well if you should say, "O Allah, bless Muḥammad and the family of Muḥammad with a blessing, *ṣalá*, that to Thee is pleasing and of his right is a fulfilment, and give him access and send him to the station of glory that Thou didst promise him, and reward him on our behalf what he is worth, and reward him on our behalf the most excellent of that with which Thou hast rewarded any prophet on behalf of his people, and bless him and all his brethren among the pro hets and among the righteous, O Thou most merciful of those showing Mercy".' You say this seven times, for it has been
(303) said, 'Whoever says it on seven Fridays seven times each Friday has obligatory for him the intercession of Muḥammad'.

[1] *Al-ummí*, says the SM, may mean 'unlettered', or 'Meccan', or, 'the one with the Fátiḥa, the Mother of the Book' (SM ii. p. 34D). Other references are Nöldeke, *Geschichte des Qorans*, p. 10; Ṭabarí, *Tafsír*, i. pp. 283, 286; Rází, *Mafátiḥ*, i. p. 381; Fleischer, *Kleinere Schriften*, by Indices.

(304) If one wishes to do more, let him bring the traditional intercession (*ṣalá*) and say, 'O Allah, cause the excellences of Thy blessing, Thy growing benefactions and the honour of Thy benevolences, mercy and felicitation to come upon Muḥammad, who is the chief of those sent by Thee, the leader of those fearing Thee, the Seal of the Prophets, the Messenger of the Lord of the worlds, the Captain of Good and the Conqueror of Righteousness, the Prophet of Mercy and the Chief of the People. O Allah, send him to a station of glory through which his nearness increases and by which his eye is refreshed and on account of which the first and the last emulate him without envy. O Allah, give him favour, excellence, honour, access, the exalted degree and the lofty, overtopping position. O Allah, give Muḥammad his request, extend him his hope, make him the first intercessor, and the first successful intercessor. O Allah, establish his argument, weigh down his balance, make effective his cause, and exalt his degree among the highest of those with Thee. O Allah, assemble us in his party and make us to be of the people of his intercession! Make us live according to his Usage, and cause us to die according to his religious party, and bring us to his watering place, and give us drink in his cup, unashamed, not regretting, not doubting, not changing, not trying others, and not tried! *Ámín!* O Lord of the Worlds!'

In short, whatever expression of the blessing one uses, even though it should be the well-known expression of the Witnessing, he is one that is saying the Blessing upon the Prophet. It is fitting that he should join to it the Seeking Forgiveness, for that also is liked on this day.

The fourth is the Recital of the Qur'án. So let him recite much of it. Let him recite the *Súrat al-*
(305) *Kahf*, Cave (xviii), especially, for it has been related from Ibn 'Abbás and Abú Huraira in a tradition traced back to the Prophet that whoever recites the *Súrat al-Kahf* on the eve of Friday or on Fridya is given a

light from where he recites it to Mecca, and he is forgiven until the next Friday, along with three days extra, and 70,000 angels intercede for him until he enters upon the morning and he is preserved from illness, disease of the stomach, pleurisy, leprosy, elephantiasis and the testing of the Antichrist.

It is liked that he finish a recital of the Qur'án on Friday and the eve of Friday, if he can, and let his finishing be in the two *rak'as* of the Dawn Worship if he has been reciting in the night, or in the two *rak'as* of the Sunset Worship, or, between the Call to Worship and the Institution of the Friday Observance,
(306) for it has great excellence. The pious, *ábidún*, used to like to recite on Friday, 'Say, He is Allah, One!'
(307) (cxii) a thousand times. It is said, 'Whoever recites it in ten *rak'as*, or twenty, does what is more excellent than an entire recital of the Qur'án'.

(308) They used to make intercession for the Prophet a thousand times. They used to say, 'O the Praise of Allah', and 'The Praise is Allah's', and 'There is no god but Allah', and 'Allah is greater', a thousand times. If he recites the six Praises on
(309) Friday or the eve of Friday it is well. It is not recorded from the Prophet that he used to recite the *súras* in their total substance except on Friday, and on the eve of Friday.

(310) He used to recite at the Sunset Worship of the eve of Friday, 'Say, O ye unbelievers!' (cix) and
(311) 'Say, He is Allah, One!' (cxii). He used to recite in the last of the evening Worships on the eve of Friday, *Súrat al-Jumú'a* (lxii) and *al-Munáfiqún*
(312) (lxiii). It is related that he used to recite them both in the two *rak'as* of the Friday Observance. He
(313) used to recite in the Morning Worship of Friday *Súrat Sajdat Luqmán* (xxxi), and *Súrat al-Dahr* (lxxvi), 'Has there come upon men?'

The fifth is the performances of the Worship. It is liked, when one enters the congregational mosque, not to sit down until he performs four *rak'as* in which he recites, 'Say, He is Allah, One' (cxii) two

hundred times, in each *rak'a* fifty times. For it is
(314) handed down from the Messenger of Allah that whoever does so will not die until he sees his place of sitting in the Garden, or it is seen for him.

He should not omit the two *rak'as* of the Greeting, even if the *imám* should be making the address, but
(315) he should be brief. The Messenger of Allah ordered that. In a *gharíb*,[1] 'strange', tradition, it is related that Muḥammad kept silent for one entering the mosque until he performed the two *rak'as*. The Kúfís[2] said, 'If the *imám* pauses for him, he performs them'.

It is liked on this day that he should perform a Worship of four *rak'as*, with the four *súras* of *al-An'ám* (vi), *al-Kahf* (xviii), *Ṭáhá* (xx), and *Yá Sín* (xxxvi). If he cannot recite them well he recites *Súrat Yá Sín*, *Súrat Sajdat Luqmán* (xxxi), *Súrat al-Dukhán* (xliv) and *Súrat al-Mulk* (lxvii). He should not omit reciting the four *súras* on the eve of Friday, for there is great excellence in them. Whoever cannot recite them well should then recite what he can do well, and it is equal to the complete recital of the Qur'án for him. He should do much of the recital of the *Súrat al-Ikhláṣ* (cxii).

It is liked that he should perform the Worship of the Praise, according to the manner that shall be
(316) mentioned in the Chapter on the Voluntary Worship, for Muḥammad said to his uncle 'Abbás,[3] 'Use it in
(317) the Worship on every Friday'. Ibn 'Abbás was wont not to omit performing this act of Worship on Friday after the passing of the meridian, and used to tell of the grandeur of its excellence. The best is

[1] *Gharíb*, 'strange', 'rare'; if a tradition is transmitted by only one definite person of later generations, it is called *gharíb* in reference to that person (*Ency. of Islam*, ii. p. 192A).

[2] The Kúfís are named after the city of al-Kúfa, founded A.H. 18 by the khalífa Umar. Muir and Weir, op. cit., p. 123; Nicholson, *Literary History of the Arabs*, p. 343.

[3] Abú al-Faḍl 'Abbás bin 'Abdalmuṭṭalib, uncle of Muḥammad (d. 32). *Ency. of Islam*, i. pp. 9 ff.

that he should devote his time up to the passing of the meridian to the Worship itself, and after the Friday Observance until mid-afternoon, to the hearing of learning, and after that until sunset, to the Praise, and the Asking of Forgiveness.

The sixth is almsgiving. It is liked on this day and excels in excellence on this day especially, for it is multiplied, except for one who asks while the *imám* is making the address, and talks during the address of
(318) the *imám*, for this is disliked. Ṣáliḥ bin Muḥammad[1] said, 'A poor man begged on Friday at the side of my father. So a man gave a bit to hand it to him,
(319) but my father did not take it from him'. Ibn Mas'úd said, 'Whenever a man begs in the mosque he is worthy not to receive. Whenever he begs on
(320) the Qur'án, do not give to him'. Of the learned there are some who dislike giving alms to beggars in the congregational mosques, who step over the necks of the people, unless he beg standing or sitting in his place without stepping over.

(321) Ka'b al-Aḥbár said, 'Whoever is present at the Friday Observance and then goes out and gives two different things of the things that are given as alms, and then returns and performs two *rak'as*, completing their Bowing, their Prostration and their humbleness, and then says, "O Allah, I ask Thee by Thy name, in the name of Allah, the Merciful and Compassionate, in the name of Him beside whom there is no God, the Living, the Self-Existent, whom neither slumber takes nor sleep", does not ask Allah anything but He gives it'.

(322) Some one of the Fathers said, 'Whoever feeds a poor man on Friday and then goes early and is early at the congregational mosque, and does not harm anyone, and then, when the *imám* gives the Salutation at the close of the Worship, says, "In the name

[1] Ṣáliḥ bin Aḥmad bin Muḥammad b. Ḥanbal al-Shaibání (son of the one in note 1, p. 76), (d. 265, 266). *Ibn Ṭagri Bardii*, ii. p. 42; De Slane, op. cit., i. p. 45.

of Allah, the Merciful and Compassionate, the Living, the Self-Existent One, I ask Thee that Thou forgive me and have mercy on me, and preserve me from the Fire", and then makes supplication for what seems good to him, is answered'.

The seventh is that he should spend Friday for the next abode. So he withdraws in it from all the works of this life, and does many *wirds*,[1] 'devotional recitals', in it. He should not begin a journey in it,
(323) for it is related that whoever makes a journey on the eve and early part of Friday has his two angels invoke curses upon him, for it is forbidden after the appearance of dawn, except when the company of fellow travellers will pass on. Some of the Fathers disliked buying water in the mosque from the water-carrier, for drinking or donating it, in order that it might not be bought in the mosque, for selling and
(324) buying in the mosque are disliked. But they said, 'There is no harm, were he to give the bit of money outside the mosque, and then drink it or donate it to others as a religious service in the mosque'.

In short, he should, on Friday, do more of his *wirds*, Recitals, and of his various good works, for whenever Allah loves a creature, He occupies him in the excellent times in excellent works. Whenever He hates him, He occupies him in the excellent times in evil deeds, that that may be more productive of pain in his punishment and more intensifying of the hate of him, because of his refusal of the blessing of the time and his violation of the sacredness of the time.

On Friday, certain *du'as*, Supplications, are liked, and mention of them will be made in the Book of *Da'awát*,[2] Supplications, if Allah will, and may Allah bless every elect creature!

[1] This is Book x of the First Quarter of the *Iḥyá'*, SM v. pp. 118 ff.; see Introduction, p. 32.

[2] This is Book ix of the First Quarter of the *Iḥyá'*, SM v; see also Introduction, p. 31.

CHAPTER VI

VARIOUS PROBLEMS WHICH CAUSE GENERAL DISTRESS AND WHICH THE DEVOTEE NEEDS TO KNOW

THE problems which are of rare occurrence we have investigated in the Books of *Fiqh*, Canon Law.

The Problem of the Slight Act: Although it does not invalidate the Worship, it is disliked, unless there is need for it. That kind of act is the repelling of a passer by and the killing of a scorpion that one fears and can kill with one or two blows, but whenever they become three, they are too many, and invalidate the Worship. Similarly one may get rid of a louse and a flea, whenever he suffers from them. Similarly, his need of scratching, which disturbs him from humble-
(325) ness. Ma'ádh used to catch a louse and a flea,
(326) during the Worship, and Ibn 'Umar used to kill a louse and a flea during the Worship, so that the blood
(327) would appear on his hand. Al-Nakha'i said, 'You catch it and disable it and there is nothing against
(328) one if he kill it'. Ibn Musaiyab said, 'He takes it
(329) and benumbs it and then throws it down'. Mujáhid[1] said, 'The most liked thing, in my opinion, is to let it alone, unless it causes one suffering, and so distracts him from his Worship, and then he should disable it enough so that it will not cause him suffering and then throw it away'.

This is a permission only, and otherwise the perfect thing is to guard against the action, even if it
(81) be slight. On that account one of them was accustomed not to brush away a fly, for he said, 'I will not

[1] He is not further defined, but is probably Abú Hajjáj Mujáhid bin Jabr (Jubair, in *Ibn Khall.*), Successor (d. 101-3 or 111). De Slane, *Ibn Khallikan*, i. p. 568; *el-Nawawi*, p. 540; Wüstenfeld, *Dahabi, Liber Classium Virorum*, iii. 18.

accustom myself to it, so that it may corrupt my Worship for me, seeing that I have heard that criminals before kings are patient under great suffering, and do not move'.

Whenever one yawns, there is no harm in putting his hand over his mouth, which is preferable. If he sneezes he says, 'O the Praise of Allah!' to himself, and does not move his tongue. If he belches, he should not raise his head to the sky. If his cloak falls, he should not rearrange it, and so with the ends of his turban, for that is disliked, unless it is necessary.

The Problem of Worship in Sandals: It is permissible, *já'iz*,[1] even though removing the sandals is easy. The permission with regard to the leather socks[2] is not on account of the difficulty of removing them, but rather, this uncleanness is pardonable. Footwear in general comes under the meaning of
(330) leather socks. The Messenger of Allah performed Worship in his sandals. Then he removed them, so the people removed their sandals. Then he said, 'Why did you remove your sandals?' They replied, 'We saw you remove yours, so we removed ours'. He said, 'Gabriel came to me to tell me that they had some dirt on them, so whenever any one of you sets out for the mosque, let him turn up his sandals, and let him look at them, and if he sees any dirt, let him scrape them on the ground, and let him Worship in them'.

(331) One of them said, 'Worship in sandals is more excellent because Muḥammad said, "Why did you remove your sandals?"' This is going too far, for he questioned them to show them the reason for his removing his sandals, since he knew that they removed theirs to be in accord with him.

[1] For *já'iz*, 'permitted', as legally indifferent acts, see Macdonald, *Development*, p. 73.

[2] The allowability of wearing leather socks and rubbing over them in the ablution is a divisive question in Islam. See Macdonald, *Development*, pp. 298, 314.

(332) 'Abdalláh bin al-Sá'ib[1] has related that the Prophet removed his sandals. So then, he did both things. But it is not fitting that one who removes his should put them on his right or his left, for that restricts the space, and cuts off the row. Rather he puts them in front of him, and does not leave them behind him, for his heart would be turning to them. Perhaps the one who thinks that Worship in them is more excellent has this idea, that is, the turning of the heart to them.
(333) Abú Huraira related that the Prophet said, 'Whenever one of you performs a Worship, let him put his
(334) sandals between his feet'. Abú Huraira said to some one else, 'Place them between your feet and
(335) do not trouble any Muslim by them'. The Messenger of Allah placed them at his left, while he was acting as *imám*. So the *imám* may do that, since no one stands at his left. It is preferable that he should not put them between his feet, for they would engage his attention, but before his feet. Perhaps
(336) that is the meaning of the tradition. Jubair bin Muṭ'am[2] said, 'A man's placing his sandals between his feet is an innovation'.

A problem. Whenever he expectorates in his Worship, his Worship is not invalidated, because it is a minor act. Whatever sound does not result from is not reckoned as speech, and is not of the form of the letters of speech, only, it is disliked. So, one must guard against it, except that the Messenger of Allah
(337) gave permission about it, since one of the Companions related that the Messenger of Allah saw in the *qibla* direction an expectoration mark, and then became very angry. Then he scraped it with a palm-branch that was in his hand, and said, 'Bring me some mixed perfume'. So he smeared over the mark with saffron. Then he turned to us and said, 'What one of you likes to be spit on in the face?' We said, 'Not one

[1] 'Abdalláh bin Sá'ib, Companion, Meccan reciter of the Qur'án. *Ibn Hajar*, ii. p. 766 f.

[2] Jubair bin Muṭ'am, Companion (d. 57-59). *Ibn Hajar*, i. p. 461.

of us'. He replied, 'Then any one of you, whenever he enters upon the Worship, has Allah between himself and the *qibla*', and, in another version, 'has Allah facing him'. So let not any one of you expectorate in front of his face, nor on his right, but to his left, or beneath his left foot, but if it should unexpectedly proceed from him, let him spit into his garment, and let him make it slight, and rub one part with another.

Another Problem. The standing of the imitator of the *imám* has *sunna*, Usage, and *farḍ*, Prescribed, aspects. The Usage is that he stand at the right of the *imám*, drawn back from him a little. A woman alone should stand behind the *imám*, although if she should stand beside the *imám*, that would not be harmful, but she would contravert the Usage. If there should be a man with her, the man should stand at the right of the *imám*, and she behind the man. He should not stand behind the row by himself, but rather enter into the row himself, or draw to himself one from the row. But if he should stand by himself, his Worship would be valid, along with dislike.

The *farḍ*, Prescribed, part is the continuity of the row, i.e. that there should be between the imitator and the *imám* a connecting bond, since they are in a company. So if they are in a mosque, that is sufficient as a connection, for it was built for that, and there is no need for continuity of row, but rather for this, that he be cognizant of the actions of the *imám*.

(338) Abú Huraira performed a Worship of an *imám* on the roof of a mosque. Whenever the follower is in the front of the mosque, in the roadway, or the open space adjoining, and there is no obstacle of masonry separating them, the nearness of the measure of the distance of the bowshot of an arrow is sufficient. There is sufficient bond in the Worship when the action of one of them reaches the other. But continuation is stipulated only when one stands in the courtyard of a house at the right of the mosque, or the left, with its

door cleaving to the mosque, and the Stipulation is that the row of the mosque extend in the courtyard's passage-way, without a break, to the court. Then the Worship of whoever is in that row and behind, is valid, but not the Worship of the one who is in front of it. This is the rule of the separated buildings, but a single building and a single court are like an open space.

Another Problem. (*a*) Whenever the late-comer arrives in time for the last of the Worship of the *imám*, that is the first of his Worship. So let him come into accord with the *imám*, and let him build upon that, and let him recite the *qunút*, Supplication, in the morning at the last of his own Worship, even though he has recited the *qunút*, Supplication, along with the *imám*.

(*b*) If he is in time for part of the Standing Posture along with the *imám*, he should not engage in the Supplications, but let him begin with the Fátiḥa, and let him do it quickly. Then, if the *imám* does the Bowing before he finishes the Fátiḥa, and he is able to catch up with him on his rising from the Bowing, let him finish it. But if he is unable, he gets into accord with the *imám* and bows when he does. A part of the Fátiḥa has the authority of the whole of it, so the Fátiḥa falls away from him because of their going ahead of him. If the *imám* bows while he is in the midst of reciting the *súra*, let him break it off.

(*c*) If he overtakes the *imám* in the Sitting or the Witnessing portions of the Worship, he says the *takbírat al-iḥrám*, and then he sits. He does not say the *takbír* of the transitions when he overtakes the *imám* in the Bowing, for he says the *takbír* a second time in the bending over, for that is a transition reckoned to belong to it, and the *takbírs* are for the original transitions in the Worship, not for incidents on account of the imitation of the *imám* on the part of the follower who is late. But he does not overtake the *rak'a* so long as he does not come to rest in bowing while the *imâm* is still within the time limit of those bowing with him. For, if his coming to rest at the Bowing is not complete until after the *imâm* has passed out of the time limit of those bowing, that *rak'a* escapes him.

A Problem. (*a*) Let anyone whom the Noon Worship escapes up to the time of mid-afternoon perform the Noon Worship first, and then the Afternoon one. But if he begins with the Afternoon Worship, that may do, but he has left what is preferable, and heedlessly risked the appearance of heterodoxy. However, if he finds an *imâm* to follow, let him perform the Afternoon Worship and then let him perform the Noon Worship after it. The Congregational Worship has first claim to performance.

(*b*) But if he performs a Worship by himself in the early part of the period, and then overtakes the Congregational Worship, he should perform the Worship in the congregation, and state the Intention of the Worship of the time, and Allah will take account of whichever one He wills.

(*c*) But if he states the Intention of a Worship that escaped, or a *taṭawwu'*, Voluntary, Worship, it is permitted.

(*d*) If he has just performed a Worship in the congregation, and then overtakes another congregation, let him state the Intention of an escaped Worship, or a *nâfl*, Supererogatory, Worship, for the repetition of the payment of the Worship in the congregation another time has no reason, and is admissible only for the sake of securing the excellence of the Congregational Worship.

Another Problem. When one has performed a Worship, and then sees on his garment some uncleanness, the most liked thing is to perform a Substitute Worship, but it is not incumbent upon him, and if he should see the uncleanness in the midst of the Worship, he casts off the garment and finishes the Worship. The most liked is beginning again. The

(330) basis for this is the story of the Prophet's taking off his sandals when Gabriel informed the Messenger of Allah that there was some uncleanness upon them, for he did not begin the Worship anew.

Another Problem. Anyone who leaves out the First Witnessing, or the *qunût*, Supplication, or leaves out the Blessing for the Messenger of Allah, in the First Witnessing, or commits a heedless act, so that the Worship becomes invalid through something determinated, or who is in doubt and does not know whether he performed a Worship of three *rak'as* or four, in these cases begins with what he is sure about, and performs two Prostrations[1] of Forgetfulness before the Salutation. And if he forgets them he performs them after the Salutation whenever he remembers after a short time. For if he performs a Prostration after the Salutation and after he has done something that invalidates his state of ceremonial cleanness, his Worship is invalid. For, after he enters upon the Prostration, it is as if he makes his Salutation out of place through forgetfulness, so validation does not result because of it and he may return to the Worship. So, for that reason, he makes a new Salutation after the Prostration. But if he remembers about the Prostration of Forgetfulness after leaving the mosque, or after a long period, it has escaped.

Another Problem. Evil suggestion during the Intention to perform the Worship. Its cause is unsoundness in the mind, or ignorance of the religious law. For, obedience to the command of Allah is like obedience to the command of anyone else, and magnifying Him is like magnifying anyone else, so far as purpose is concerned. Anyone who has a learned man come to him, rises for him. Then were he to say, 'I have the intention to rise and stand, magnifying the entrance of the honourable Zaid, on account of his excellence, synchronizing my

[1] For this see Introduction, p. 29.

action with his entrance, turning to him with my face', he would be weak-minded. Nay, but as he sees him, and becomes aware of his excellence, the impulse to magnify rises in him of itself, and makes him stand up, and he becomes a magnifier, except when he rises for some other occupation, or rises in a state of unmindfulness.

The Stipulation for the Worship to be 'noon', 'a regular payment', and 'prescribed', so that the obedience may be complete, is like the stipulation for the standing of the host to be united with the entrance of the learned man, along with facing the one coming in, and along with the non-existence of any other motive but that, and united with the purpose of magnifying him by means of the standing up, in order that the standing up may be a magnifying. For, if he were to stand up, turning his back, or wait and then stand up after awhile, he would not be a magnifier.

Next, these qualities must needs be known and intended by the worshipper. Next, their presence in the self does not occupy so long as a single moment, but only the setting in order of the expressions which indicate them is long, whether it be the utterance of them by the tongue or the thinking of them in the heart. So, whoever does not understand the Intention of the Worship after this sort, does not understand what intention is. For there is nothing more in it but that you were summoned to perform the Worship at a certain time, and you responded favourably and stood up to perform it. So, distraction through evil suggestions from Satan is sheer ignorance, for these purposes and these knowledges are united in the self in one state, and are not separated out into individual elements in the mind in such a way that the self may gaze upon and consider them, for there is a difference between the presence of a thing in the self and differentiating it in the thought. Presence is the opposite of absence and unmindfulness, even though it is not differentiated. For, anyone who has knowledge of an originated thing, for instance, knows it in one knowledge and one state, but this knowledge includes knowledges which are present even though they are not differentiated. For, anyone who has knowledge of an originated thing, has knowledge of the existent and the non-existent, and of coming before and coming after, and time, and knows that the coming before belongs to non-existence and coming after to existence. These knowledges are comprised under the knowledge of the originated thing, by the proof that anyone who has knowledge of an originated thing and has no further knowledge about it, and, were he asked, 'Did you know the coming before only, or the coming after, or non-existence, or the preceding of the non-existence, or the coming after of the existence, or time, which is divided into past and future?' should reply, 'I have never known it', would be a liar, and his speech would be contradictory to his saying, 'I know the originated thing'.

From ignorance of this point distraction is aroused. Then indeed the distracted man imposes on himself the task of making present in his heart that it is a noon-time act, and that it is a performance of a duty at its appointed time, and that it is prescribed, all in one state, differentiated into its various expressions while he observes them, which is absurd. Were he to impose that task on himself in standing up for a learned man, it would be impossible for him. So, by this knowledge, distraction is warded off, and it is simply that he knows that obedience to the command of Allah in the Intention is like obedience to the command of some one else.

Furthermore, I add to it, by way of facilitation and permission, and say, Were the one who is distracted not to understand what the Intention is without the presence of these things separately, and were he not to picture within himself the obedience of a single act, and were he to present the whole of that during the *takbîr*, from its beginning to its end, so that he would not finish the *takbîr* without having secured the Intention, he should let that suffice him. We would not burden him with the task of joining the whole to the beginning of the *takbîr* or to the end of it, for that would be an excessive burden. Had that been commanded, a question about it would have occurred to the first believers, and one of the Companions would have been distracted in the Intention. So, the absence of the occurrence of that is a proof that the command is on an easy basis. Therefore it is fitting that the one who is distracted should be content with whatever way is made easy for him, so that it may become habitual for him, and distraction may leave him. He should not demand of himself meticulous precision in that, for the effort to be precise increases distraction. We have mentioned in the '*Fatwâs*',[1] aspects of the precise requirements in the analysis of the cognitions and purposes connected with the Intention. These the learned need to know. But as for the generality of men, perhaps it would hurt them to hear them, and arouse distractions. So, for that reason, we have left them out of the present discussion.

Another Problem. It is fitting that the follower should not precede the *imâm* in the Bowing and the Prostration and the rising up from them, or in the rest of the acts, and should not do them at the same time with him, but follow him, and follow his pattern, for this is the meaning of *al-iqtidâ'*, 'the imitation'. If he should do them at the same time with him intentionally, his Worship would not be invalid, just as if he were to stand by his side without being back of him. But if he were to precede him in any Element, then, as regards the invalidation of his Worship, there is disagreement. It would not be far out to judge it invalid, comparing

[1] This is a collection of 190 *fatwâs*, 'judgements', and is mentioned in SM i. p. 42.

it with the case when he is in advance of the *imám* in position. Nay, rather, this is preferable, for the Congregational Worship is an imitation in act, but not in position, and following the *imám* in act is more important. The Stipulation to leave the position in advance of the *imám* is only to facilitate following in act and to secure the appearance of following, since that which is suitable for the one imitated is to be in advance. So, to be in advance of him in act has no justification, unless it is some forgetfulness. Therefore the Messenger of Allah
(339) expressed strong disapprobation of it, for he said, 'Is not he who raises his head before the *imám* does, afraid that Allah will turn his head into the head of a donkey?'

As for being behind one Element, that does not invalidate the Worship. That is that the *imám* should take the erect position after his Bowing, while the follower has not yet bowed. But, being behind to this extent is disliked. If the *imám* places his forehead upon the ground while he has not finished up to the time-limit of those bowing, his Worship would be invalid. Likewise, if the *imám* places his forehead for the second Prostration while he has not performed the first Prostration.

Another Problem. It is incumbent upon one who is present at the Worship, whenever he sees a mistake of some one else in his Worship, to charge him and express disapprobation of him. If it issued from an ignorant one, he should accompany the ignorant one and instruct him. Examples of this are the command to rectify the rows and to prevent standing alone outside the row, and the disapprobation of one who raises his head before the *imám*, and so on.
(340) Muḥammad has said, 'Woe be to the one who knows, proceeding from him who does not know, when he does not instruct him!' Ibn Mas'úd said, 'Whoever sees one making a mistake in his Worship
(341) and does not forbid him, is a sharer in his sin'. It is

related from Bilál bin Sa'd[1] that he said, 'A mistake when it is unapparent, does not harm any but its maker, but whenever it is made apparent and is not
(342) changed, it harms the people'. It occurs in Tradition that Bilál[1] used to rectify the rows and strike men's
(343) tendons of Achilles with a whip. It is related from 'Umar that he said, 'Find out about your brethren in your Worship, and whenever you have found out about them, if they are ill, visit them, and if they are well, remonstrate with them, by expressing disapprobation of one who has left the Congregational Worship'.

It is fitting that he should not act gently about it.
(344) The first believers used to go far in this, in so much that one would carry a bier to some who turned their backs on the Congregational Worship, pointing to the fact that the dead are the ones who may remain away from the Congregational Worship, and not the living.

Whoever enters the mosque should make for the right side of the row. For that reason the men
(345) pressed together for it in the time of the Messenger of Allah, in so much that is was said to him, 'The left side is unused'. So he said, 'The one who builds up the left side of the mosque has two portions of reward'. Whenever anyone finds a lad in a row, and does not find a place for himself, he should oust him and occupy it, I mean, whenever he has not attained to the age of puberty.

So this is what we have wished to mention of the problems that are a common cause of distress. There will follow the rules for the separate performances of the Worship in the *Book of Wirds*, 'Devotional Recitals', if Allah will.

[1] Bilál bin Sa'd, Story-teller, Successor (d. 120). *Ibn Ṭagri Bardii*, i. p. 230; *Tajríd Asma' al-Ṣaḥábá*, p. 69.

CHAPTER VII

SUPEREROGATORY PERFORMANCES OF THE WORSHIP

KNOW that the performances of the Worship that are not *farḍ*, Prescribed, are divided into three parts: the *sunna*, Usage, the *mustaḥabb*, Liked, and the *taṭawwu'*, Voluntary.

We mean by the *sunna*, Usage, those of which it is handed down from the Messenger of Allah that he consistently performed them, such as the *rátiba*, Fixed, performances following the *farḍ*, Prescribed, performances of the Worship; the *ḍuḥá*, Forenoon, Worship; the *witr*, Odd, Worship; the *tahajjud*, Night, Worship and others, for the word *sunna* 'usage', is an expression of 'the way that has been walked in'.

We mean by the *mustaḥabb*, Liked, those whose excellence Tradition has reported, but the consistent performance of which has not been handed down, as we shall repeat in the Worship of the Days and Nights of the Week, and such as the Worship on going out of a dwelling, and entering it, and such like.

We mean by the *taṭawwu'*, Voluntary, Worship those that come after that, which no tradition reports in particular, but which a creature does voluntarily, in as much as he is desirous of communion with Allah through a Worship whose excellence the religious law reports in a general way, and by which he shows himself to be free giver, since he was not urged to that Worship in particular, although he is urged to Worship in general, and *taṭawwu'*, 'voluntary', is an expression for a gift freely given.

I have named the three divisions *náfl*, 'supererogatory', because 'supererogatory' is 'additional', and the whole of them are additional to the *farḍ*, Prescribed, performances of the Worship.

The expressions *náfila*, 'supererogatory', *sunna*, 'usage', *mustaḥabb*, 'liked', and *taṭawwu'*, 'voluntary', we desired to use in a technical sense, to define these meanings, and it is no sin for anyone to change this technical use, and there is no strictness about the terms that may be used after their meanings are understood.

Each one of these three classes has degrees of excellence that differ from one another, in accordance with whatever any traditions and records say about them and their excellence, and in accordance with the duration of the continuance of the Messenger of Allah; and in accordance with the trustworthiness and repute of the traditions which have come down about them. For that reason it is said, 'The Usages of the Congregational Worship are more excellent than the Usages of the individual Worship. The most excellent of the congregational Usages is the Worship of the Two Feasts; then the Eclipse of the Sun; then the Request for Rain. The most excellent of the individual Usages is the Odd Worship; then the two *rak'as* of the Dawn; then the Fixed Worship which comes after these two, according to their differences'.

Know that the Supererogatory Worships, with regard to their connection with the circumstances on which they depend, are divided into: (*a*) those dependent upon causes, such as the Eclipse of the Sun, and the Request for Rain; (*b*) those dependent upon seasons. Those dependent upon seasons are divided into (1) what is repeated with the recurrence of day and night, or (2) with the recurrence of the week, or (3) with the recurrence of the year. In all, there are four classes.

Class One: Those that are Repeated with the Recurrence of the Days and Nights

These are eight in number: Five are the Fixed performances of the five Prescribed performances of the Worship, and three more after them are the

Forenoon Worship, the Enlivening of what comes between the two Evening Worships and the Night Worship.

(*a*) The first is the *râtiba*, Fixed, performance of the
(346) morning, which is of two *rak'as*. The Messenger of Allah said, 'The two *rak'as* of the dawn are better than this life and what is in it'. Its time begins with the appearance of the true dawn, which is that whereof the light spreads in the horizon, rather than the first or false dawn. The apprehension of that by the physical sight is difficult at the beginning of it, unless one learns the mansions of the moon or knows the conjunction of its appearance with the stars visible to the sight, and so deduces it from the stars. He may know it from the moon on two nights of the month, for the moon rises at dawn on the night of the twenty-sixth, and the morning appears at the setting of the moon on the night of the twelfth of the month. This is what is usual, but an irregularity enters it in some of the signs of the zodiac, and the explanation of that is lengthy. The learning of the mansions of the moon is one of the important duties of the devotee, so that he may observe by it the measurements of the times at night and in the morning.

The time of the two *rak'as* of the dawn elapses with the passing of the time of the Prescribed Worship of the morning, which is at the appearance of the sun. But the Usage is the payment of them before the Prescribed Worship. So, if one enters the mosque while the Worship has been instituted, let
(347) him engage in the Prescribed Worship, for Muḥammad said, 'Whenever the Worship is instituted, there is no Worship except the Prescribed'. Then whenever he finishes the Prescribed, he stands up for those two *rak'as*, and performs them. The true view is that they are a payment so long as they occur before the appearance of the sun, for they follow upon the Prescribed Worship according to its time, and the order between them is a Usage in making one precede and the other follow only when-

ever he does not come upon a congregation. Whenever he does come upon a congregation, the order is reversed, but they remain a payment.

The liked thing is that he perform them at home, and be quick in them. Then he enters the mosque and performs the Worship of the two *rak'as* of the Greeting of the Mosque, and then sits down and does not perform a Worship until he performs the Prescribed Worship. During the time between the Morning Worship and the appearance of the sun the most liked thing is the *dhikr*, 'invocation', and *fikr*, 'meditation', and confining oneself to the two *rak'as* of the dawn and the Prescribed Worship.

(*b*) The second is the Fixed Worship of noon, which consists of six *rak'as*; two come after the Noon Prescribed Worship, which is also a *sunna mu'akkada*, 'confirmed usage', and four come before it, which are also a Usage, although they are inferior
(348) to the two that come last. Abú Huraira related from the Prophet that he said, 'Whoever performs a Worship of four *rak'as* after the sun's passing the meridian, reciting well in them, and doing their Bowing and their Prostration well, has worshipping with
(349) him 70,000 angels, asking forgiveness for him until the night'. Muḥammad was wont not to miss four *rak'as* after the sun's passing the meridian, prolonging them, and said, 'The doors of heaven are open at this hour, so I like some work to rise for me then'. Abú Aiyúb the Helper[1] related it, and was alone in hand-
(350) ing it down. What Umm Ḥabíba, the wife[2] of the Prophet, related, proved this also: 'He said, "Whoever performs every day a Worship of twelve *rak'as*, exclusive of the Prescribed, has built for him a house in the Garden; two *rak'as* before the Dawn Worship; four before the Noon; two *rak'as* after it; two *rak'as* before the Afternoon, and two after the Sunset Worships"'.

[1] Abú Aiyúb Khálid bin Zaid al-Anṣárí (d. 52). *Ibn Saad*, iii. 2. p. 49 f.; *Ency. of Islam*, i. p. 75.

[2] Umm Ḥabíba, daughter of Abú Sufyán, and one of Muḥammad's wives (d. 44). *Ibn Saad*, viii. pp. 68 ff.

(351) Ibn 'Umar said, 'I have preserved from the Messenger of Allah " on every day ten *rak'as* " ', and he mentioned what Umm Ḥabība mentioned, except the two *rak'as* of Dawn, for he said, 'That was an hour in which the Messsenger of Allah was wont not to be visited, but my sister, Ḥafsa,[1] has told me that he used to perform a Worship of two *rak'as* in her house and then go out'. He said in his tradition, 'Two *rak'as* before the Noon, and two *rak'as* after the Evening Worships'. So the two *rak'as* before the Noon have become better confirmed than the whole four.

The time of that begins with the passing of the meridian. The passing is known by the lengthening of the shadow of people standing erect, inclining to the direction of the east, since the shadow of a man falls to the side of the west at the appearing of the sun, being long. So the sun continues to rise, while the shadow grows less, and swerves from the direction of the west until the sun reaches the utmost degree of its elevation, this being the measure of mid-day, and that is the utmost degree of the shortness of the shade. Then, when the sun passes from the utmost degree of elevation, the shadow begins to lengthen. Then, whenever the increase becomes appreciable to the sense, the time of noon begins. One knows of a surety that the passing of the meridian according to the knowledge of Allah occurred before it, but duties are not connected with anything except what comes under the observation of the sense. The amount of the shade remaining, which is cast from a man, goes on increasing, being long in winter and short in summer. The utmost degree of its length is when the sun reaches the first of Capricorn,[2] and the utmost degree of its shortness is at its reaching the first of Cancer.[3] One may know that by means of persever-

[1] Ḥafṣa, daughter of the khalīfa 'Umar, wife of Muḥammad (d. 45). *Ency. of Islam*, ii. p. 216.

[2] Capricorn, eighth sign of the zodiac.

[3] Cancer, fourth sign of the zodiac.

ance and measurements. Of the methods at hand for making sure, for him who is excellent at taking observations of the stars, one is that he should note the axis of the north at night, and place upon the earth a square board in a symmetrical position, so that the one of its sides towards the polar-axis is in a position so that, if you were to suppose a stone fell from the axis to the earth, and then suppose a line were extended from the place where the stone fell to the side of the board which is near it, then the line would form upon the board two right angles, that is, the line would not be inclining to either one of the two sides. Then you erect a post upon the board, vertically and symmetrically, in the place of the mark (*o*), which is opposite the polar-axis. Its shade falls upon the board at the first part of the day, inclining towards the direction of the west on the side of line (*a*). Then it continues to incline until it superimposes itself on line (*b*), so that, as it moves, could its end be extended, it would reach in a straight line to the place of the falling of the stone, and it would be parallel to the east and the west sides of the board, inclining to neither one of them. Then, when its inclination to the west side ceases, the sun reaches the utmost degree of its elevation, and then, when the shadow swerves from the line which is upon the board to the

The East side.

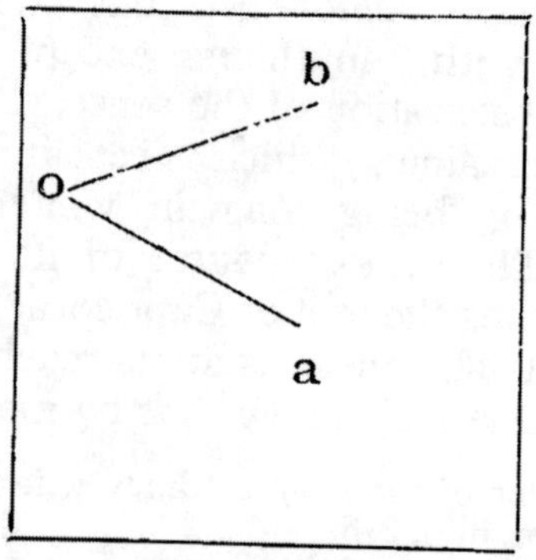

The West side.

east side, the sun has passed the meridian. This is apprehended by the sense, giving assurance of the time which is near to the beginning of the passing of the meridian as it is in the knowledge of Allah. Then you make a mark at the end of the shade when it swerves, and so, when the shadow from the mark becomes like the post itself in length, the time of *'aṣr*, mid-afternoon, begins. There is no harm in having this amount of knowledge of the passing of the meridian. As in drawing on previous page.

(*c*) The third is the Fixed Worship of mid-after-
(352) noon. It is four *rak'as* before the Mid-afternoon Worship. Abú Huraira related from the Prophet that he said, 'Allah has mercy upon any creature who performs a Worship of four *rak'as* before the Mid-afternoon Worship'. So, doing that in the hope of participating in the request[1] of the Messenger of Allah is liked with a confirmed liking, for his request is certainly answered affirmatively. But his consistent performance of the Usage Worship before mid-afternoon was not like his consistent performance of the two *rak'as* before the Noon Worship.

The fourth is the *rátiba*, Fixed, Worship of sunset. It is two *rak'as* after the Prescribed Worship. The narratives do not agree about them. But as regards two *rak'as* before it, between the *mu'adhdhin's* Call to the Worship and the *mu'adhdhin's* Institution of the Worship, by way of losing no time, this has been handed down from a company of the Companions, such as Ubai bin Ka'b, 'Abáda bin Ṣámit,[2] Abú Dharr and Zaid bin Thábit[3] and others.
(353) 'Abáda, or someone else, said, 'Whenever the *mu'adhdhin* gave the Call to Worship at sunset the

[1] In the *Durra*, al-Ghazzálí relates a tradition that on Resurrection Day Muḥammad's supplication will be, 'My people! My people! O my Lord! Give them peace!' Gautier, *Ad-Dourra al-Fákhira*, p. 68 (Arabic text).

[2] 'Abáda bin Ṣámit (d. 34). *Ibn Hajar*, ii. pp. 661 ff.

[3] Abú Sa'd Zaid bin Thábit b. al-Dahhák al-Anṣárí, compiler of the Qur'án. Muir, *Caliphate*, p. 151 f.; De Slane, *Ibn Khallikan*, i. p. 372.

Companions of the Messenger of Allah vied together in hastening to the columns to perform the Worship
(354) of two *rak'as*. One of them said, 'We used to perform the Worship of two *rak'as* before sunset so that someone would come in and would suppose that we had performed the Worship and would ask, "Have you performed the Worship of the sunset?"' That is included in the general application of the
(355) statement of Muḥammad, 'Between every two calls[1] to Worship there is a time of Worship, for whoever
(356) is willing'. Aḥmad bin Ḥanbal used to perform them and then the people remonstrated with him, so he abandoned them. Then he was asked about that, so he said, 'I did not see the people performing them so I abandoned them'. And he said, 'If a man performs them in his house, or a place where the people would not see him, that would be well'.

The time of the setting of the sun begins at the disappearance of the sun from the sight in level countries which are not encompassed by mountains. If they are encompassed by mountains in the direction of the west, one pauses until he sees the approach of darkness on the side of the east.
(357) Muḥammad said, 'Whenever night approaches from there and day departs from there, the one fasting enters upon the time of the breaking of the fast'.

The most liked thing is to lose no time in performing the Worship of sunset especially. If you delay and perform the Worship before the disappearance of the red after-glow, it would be a payment of the Worship in the prescribed time, but it is disliked. 'Umar delayed the Worship of sunset one night until stars appeared, so he freed a slave. Ibn 'Umar delayed it until two stars appeared, so he freed two slaves.

The Fixed performance of the last Evening Worship is four *rak'as* after the Prescribed Evening Worship.
(358) 'Â'isha said, 'The Messenger of Allah used to perform

[1] The *âdhân*, Call, and the *iqâma*, Institution, explains the SM.

a Worship of four *rak'as* after the last Evening Worship. We would then sleep'.

Some of the learned chose from the whole body of the traditions to hold that the number of the *rátiba*, Fixed, Worships was seventeen, like the number of the Prescribed Worships: two before the Morning, four before the Noon, and two after it, four before the Afternoon, and two after the Sunset, and three after the last Evening Worship, this being the Odd Worship. When the traditions which have come down about this are known, there is no sense
(359) in conjecturing about it. For Muḥammad has said, 'The Worship is the best task, so, whoever will, does much, and whoever will, does little'.

So then the choice of every devotee from these Voluntary Worships is in the measure of his desire for good. So it has appeared in what we have mentioned that some of them are better confirmed than others, and to abandon the better confirmed ones is certainly less desirable. The Prescribed Worships are completed by the Supererogatory ones, and so to the one who does not seek much of them for himself it will soon happen that his Prescribed Worships will not be sound without a restorer.

(360) The sixth is the *witr*, Odd, Worship. Anas bin Málik said, 'The Messenger of Allah used to perform a *witr* Worship after the Evening Worship with three *rak'as*, reciting in the first, 'Say the Praise of the name of thy Lord Most High!' (Qur'án lxxxvii), and in the second, 'Say, O ye Unbelievers' (cix), and in the third, 'Say, He is Allah, One' (cxii).

(361) It occurs in Tradition that Muḥammad used to perform, after the *witr* Worship, a Worship of two *rak'as* in a sitting position, and in some of them it is said, 'sitting cross-legged'. In some traditions it is
(362) said, 'When he wished to get into his bed, he dragged himself to it, and performed a Worship of two *rak'as* before he lay down, reciting in them, "When the earth quakes" (xcix), and *Súrat al-Takáthur*' (cii), and in another account, 'Say, O ye Unbelievers!' (cix).

The *witr* Worship is permissible unconnected and connected with one and two Salutations.[1] The Messenger of Allah performed an Odd Worship with one and three and five, and so on, with odd numbers up to eleven *rak'as* (the narrative about thirteen is uncertain), and in an exceptional[2] tradition, seventeen *rak'as*. These *rak'as*, I mean what we have called as a whole the *witr*, Odd, Worship, were Muḥammad's Worship at night, and are the *tahajjud*, Night, Worship. The Night Worship is a confirmed *sunna*, Usage, and its excellence will appear in the *Book of Wirds*, 'Devotional Recitals'.

With regard to the most excellent there is disagree-
(363) ment, for it is said, 'To perform a single *rak'a* is more excellent, since it is validated that Muḥammad used to perform consistently the Odd Worship with a single *rak'a*'.

(364) It is said, 'The connected *witr* Worship is more excellent to avoid the appearance of contradiction' [of the views of others]. Especially the *imám*, since one who does not consider that a single *rak'a* is a Worship may sometimes be led by him, if he performs a connected Worship, should state the Intention of performing a *witr* Worship by means of the whole. If he confines himself to one *rak'a* after the two *rak'as* of the *sunna* Evening Worship, or after the Prescribed Evening Worship, he states the Intention of performing the *witr* Worship, and it is valid, because the Stipulation of the *witr* Worship is that it should be in itself odd in number, and that it should make whatever else that went before it odd, and so, it would make the Prescribed Worship a *witr* Worship.

[1] That is, the connected is with one Salutation, and the unconnected is with two. The SM explains that this construction is an instance of chiasmus. Lane, *Lexicon*, p. 3011B, gives the varieties of *laff wa nashr*, the 'inversion' of Latin, of which the above is called, *ma'kús*, *mushawwash* or *ghair murattab*. An example of the *murattab* variety occurs in Qur'án xxviii. 73. See further in Mehren, *Rhetorik der Araber*, pp. 69, 114 (Arabic text).

[2] *Shádhdh*, 'having a single ascription attested by a (single) Sheykh, whether he be trustworthy or not' (Lane, *Lexicon*, p. 1522B).

Were he to perform the *witr* Worship before the Evening Worship it would not be valid, that is, would
(365) not secure the excellence of the *witr* Worship, which is better for him than the choice parts of the flock, as the tradition about it says. And if not, the single *rak'a* is valid at whatever time it may be performed. It is not valid before the Evening Worship only because it violates the Agreement of the people concerning the act, and because what becomes a *witr* Worship by means of it does not precede it.

But whenever one wishes to perform a *witr* Worship of three *rak'as* unconnected with a *farḍ* or *sunna* Worship,[1] consideration is in place in regard to the statement of his Intention about the two *rak'as*. For, if he states the Intention of performing, by means of them, *tahajjud*, Night, Worship or the *sunna*, Usage, Evening Worship, it would not be of the *witr* class. But, if he should state the Intention to perform the *witr* Worship, it would not in itself be a *witr* Worship, for the *witr* Worship would be only what comes after it. But the most obvious thing is that he should state the Intention of the *witr* Worship as he states the Intention of the *witr* Worship in the three unconnected ones. But the *witr* Worship has two meanings: one of them is that it should in itself be odd in number, and the other is that it should begin to be made a *witr* Worship by what comes after it. So the total of the three would be a *witr* Worship, and the two *rak'as* would be part of the total of the three, except that its quality of being a *witr* Worship would depend upon the third *rak'a*. If he resolves to make a *witr* Worship of the two of them, by means of a third, it is for him to state the Intention of performing a *witr* Worship by means of them, for the third *rak'a* is a *witr* in itself, and is one that renders other than itself *witr*, while the two *rak'as*, do not make others a *witr* and they are not in themselves *witr*, but they are made *witr* by others.

[1] The SM adds, 'and therefore with two Salutations'

It is fitting that the *witr* Worship should be the last Worship of the night, so it occurs after the *tahajjud*, Night, Worship. The excellences of the *witr*, Odd, Worship and the *tahajjud*, Night, Worship and the manner of the order between the two of them will come in the *Book of the Order of the Wirds*, 'Devotional Recitals'.

The seventh is the *ḍuḥá*, Forenoon, Worship. Now, consistent performance of this is one of the most dutiful and excellent of acts. As for the number of its *rak'as*, the most, in what is handed down about
(366) it, is eight *rak'as*. Umm Hání',[1] the sister of 'Alí bin Abú Tálib, related that Muḥammad performed a Forenoon Worship of eight *rak'as*, prolonging them and doing them well, but no one else has handed down
(367) this amount. But 'Á'isha has mentioned that Muḥammad used to perform the Forenoon Worship with four *rak'as* and add whatever Allah willed that he should add. So, she did not prevent additional, that is, he used consistently to do four, and not less
(368) than that, and perhaps additional. It is related in a *mufrad*[2] tradition, 'with a single authority', that the Prophet used to perform the Forenoon Worship with six *rak'as*.

(369) As for its time, 'Alí related that Muḥammad used to perform the Forenoon Worship with six *rak'as* at two times: one, when the sun appears and advances he would get up and perform two *rak'as*, which is the first part of the second of the *wirds*, Portions, of the Day, as shall appear later.[3] When the sun brightens up and is in a fourth of the sky on the side of the east, he would perform four. But the first is whenever the sun mounts only the measure of half a lance, and the second is whenever a fourth of the day goes, in correspondence with the Afternoon Worship, for its time is when a fourth of the day

[1] Umm Hání', sister of 'Alí bin Abú Ṭálib (note 1, p. 58), wife of Muḥammad. *Ibn Saad*, viii. pp. 32, 108; *Ibn Hajar*, iv. p. 718.

[2] *Mufrad*, 'solitary, separate from others'. Lane, *Lexicon*, p. 2364A.

[3] This is at SM v. pp. 140 ff.

remains. Noon is at the middle of the day, and the Forenoon Worship is at the middle point between the appearance of the sun and its passing the meridian, just as mid-afternoon is at the middle point between the passing of the meridian and the setting of the sun. This is the most excellent of the times. From the time of the ascent of the sun until what comes before its passing of the meridian, is, in brief, a time for the Forenoon Worship.

The eighth is the Enlivening of what comes between the two Evening Worships, and this is a *sunna*
(370) *mu'akkada*, Confirmed Usage. From what is on record concerning the practice of the Messenger of Allah between the two Evening Worships, its number
(371) is six *rak'as*. This Worship has great excellence. It is said, 'It is what is referred to in the saying of Allah, "Their sides withdraw from the couches"' (xxxii.
(372) 16). It has been related from Muḥammad that he said, 'Whoever performs Worship between the Sunset and the Evening performs one that is a Worship of
(373) "those who return to Allah"'.[1] Muḥammad said, 'For him who secludes himself during the time between the Sunset and the Evening Worships in a congregational mosque, not speaking except in worship,[2] or in recital of the Qur'án, there is obligation on Allah to build in the Garden two palaces, the extent of each one of them being a hundred years' journey, and set out for him between them a plantation which would contain the people of this life walking about in it'. The rest of its excellences will appear in the *Book of the Wirds*, 'Devotional Portions', if Allah will.

Class Two: Those that are Repeated with the Recurrence of the Weeks

These are the performances of the Worship of the days and nights of the weeks, for every day and every night.

[1] The reference is to Qur'án xvii. 26, 27.
[2] The SM defines *al-ṣalá* here as simply *al-du'á'*, 'supplication'.

(*a*) As for the days, we will begin in them with Sunday.

(374) (1) Sunday. Abú Huraira related from the Prophet that he said, 'Whoever performs a Worship of four *rak'as* on Sunday, reciting in each *rak'a* the Fátihat al-Kitáb (i) and the verses beginning "The Messenger believed" (ii. 285) once, has Allah write for him good deeds according to the number of all the Christians, men and women, and Allah gives him the reward of a prophet, and records for him a Pilgrimage and minor visit to the Ka'ba, and records for him in every *rak'a* a thousand Worships, and Allah gives him in the Garden for every consonant a city of excellent musk'.

(375) It is related from 'Alí bin Abú Ṭálib from the Prophet that he said, 'Assert belief in the unity of Allah with much Worship on the One Day,[1] for Allah is One, and has no associate, for whoever performs a Worship on Sunday, after the Noon Worship, of four *rak'as* after the Prescribed and the Usage *rak'as*, reciting in the first, the Fátiḥat al-Kitáb (i), and "The Sending[2] Down of the Book of the Súrat al-Sajda" (xxxii), and "He is blessed in whose hand is the Dominion" (lxvii), and then gives the Witness and the Salutation, and then stands up and performs the Worship of the other two *rak'as*, reciting in them the Fátiḥat al-Kitáb (i), and Súrat al-Jumú'a (lxii), and makes a request of Allah for what he needs has a right upon Allah to satisfy his need'.

(376) (2) Monday. Jábir[3] related from the Messenger of Allah that he said, 'Whoever performs a Worship on Monday at the advance of the day, of two *rak'as*, reciting in each *rak'a* the Fátiḥat al-Kitáb (i) once and the Throne Verse (ii. 256) once, and 'Say, He is

[1] This is the name of Sunday in Arabic.

[2] There are five other *súras* that begin with *tanzíl*, 'sending down', viz. xxxix, xl, xli, xlv and xlvi.

[3] Jábir bin 'Abdalláh the Helper (d. 74). *Ḥaji Khalfae Lexicon*, ii. pp. 332, 334.

Allah, One" (cxii), and the two Seekings for Refuge (cxiii, cxiv) once each, and then when he says the Salutation, says the Seeking of Forgiveness ten times, and says the Blessing upon the Prophet ten times, has Allah forgive him his sins, all of them'.

(377) Anas bin Málik related from the Prophet that he said, 'Whoever performs a Worship on Monday of twelve *rak'as*, reciting in every *rak'a* the Fátihat al-Kitáb (i) and the Verse of the Throne (ii. 256) once, and then, when he finishes, recites, "Say, He is Allah, One" (cxii) twelve times, and says the Seeking of Forgiveness twelve times, will be called on Resurrection Day: "Where is Such a one, son of Such a one. Let him stand! and let him take his reward from Allah." Then the first reward given will be a thousand robes, and he will be crowned and it will be said to him, "Enter the Garden!" Then there will meet him a hundred thousand angels, each angel with a gift, escorting him so that he visits in turn a thousand palaces of light, shining brightly'.

(378) (3) Tuesday. Yazíd al-Raqáshí related from Anas bin Málik that he said, 'Muhammad said, "Whoever performs on Tuesday a Worship of ten *rak'as* at the middle of the day," and in another tradition, "at the advance of the day, reciting in each *rak'a* the Fátihat al-Kitáb (i) and the Verse of the Throne (ii. 256) once, and, "Say, He is Allah, One" (cxii) three times, does not have a sin recorded against him for seventy days, and if he dies up to seventy days, he dies a martyr, and is forgiven the sins of seventy years'.

(379) (4) Wednesday. Abu Idrís al-Khawlání[1] related from Ma'ádh bin Jabal that he said, 'The Messenger of Allah said, "Whoever performs a Worship on Wednesday of twelve *rak'as* at the advance of the day, reciting in each *rak'a* the Fátihat al-Kitáb (i) and the Verse of the Throne (ii. 256) once, and 'Say,

[1] Abú Idrís al-Khawlání (d. 80). *Annales at-Tabari*, ii. pp. 205. 855.

He is Allah, One' (cxii) three times, and the two Seekings for Refuge (cxiii, cxiv) three times, has an angel call him at the Throne, 'O 'Abdalláh! Begin the work anew, for Allah has forgiven you whatever sins have gone before, and Allah has removed from you the punishment of the grave as well as its straitness and its darkness, and has removed from you the hardships of the Resurrection', and there is sent up for him for that day the work of a prophet"'.

(380) (5) Thursday. From 'Ikrima from Ibn 'Abbás it is related that he said, 'The Messenger of Allah said, "Whoever performs a Worship of two *rak'as* on Thursday, between the Noon and the Afternoon Worships, reciting in the first the Fátiḥat al-Kitáb (i) once, and the Verse of the Throne (ii. 256) a hundred times, and in the second the Fátiḥat al-Kitáb once, and, 'Say, He is Allah, One' (cxii) a hundred times, and recites the Blessing upon Muḥammad a hundred times, has Allah give him the reward of one who fasts the three months of Rajab, Sha'bán and Ramaḍán, and he has the reward like that of a pilgrim to the House, and has written for him good deeds according to the number of every one who believes in Allah and trusts Him"'.

(381) (6) Friday. It is related from 'Alí bin Abú Ṭálib from the Prophet that he said, 'Friday is a Worship in its totality. There is no believing creature who gets up when the sun rises and advances the measure of a lance or more than that, and then performs the ablution well, and then performs the Worship of Praise of the forenoon with two *rak'as*, with faith and belief, but has Allah record for him two hundred good deeds, and erase from him two hundred evil deeds, and whoever performs a Worship of four *rak'as* has Allah exalt him four hundred degrees in the Garden, and whoever performs eight *rak'as* has Allah exalt him in the Garden eight hundred degrees and forgive him his sins, all of them, and whoever performs twelve *rak'as* has Allah record for him two thousand and two hundred good deeds and erase from him

two thousand and two hundred evil deeds, and has Allah exalt him in the Garden two thousand and two hundred degrees.'

(382) From Náfi' from Ibn 'Umar from the Prophet it is related that he said, 'Whoever enters the congregational mosque on Friday and then performs a Worship of four *rak'as* before the Worship of the Friday Observance, reciting in every *rak'a* the Praise (i), and, "Say, He is Allah, One" (cxii) fifty times, will not die until he sees his place of sitting of the Garden or it is seen for him'.

(383) Saturday. Abú Huraira related that the Prophet said, 'Whoever performs a Worship on Saturday of four *rak'as*, reciting in each *rak'a* the Fátiḥat al-Kitáb once and, "Say, He is Allah, One", three times, and when he finishes, recites the Verse of the Throne (ii. 256), has Allah record for him, for every consonant a Pilgrimage, and minor visit to the Ka'ba and raise up for him the reward of a year of fasting during its days, and of standing for Worship during its nights and has Allah give him for every consonant the reward of a martyr, and he is under the shade of the Throne of Allah with the prophets and martyrs'.

(384) (*b*) As for the nights.

(1) The eve of Sunday. Anas bin Málik related concerning the eve of Sunday that Muḥammad said, 'Whoever performs a Worship on the eve of Sunday of twenty *rak'as*, reciting in every *rak'a* the Fátiḥat al-Kitáb (i) and, "Say, He is Allah, One" (cxii) fifty times, and the two Seekings for Refuge (cxiii, cxiv) each once, and says the Seeking of Forgiveness of Allah a hundred times, and says the Seeking of Forgiveness for himself and for his parents a hundred times, and says the Blessing upon the Prophet a hundred times, and renounces[1] his claiming of any power and strength, and seeks the protection of Allah, and then says, "I bear witness that there

[1] That is, by saying, 'There is no power and no strength but in Allah'.

is no god but Allah, and I bear witness that Adam[1] is the sincere friend of Allah and His original formation, and Ibráhím is the cordial friend of Allah, and Moses[2] is the interlocutor of Allah, and 'Ísá is the Spirit of Allah, and Muḥammad is the beloved of Allah", has reward in accordance with the number of those who assert Allah has a son, and those who do not assert that Allah has a son, and Allah raises him along with the faithful on Resurrection Day, and he has a right upon Allah to admit him into the Garden with the prophets'.

(385) (2) The eve of Monday. Al-A'mash[3] related from Anas bin Málik that he said, 'The Messenger of Allah said, "Whoever performs a Worship on the eve of Monday, with four *rak'as*, reciting in the first the 'Praise belongs to Allah' (i) and, 'Say, He is Allah, One' (cxii) ten times, and in the second, the 'Praise belongs to Allah', and, 'Say, He is Allah, One' twenty times, and in the third the 'Praise belongs to Allah', and, 'Say, He is Allah, One' thirty times, and in the fourth, the 'Praise belongs to Allah', and, 'Say, He is Allah, One' forty times, and then says the Salutation, and recites, 'Say, He is Allah, One' seventy-five times, and says the Seeking of Forgiveness of Allah for himself and his parents seventy-five times, and then makes his request of Allah, has a right upon Allah to give him his request that he asked"'. This is called 'the Worship of Need'.[4]

(386) (3) The eve of Tuesday. 'Whoever performs a Worship of two *rak'as*, reciting in each *rak'a* the Fátiḥat al-Kitáb and, "Say, He is Allah, One", and

[1] Adam; Hughes, *Dictionary of Islam*, p. 9; *Ency. of Islam*, i. p. 296 (under Ḥawwá).

[2] The Biblical Moses. Qur'án passages and commentators' remarks are given in Hughes' *Dictionary*, pp. 356 ff.

[3] Abú Muḥammad Sulaiman bin Mihrán al-A'mash (d. 148). De Slane, op. cit., i. pp. 587 ff.

[4] This is the eighth of the Occasional, *náfl*, Worships mentioned by al-Ghazzálí; see Translation, p. 221.

the two Seekings for Refuge (cxiii, cxiv) fifteen times, and recites, after the saying of the Salutation, fifteen times, the Verse of the Throne (ii. 256) and says the Seeking of Forgiveness of Allah fifteen times, has great reward, and substantial recompense'.

(387) It is related from 'Umar from the Prophet, that he said, 'Whoever performs a Worship on the eve of Tuesday, with two *rak'as*, reciting in each *rak'a* the Fátiḥat al-Kitáb once, and "Verily, We sent it down" (xcvii), and, "Say, He is Allah, One", seven times, has Allah free his neck from the Fire, and on Resurrection Day, be his leader and guide into the Garden'.

(388) (4) The eve of Wednesday. Fáṭima related from the Prophet, that he said, 'For everyone who, on the eve of Wednesday, performs a Worship of two *rak'as*, reciting in the first the Fátiḥat al-Kitáb once, and, "Say, I seek refuge in the Lord of the dawn" (cxiii) ten times, and in the second, the Fátiḥat al-Kitáb once, and, "Say, I seek refuge in the Lord of mankind" (cxiv) ten times, then, after the Salutation, says the Seeking of Forgiveness of Allah ten times, and says the Blessing upon Muḥammad ten times, there will descend from every heaven seventy thousand angels, recording his reward until the Day of Resurrection'.

(389) In another tradition,[1] 'Sixteen *rak'as*, reciting after the Fátiḥa whatever Allah may will, and reciting in the last two *rak'as* the Verse of the Throne thirty times, and in the first two thirty times, "Say, He is Allah, One," he intercedes for ten of the people of his household, all of whom deserve the Fire'.

(390) Fáṭima is related to have said, 'Muḥammad said, "Whoever, on the eve of Wednesday, performs a Worship of six *rak'as*, reciting in every *rak'a* after the Fátiḥa, 'Say, O Allah, Possessor of the Dominion' (iii. 25) to the end of the verse, and when he finishes his Worship, says, 'May Allah requite Muḥammad

[1] This is placed after Tradition No. 390 in the margin of the SM edition, and is omitted from his text.

his desert on our behalf', has forgiven him the sins of seventy years, and has recorded for him freedom from the Fire"'.

(391) (5) The eve of Thursday. Abú Huraira said, 'The Messenger of Allah said, "Whoever, on the eve of Thursday, between the Sunset and the Evening Worships, performs a Worship of two *rak'as*, reciting in each *rak'a* the Fátiḥat al-Kitáb and the Verse of the Throne five times, and 'Say, He is Allah, One', five times, and then, when he finishes his Worship, says the Seeking of Forgiveness of Allah fifteen times, and puts his reward to the credit of his parents, repays the right of his parents upon him, even though he was undutiful to them, and Allah gives him what is given the righteous and the martyrs"'.

(392) (6) The eve of Friday. Jábir said, 'The Messenger of Allah said, "Whoever, on the eve of Friday, between the Sunset and the Evening Worships, performs a Worship of twelve *rak'as*, reciting in every *rak'a* the Fátiḥat al-Kitáb once and, 'Say, It is! Allah is One!' eleven times, is regarded as if he had performed a creature's service to Allah for twelve years, fasting all its days and standing for Worship all its nights"'.

(393) Anas said, 'The Prophet said, "Whoever performs, on the eve of Friday, the last Evening Worship in the congregation, and performs the Worship of the two *rak'as* of the *sunna*, Usage, and then performs after them a Worship of ten *rak'as*, reciting in every *rak'a* the Praise (i) and, 'Say, He is Allah, One' (cxii), and the two Seekings for Refuge (cxiii, cxiv) each once, and then performs a *witr*, Odd, Worship of three *rak'as*, and then sleeps on his right side with his face toward the *qibla*, will have it as if he had enlivened the Night of Decree"'.

(394) Muḥammad said, 'Do much of the Asking of Blessing on me on the Night of Eager Desire and the Day of Brightness, that is, on the eve of Friday and on Friday'.

(395) (7) The eve of Saturday. Anas said, 'The Messenger of Allah said, "Whoever, on the eve of Saturday, between the Sunset and the Evening Worships, performs a Worship of twelve *rak'as*, has built for him a palace in the Garden, and it is as if he has given alms to every believer, man and woman, and is innocent of Judaism, and has a right[1] upon Allah to forgive him"'.

Class Three. Those Performances of Worship that are Repeated with the Recurrence of Years

There are four of this class: the Worship of the Two Feasts, the *taráwíḥ*, 'rest-giving', Worship of Ramaḍán, the Worship of Rajab and the Worship of the middle of Sha'bán.

(*a*) The first is the Worship of the Two Feasts. It is a *sunna mu'akkada*, Confirmed Usage, and one of the distinctive rites of al-Islám. It is fitting that seven things should be observed in it.

(1) The first is that the *takbír* is in series of three, so he says, 'Allah is greater! Allah is greater! Allah is greater indeed!' and 'Much praise belongs to Allah', and 'Praise belongs to Allah morning and evening! There is no god but Allah only! He has no associate! we devote to Him our religion sincerely; even though the unbelievers disapprove!'

One begins with the *takbír* on the eve of the Feast of the Breaking of the Fast of Ramaḍán until the beginning upon the Worship of the Feast. In the second Feast he begins the *takbír* after the morning of the Day of 'Arafa until the end of the day of the thirteenth, and this is the most perfect of the statements. He repeats the *takbír* after the Prescribed Worship and after the Supererogatory Worship, the one after the Prescribed being better confirmed.

[1] The SM explains this as 'by way of the favour and grace of Allah'.

(2) The second is that when he gets up in the morning of the day of the Feast he bathes, and adorns and perfumes himself, as we have mentioned regarding the Friday Observance.[1] The cloak and the turban are most excellent for men, and let boys avoid silk, and the aged adornment, on going out.

(396) (3) The third is that he leaves one way and returns another. So did the Messenger of Allah. Muḥammad used to command the unmarried girls and those who wore veils to be sent out.

(4) The fourth is that it is liked to go out to the desert, except in Mecca and Jerusalem. But if it should be a rainy day, there is no objection to Worship in the mosque. It is permissible on a clear day for the *imám* to command a man to perform the Worship with those who are unable to go out in the mosque and himself go out with the able, saying the *takbír* on the way.

(5) The fifth is that he observes the time. For the time of the Worship of the Feasts is between the rising of the sun and its passing the meridian, and the time of slaughtering for the sacrifices is after the rising of the sun and the length of time it takes for two addresses and two *rak'as* until the close of the thirteenth day. It is liked to hasten the Worship of the *aḍḥá*, Sacrifices, on account of the slaughtering, and to delay the Worship of the Breaking of the Fast for the sake of distributing the alms of the *fiṭr*, Breaking of the Fast, before the Worship. This is a Usage of the Messenger of Allah.

(6) The sixth is about the manner of the Worship. Let the people go out saying the *takbír* on the way, and when the *imám* reaches the place of Worship, he should not sit down and should not perform any *náfila* Worship. The people have the right to perform *náfila* Worship.[2] Then the crier should

[1] See pp. 150 ff. of the Translation.

[2] The other texts read, 'the people should stop performing the *náfila* Worship'.

cry, 'The Worship is gathering!' The *imám* leads them with a Worship of two *rak'as*, saying the *takbír* in the first, except the *takbírat al-iḥrám* and of the Bowing, seven times, saying between every two *takbírs*, 'O the Praise of Allah!' and 'The Praise belongs to Allah!' and 'There is no god but Allah!' and 'Allah is greater!' and says, 'I have turned my face toward Him who originally divided the heavens and the earth!' after the *takbír* of the Opening of the Worship. He should postpone the Seeking of Refuge until after the eighth *takbír* and recite Súrat Qáf (l) in the first *rak'a* after the Fátiḥa and recite 'The Hour drew near!' (liv) in the second *rak'a*. The extra *takbírs* in the second are five in number, apart from the *takbír* of the Standing Posture and the Bowing, and between every two *takbírs* are what we have mentioned. Then he gives the two addresses, sitting down between them. He whom the Worship of the Feast escapes performs a Substitute for it.

(397) (7) The seventh is that he sacrifices a sheep. The Messenger of Allah sacrificed two fine sheep, and slaughtered them with his own hand, and said, 'In the name of Allah',[1] and 'Allah is greater! This is for me and any of my people who does not
(398) sacrifice!' Muḥammad said, 'Whoever sees the crescent of the moon of the month of Dhú al-Ḥijja, and desires to sacrifice, should not take off any
(399) of his hair or finger nails'. Abú Aiyúb the Helper said, 'A man used to sacrifice, in the time of the Messenger of Allah, a ewe, for the sake of his household and they used themselves to eat and to feed others'. One has the right to eat from the sacrifice after three days and more. The permission for it came after the prohibition of it.

(400) Sufyán al-Thawrí said, 'It is liked for one to perform a Worship, after the Feast of the Breaking of the Fast, of twelve *rak'as*, and after the Feast of the

[1] Note that 'the Merciful and Compassionate' is omitted on this occasion.

Sacrifice, of six *rak'as*', and he said, 'It is one of the Usages'.

(*b*) The second is the *taráwíḥ*, Rest-giving, Worship of Ramaḍán. It consists of twenty *rak'as.* The manner of performing it is well known. It is a Confirmed Usage, although it is inferior to the Worship of the Two Feasts. There is disagreement as to whether congregational or individual Worship is more
(401) excellent in this Worship. The Messenger of Allah went to it two or three nights in the congregation.
(402) Then he did not go out, and said, 'I fear that it may be made obligatory upon you'. 'Umar gathered the people to it in congregation, in as much as it was safe from becoming obligatory through the cessation of the revelation.[1] So it was said, 'The congregational observance of it is more excellent because of the action of 'Umar, and because congregating together is a blessing and has excellence, as is evidenced by the Prescribed Observances, and because one, perhaps, would be lazy alone, and be zealous under the observation of a congregation'.

It is also said, 'The performance of it alone is more excellent because this is a *sunna*, Usage, that is, not one of the Rites of the religion, like the Two Feasts. So its affiliation with the Worship of the Forenoon and the Greeting of the Mosque is preferable, seeing that (*a*) congregational observance has not been made a law in them, and (*b*) that the custom has come to be that a group enters a mosque together and yet they do not perform the Worship of the Greeting of the Mosque in congregation, and (*c*)
(403) on account of the saying of Muḥammad, 'The superiority of the Voluntary Worship over the Worship in the mosque is like the superiority of the performance of the *maktúb*, Prescribed, Worship in the mosque over the performance of the Worship in the house'.
(404) It is related that Muḥammad said, 'Worship in

[1] That is, after the death of Muḥammad.

this my[1] mosque is more excellent than a thousand performances of Worship in any other mosque, and Worship in the inviolate mosque[2] is more excellent than a thousand performances of the Worship in my mosque, and, more excellent than all of that, is the Worship of a man who performs in the corner of his house a Worship of two *rak'as* that no one knows about except Allah'. This is because hypocrisy and affectation perhaps draw near to one in a congregation, and he is in safety against it alone. So this is what is said about it, and the preferred conclusion is that the congregational observance is more excellent, as 'Umar considered. In some of the *náfila* Worships congregational observance was made the law, and this Worship is worthy to be among the rites of the religion that are apparent.

As for taking account of hypocrisy in a congregation, and laziness when alone, this is a turning aside from the consideration purposed in the excellence of the congregation, in so far as it is a Congregational Worship. It is as though he who holds that position were saying, 'The Worship is better for one than abandoning it, out of laziness', and 'Singleness of devotion is better than hypocrisy'. So, let us consider the question in the case of him who has confidence in himself, that he will not be lazy, even though he is by himself, and will not be hypocritical, even though he is present with a congregation, and then, which of them is more excellent? In that case the opinion will turn between the blessing in a congregation, and the increase of the strength of one's singleness of devotion and presence of the heart when by oneself. So it is permissible that there should be some hesitancy with regard to the superiority of one of them over the other.

Among the acts that are liked there is the *qunút*, Supplication, in the *witr* Worship in the latter half of Ramaḍán.

[1] In al-Madina. [2] In Mecca.

(*c*) As for the Worship of Rajab, it has been related *isnâdan*, with a 'traced' chain of witnesses, from the
(405) Messenger of Allah, that he said, 'There is no one who fasts the first Thursday in Rajab and then performs a Worship between the first Evening Worship and the nightfall, of twelve *rak'as*, separating every two *rak'as* with a Salutation, reciting in each *rak'a* the Fátiḥat al-Kitáb once, and, "Truly, We sent it down on the Night of Decree" (xcvii) three times, and, "Say, He is Allah, One" (cvii) twelve times, and then, when he finishes his Worship, asks the Blessing for me seventy times, saying, "O Allah, bless Muḥammad, the unlettered Prophet, and his family!" and then performs a Prostration, and, while in prostration says, "Praiseworthy, Holy, Lord of the angels and the spirit!" and then raises his head and says, seventy times, "O Lord, forgive and have mercy and pass over what Thou knowest! Verily, Thou art the Most Mighty and the Most Wise and Kind!" and then performs another Prostration and says in it what is similar to that which he said in the first Prostration, and then makes request for what he needs, in his Prostration, but will have it performed.'
(406) Muḥammad said, 'There is no one who performs this Worship without having Allah forgive all his sins, even though they are like the froth of the sea, and the number of the sand, and the weight of the mountains, and the leaves of the trees, and there shall be intercession on behalf of seven hundred of his household of those who have deserved the Fire'

So, this Worship is liked, and we have set it forth is this section only because it is repeated with the recurrence of the years, although its degree does not approximate the degree of the Rest-giving Worship and the Worship of the Two Feasts, because a single line[1] of authority has handed this Worship down. But I saw the people of Jerusalem, all of them, con-

[1] Áḥád 'single line of tradition'. These are traditions given by only one authority. *Ency. of Islam*, ii. p. 192A.

sistently perform it, and not allow it to be abandoned, so I desired to set it forth.

(407) (*d*) As for the Worship of Sha'bán. On the eve of the fifteenth of this month one performs a Worship of a hundred *rak'as*, every two *rak'as* with a Salutation reciting in every *rak'a* after the Fátiḥa, 'Say, He is Allah, One', eleven times, and, if he will, he performs ten *rak'as*, reciting in each *rak'a* after the Fátiḥa one hundred times, 'Say He is Allah, One', for this also is related in the totality of the performances of the Worship. The Fathers used to perform this Worship, and call it the 'Good Worship', and to gather together for it, and perhaps they performed it in con-
(408) gregation. It is related from al-Ḥasan that he said, 'Thirty of the Companions of the Prophet reported to me that whoever performs this Worship on this night has Allah look upon him seventy times, and perform for him with each look seventy needs, the least of which is forgiveness'.

Class Four: The *Náfila*, Supererogatory, Worships that Depend upon Occasional Causes, and do not Depend upon Appointed Times

These are nine in number: The Worship of the Eclipse[1] of the Moon, and of the Eclipse of the Sun, of the Request for Rain, of the Greeting of the Mosque, the Two *Rak'as* between the Call to Worship and the Institution of the Worship, the Two *Rak'as* upon leaving the house and entering it, and the like. So we will mention those of them that occur to us now:

(409) (1) The first is the Worship of the Eclipse. The Messenger of Allah said, 'The sun and the moon

[1] The SM lists five different interpretations of *kusúf* and *khusúf*: *kusúf* is the change to blackness, while *khusúf* is the decrease of blackness; (2) both apply to the departure of light from the sun and moon, with *kusúf* at its beginning and with *khusúf* at its end; (3) *kusúf* applies to the departure of all the light, with *khusúf* for departure of part of the light; (4) *khusúf* for the departure of all the colour, with *kusúf* for the change of all the colour; (5) is the application of *kusúf* to the sun and *khusúf* to the moon. SM iii. p. 427 c.; cf. Lane, *Lexicon*, p. 738B.

are two of the signs of Allah; they do not come into eclipse on account of the death or of the life of anyone, so whenever you see that, seek refuge in fear to the remembrance of Allah and to Worship'. He said that when his boy Ibráhím died while the sun was in eclipse, and the people thereupon said, 'It was in eclipse only on account of his death'.

Consideration will now be given to its manner and its time. As for the manner, whenever the sun is in eclipse, in a time when the Worship is disliked or not disliked, there should be a Call to Congregational Worship, and the *imám* should lead the people in a Worship of two *rak'as* and bow in each *rak'a* two times, with the former of both of them longer than the latter of them, but he should not speak audibly. He recites in the first *rak'a*, from the Standing Posture of the first *rak'a*, the Fátiḥa and 'The Cow' (ii), and in the second, the Fátiḥa and 'The Family of 'Imrán' (iii), and in the third, the Fátiḥa and 'The Women' (iv), and in the fourth, the Fátiḥa and 'The Table' (v), or that amount of the Qur'án, from whatever place he wishes. Were he to confine himself to the Fátiḥa in each *rak'a*, that would suffice him. Were he to confine himself to the short *súras*, there would be no harm, because the purpose of the prolongation is the continuance of the Worship until the clearance of the sun or moon after the eclipse. He says 'The Praise' in the first to the amount of a hundred verses, and in the second to the amount of eighty verses, and in the third to the amount of seventy verses, and in the fourth to the amount of fifty verses.

Let the Prostration be equal to the length of the Bowing in each *rak'a*. Then he delivers two addresses after the Worship, with a period of sitting between them. He commands the people to give alms, to free slaves, and to repent.

He does likewise in the eclipse of the moon, only in it he speaks audibly, since it is at night.

As for the time, it is at the beginning of the

eclipse until the completion of the clearance. The time for it also ends when the sun sets while in eclipse. The Worship of the Eclipse of the Moon passes when the disk of the sun appears, since it cancels the dominion of the night, but it does not pass with the setting of the moon while it is eclipse, since the whole night is the dominion of the moon. But if it clears in the midst of the Worship, one completes it quickly. Whoever overtakes the second Bowing with the *imâm* has that *rak'a* escape him, for the fundamental thing is the first Bowing.

(2) The second is the Worship of the Petition for Rain. So, when the streams are lost in the earth, and the rains are cut off, or a canal collapses, it is liked for the *imâm* to command the people first to fast three days, and do what they are able in giving alms, and to cease from injustices, and to repent from disobedience, and then go out with them on the fourth day, along with the aged and the youths, all having cleansed themselves, in shabby and humble clothes, humbling themselves, in contrast to the feast days. It is said, 'It is liked to take out the animals, because of their sharing the need, and because of the
(410) saying of Muḥammad, "Were it not for the young nursing, and the elders bowing and the cattle feeding, there would surely be poured upon you punishment"'.

Were the non-Muslim people[1] under Muslim authority also to go out, distinguished by their marks, they should not be prohibited. Then, when they have all gathered together at the spacious place of Worship in the plain, the Call to Congregational Worship is given. Then the *imâm* performs a Worship of two *rak'as* with them, like the Worship of the two Feasts, without the *takbîr*. Then he

[1] The *ahl al-dhimma* are the people of a conquered country who do not embrace Islam and are not enslaved, but are guaranteed life, liberty and modified property rights, with certain duties toward Muslims. *Ency. of Islam*, i. p. 958 f.

delivers two addresses, with a brief sitting between them, and lets the Seeking for Refuge be the main part of the two addresses. It is fitting that, in the middle of the second address he should turn his back to the people and face the *qibla*, and turn his cloak upside down at this time, drawing a good omen from the changing of the state. So did the Messenger of Allah. So he makes its upper part become the lower part, and what was on the right side appear on the left side, and what was on the left side appear on the right side. So shall the people do.

Then they make a Supplication at this time inaudibly. Then the *imám* faces them and makes the address. They leave their cloaks turned as they were until they take them off when they take off their clothes. He says, in the Supplication, 'O Allah, Thou hast commanded us to make Supplication to Thee, and hast promised us Thine answer: so we have supplicated Thee, as Thou hast commanded us, and now answer us as Thou hast promised us! O Allah, bestow upon us forgiveness of what we have committed, and Thine answer in providing us water and in abundance of our apportioned sustenance.' There is no harm in making supplication at the various performances of Worship during the three days preceding the going out. This Supplication has Proprieties and inward Stipulations, consisting of repentance and the restitution of wrongs and of other things, and that will follow in the Book of *Da'awát*, Supplications.

(3) The third is the Worship at Funerals. Its manner is well known. The most comprehensive
(411) Supplication handed down is what is related in the *Ṣaḥíḥ* of al-Bukhárí[1] from 'Awf bin Málik.[2] He said, 'I saw the Messenger of Allah perform a Worship at a funeral and I preserved this much of his supplication, "O Allah, forgive him, have

[1] Al-Bukhárí, *Ency. of Islam*, i. p. 783 f.
[2] 'Awf bin Málik al-Ashja'í (d. 73), *el-Nawawi*, p. 489 f.

mercy on him, preserve him, pardon him, make his descent honourable, enlarge his entrance, wash him in water and snow and hail, cleanse him from sins, as one cleans a white garment of defilement, and change him to an abode better than his present abode, to a family better than his present family, and a mate better than his present mate. Place him in the Garden and rescue him from the punishment of the Grave, and from the punishment of the Fire! " so that', said 'Awf, 'I desired that I were myself that dead man'.

It is fitting that one who overtakes the second *takbîr* should observe the order of the Worship by himself, and say the *takbîrs*, with the *takbîrs* of the *imâm*, and when the *imâm* says the Salutation, he should perform a substitute for the *takbîr* which escaped him, as is done by one late, for, were he to get ahead in saying the *takbîrs* there would not remain any meaning to the imitation of the *imâm* on the part of the worshipper in this Worship, since the *takbîrs* are the apparent Elements, and worthy to have the standing of the *rak'as* in the rest of the Worships. This is to me the best regarded view, although some other than this is possible. The traditions that have appeared regarding the excellence of the Worship at funerals and the escorting of them are well known, so we will not be long by setting them forth. How should its excellence not be great, since it is one of the *farḍ kifâya*[1] Worships, i.e. of general obligarion, and since it becomes supererogatory only to him for whom it does not become *farḍ 'ain*, i.e. a personal obligation, through the presence of someone else. So then, one obtains by it the excellence of a *farḍ kifâya* Worship, although it is not a *farḍ 'ain* only because they altogether have undertaken to perform what is of general obligation, and thereby have removed the guilt of neglect from others. So

[1] For the *farḍ al-'ain* and *farḍ al-kifâya*, see *Ency. of Islam*, ii. p. 61.

that is not like a Supererogatory Worship which does not remove a Prescribed duty from anyone.

The desire for a great congregation is liked, seeking blessing by means of a great number of solicitudes and supplications, and because of its possible inclusion of someone whose supplication is answered, in
(412) accordance with what Kuraib[1] related from Ibn 'Abbás, to the effect that a son of his died, so he said, 'O Kuraib, see how many men have gathered together for him'. He said, 'So I went out and behold, many men had gathered together for him, so I told him. So he said, 'Would you say they are forty?' I said, 'Yes'. He said, 'Take him out then, for I heard the Messenger of Allah say, "No Muslim dies with forty men, who do not make anything to be an associate with Allah, performing the Worship of his funeral, but Allah welcomes their intercession for him"'.

When he escorts the funeral and reaches the cemetery or enters it, at first he says, 'The Peace is upon you, O people of these abodes, of the believers and Muslims, and may Allah have mercy upon those of us who are coming soon, and those who are coming later, for we, if Allah will, are to meet you!'

It is preferable that he should not depart until the dead man is buried. Then, when the grave is made over the dead man, he stands near it and says, 'O Allah, Thy creature has returned to Thee, so have mercy upon him, and show mercy to him! O Allah, remove the earth from his two sides, and open the gates of heaven to his spirit, and receive him unto Thyself with a beautiful welcome, and, if he is a well-doer, double for him his good deeds; and, if he is an evil-doer, pass[2] by his evil deeds'.

(4) The fourth: the Greeting of the Mosque is a Worship of two *rak'as* and more. It is a Confirmed Usage, so that it does not fall away, even though the

[1] Abú Rishdin Kuraib bin Abú Muslim al-Ḥijází (d. 98). *El-Nawawi*, p. 520.

[2] The marginal text reads, 'requite him'.

imám is making the address on Friday, and the obligation of listening to the speaker is itself Confirmed. If he occupies himself with a Prescribed Worship, or performs a Substitution Worship that is due from him, the Worship of Greeting is thereby performed, and he gets the reward, since the purpose is that the beginning of his entrance should not be without the religious service especially belonging to the mosque, so performing the right of the mosque.

For this reason it is disliked for him to enter a mosque without having performed the ablution. So, if he enters to cross over or sit down, let him say, 'Oh, the Praise of Allah!' and 'Praise belongs to Allah!' and 'There is no god but Allah!' and 'Allah is greater!' saying them four times. It is said that they equal two *rak'as* in excellence.

The school of al-Sháfi'í holds that the Greeting is not disliked in the times when the Worship ordinarily is disliked, which are (1) after mid-afternoon, (2) after the morning, (3) at the passing of the meridian, (4) at the rising, and (5) at the setting of the sun, in
(413) accordance with the tradition that is related, that Muḥammad performed a Worship of two *rak'as* after mid-afternoon, and he was asked, 'Did you not forbid us to do that?' So he said, 'They are two *rak'as* that I was wont to perform after noon, and the deputation pre-occupied me from them'.

This tradition provides two lessons. One of them is that dislike is limited to Worship that has no cause. The weakest of causes is performing Substitutions of *náfila* Worships, since the *'ulamá'*, learned, have disagreed about the questions, whether (*a*) *náfila*, Worships may have Substitution performances, and (*b*) whenever one performs a Worship similar to a *náfila* that has escaped him, that is a Substitution performance or a Payment. So, when dislike is negated by the weakest of causes, much more is it true that it is negated by entering a mosque, which is a strong cause. For that reason the Worship at funerals is not disliked whenever it comes, and neither is the Worship of the Eclipse and of the Request for Rain, at these times, since they have causes.

The second lesson is the Substitution of the *nâfila* Worship, since the Messenger of Allah performed that. We have, in regard to it, a fine example.

(414) 'Â'isha said, 'The Messenger of Allah, whenever sleep or illness overcame him, so that he did not rise that night, used to perform a Worship of twelve *rak'as* at the first part of the day'.

The learned have said, 'Whoever is at *nâfila* Worship and has the response to the *mu'adhdhin* escape him, should perform the Substitute of it, and give the response when he says the Salutation, even though the *mu'adhdhin* has stopped. There is now no meaning to the objection of anyone who says, 'That is like the first case, and he does not give a Substitute response', since, were this objection true, the Messenger of Allah would not have performed them as a Worship in a disliked time. Yes indeed, whoever has a *wird*, Devotional Recital, to perform, and has some excusable thing hinder him from it, should not permit himself to omit it, but should make it up at some other time, so that he may not incline himself to ease and comfort, for some good will overtake him in the way of the warfare of the soul and also because Muḥammad

(415) said, 'The deed most liked before Allah is the most constant one, even though it be small'. So he should purpose by that method not to be remiss in persevering in his deed.

(416) 'Â'isha related from the Prophet that he said, 'Allah hates whoever serves and worships Allah and then abandons his religious service'. So then, let him beware of entering under the threat. The thing confirmed by this tradition is that Allah hated him, and he abandoned it out of weariness, for were it not for the hatred of Allah and his separation [from the mercy of Allah[1]], weariness would not have overcome him.

[1] This is added by the SM.

(5) The fifth is the Two *Rak'as* after the *wuḍú'*, Ablution. They are liked because the ablution is a means of access, the purpose of which is the Worship, while the defilements are hindrance, for many a time the defilement happens to occur before the Worship, so the state of ablution is broken, and the endeavour is lost. Hastening to the Two *Rak'as* is a paying of the purpose of the ablution before it passes away.

That it is liked is known from the tradition of
(417) Bilál, since Muḥammad said, 'I entered the Garden and then saw Bilál in it, so I said to Bilál, "By what means did you precede me to the Garden?" So Bilál answered, "I do not know of anything except that I do not perform a new ablution without performing a Worship after it of two *rak'as*".'

(6) The sixth is the Worship of two *rak'as* upon
(418) Entering the House and upon Leaving it. Abú Salama[1] related from Abú Huraira: 'He said, "The Messenger of Allah said, 'When you leave your house perform a Worship of two *rak'as* which will protect you from the exit of evil, and when you enter the house, perform a Worship of two *rak'as* which will protect you from the entrance of evil'". This means that every event of importance should begin with it. For this reason, there have come down two *rak'as* at the time of the *iḥrám* [in the Pilgrimage, or minor pilgrimage] and two *rak'as* at the beginning of a journey, and two *rak'as* upon returning from a journey, in the mosque before entering the house, since all that is handed down as the practice of the Messenger of Allah.

Some of the righteous, whenever they ate anything, used to perform a Worship of two *rak'as*, and when they drank anything, to perform a Worship of two *rak'as*, and so in everything that happened to them. It is fitting that one should seek the blessing

[1] Abú Salama bin 'Abdalraḥmán bin 'Awf, *faqíh* and *imám* (d. 94). Wüstenfeld, *Dahabi, Liber Classium Virorum*, ii. 29.

of Allah at the beginning of things by the mention of Allah. They, the beginnings of things, are of three orders: one of them is repeated frequently, as eating and drinking, so he begins it with,
(419) 'In the name of Allah'. Muḥammad said, 'Every matter of importance that is not begun with "In the name of Allah the Merciful and Compassionate", is maimed'.

The second order is that which is not of frequent occurrence, but which has importance, such as the contracting of marriage, and the beginning of advice and counsel, and then the liked thing in that is that it should be preceded by 'The Praise of Allah'. Then the one who does the marrying says, 'Praise belongs to Allah', and 'I invoke a blessing upon the Messenger of Allah. I have married you to my daughter.' The one who receives her says, 'The praise belongs to Allah', and 'I invoke a blessing upon the Messenger of Allah. I have accepted this marriage.'

It was the custom of the Companions in the beginning of the execution of a message, and the giving of advice and counsel to say the Praise first.

The third is that order which does not occur frequently, but, when it does occur, has permanence and has importance, such as a journey, and the purchase of a new house, and the act of *iḥrám*, 'separation', and similar things. Then it is liked to do two *rak'as* on account of it first. The least important of them is the leaving of the house and entering it, for they are a kind of short journey and return.

(7) The seventh is the Worship for Prospering. Whoever is anxious about a matter, and does not know how it will end, and does not know whether it is better to leave it or to proceed upon it, has been commanded by the Messenger of Allah to perform a Worship of two *rak'as* apart from the Prescribed, reciting in the first the Fátiḥat al-Kitáb, and 'Say, O ye unbelievers' (cix), and in the second the Fátiḥa and 'Say, He is Allah, One' (cxii), and then, when he

finishes, to make his supplication, and say, 'O Allah, I ask of Thee prospering by Thy knowledge, and ask Thee to give me power by Thy power, and I ask Thee of Thy great favour, for verily, Thou hast power and I do not have power, and dost know, and I do not know, and Thou art the Knower of the unseen. O Allah, if Thou dost know that this matter is the best for me, in my religion and this life of mine, and the end of this matter of mine, both soon and late, bring it to pass for me, and bless me in it, and then make it easy for me. If Thou dost know that this affair will be bad for me in my religion and this life of mine, and likewise its end, both soon and late, turn me away from it and turn it away from me, and bring to pass for me the best, wherever it may be. Verily Thou art powerful over everything!' Jábir bin
(420) 'Abdalláh related it. He said, 'The Messenger of Allah used to teach us the Worship of Prospering in all affairs, as he used to teach us the *súra*.'

(421) Muḥammad said, 'Whenever any one of you is anxious about an affair, let him perform a Worship of two *rak'as*. Then let him mention the affair, and offer a supplication according to what we have mentioned'.

(8) The eighth is the Worship of Need. Whenever a man's breast oppresses him and necessity in what is beneficial in his religion and this life constrains him to a matter hard for him, let him perform
(422) this Worship, for it was related from Wuhaib bin al-Ward[1] that he said, 'Among the supplications which are not refused is this, that a creature should perform twelve *rak'as*, reciting in each *rak'a* the Mother of the Book (i), and the Verse of the Throne (ii. 256), and "Say, He is Allah, One" (cxii), and when he finishes, bows down in prostration and then says, "O the Praise of Him who wears might as a garment", and says in it, "O the Praise of Him who

[1] Abú Umaiya Wuhaib bin al-Ward (d. 153). *Ibn Ṭagri Bardii*, i. p. 412; *el-Nawawi*, p. 620.

wraps Himself in glory, and is bountiful in it! O the Praise of Him who numbers everything by His knowledge! O the Praise of Him to whom alone Praise belongs! O the Praise of the Possessor of boon and favour! O the Praise of the Possessor of might and bounty! O the Praise of the Possessor of power! I ask Thee, by the mighty articulations of Thy Throne, and the utmost degree of mercy of Thy Book, and by Thy greatest name, and Thy highest greatness, and Thy universal, perfect Words, which no righteous one or sinner passes beyond, to bless Muḥammad and the family of Muḥammad," and then asks his need which has no disobedience in it, and he will be answered, if Allah will.'

Wuhaib said, 'It has reached us that it used to be said, "Do not teach it to your unintelligent people, for they will assist one another by means of it in disobedience to Allah"'.

(423) One of the wise has said,[1] 'Whoever gives four *rak'as*, is not denied four; whoever gives thanks, is not denied increase; and whoever gives repentance, is not denied acceptance; and whoever gives the Worship of Prospering, is not denied good; and whoever gives counsel, is not denied correctness'.

(9) The ninth is the Worship of the Praise. This Worship is transmitted by Tradition to be done at random, and does not belong to any particular time or any particular occasion. It is liked that the week should not be free from it one time, or the month
(424) once, for 'Ikrima has related from Ibn 'Abbás that Muḥammad said to 'Abbás bin 'Abdalmuṭṭalib, 'Do I not present you, do I not grant you, do I not give you something for which Allah forgives you your sin when you do it, first and last, old and new, mistaken and intentional, secret and open? You perform a Worship of four *rak'as*, reciting in every *rak'a* the Fátiḥat al-Kitáb and another *súra*, and when you finish the Recital in the first *rak'a*, while you are

[1] In the Cairo 1334 edition this appears at the end of Class 7.

standing, you say, "O the Praise of Allah!" and "The Praise belongs to Allah!" and "There is no god but Allah!" and "Allah is greater!" fifteen times. Then you bow and then say them ten times while bowing. Then you raise your head and say them ten times. Then you prostrate and say them ten times. Then you raise your head and say them ten times sitting. Then you prostrate and say them ten times. Then you raise your head and say them ten times, and that makes seventy-five times in every *rak'a.* You should do that in the four *rak'as.* If you are able to perform it every day, do so. But if you do not do it every day, then on every Friday once. But if you do not do it every Friday, then in every month once. But if you do not do so, then in every year once.'

(425) In another tradition it states that one should say in the first *rak'a* of the Worship, 'Thine is the Praise, O Allah!' and 'By Thy Praise!' and 'Thy name is blessed!' and 'Thy greatness is exalted!' and 'Thy names are Hallowed!' and 'There is no God but Thee!' Then he says the Praise (i) fifteen times before the Recital and ten times after the Recital, and the rest as has preceded, ten each, and does not say the Praise (i) after the last Prostration while sitting down. This is the most beautiful, and it is the choice of Ibn Mubárak.[1] The sum of the two narratives is three hundred Praises. If he performs them in the daytime he does it with one Salutation. If he does it at night, then to do it with two Salutations is better, since it appears that the Worship at night

(426) should be by twos. If h adds after the Praise, His saying, 'There is no power and no strength but in Allah the High, the Great', that is well, for that has come down in some of the narratives.

Now these are the Worships that have been handed down. None of these *náfila*, Supererogatory, Wor-

[1] Abú 'Abdalraḥmán 'Abdalláh bin Mubárak b. Wáḍiḥ al-Hanzalí (d. 181), celebrated jurisconsult and ascetic. SM i. pp. 208 ff.; De Slane, *Ibn Khallikan*, ii. p. 12 f.

ships is liked in the disliked times, except the Worship of the Greeting of the Mosque. As for what we have set forth after the Greeting of the Mosque about the Two *Rak'as* of the Ablution, and the Worship of the Journey and the Leaving of the House and the Prospering, they are not allowable, for the prohibition against them is confirmed, and these causes are weak and do not reach the degree of importance of the Eclipse, and the Request for Rain, and the Greeting of the Mosque.

I have seen someone of the Ṣúfís performing the Two *Rak'as* of the Ablution in the disliked time, and it is utterly absurd, for the ablution is not the cause for the Worship, but rather, the Worship is the cause for the ablution. So it is fitting that he should perform the ablution for the Worship, not that he should perform the Worship because he does the ablution, for it would then be the case that every one who has defiled himself who wishes to perform a Worship in a disliked time, would only have to do the ablution, and perform the Worship, and then there would remain no meaning to dislike.

It is not fitting that he should state the Intention to perform the Two *Rak'as* of the Ablution as he states the Intention to perform the Two *Rak'as* of the Greeting of the Mosque. Rather, when he does the ablution, he performs *tatawwu'*, Voluntary, *rak'as* in order that his ablution may not be unemployed, as Bilál used to do, for it is indeed purely voluntary, occurring after the ablution.

The tradition of Bilál does not indicate that the ablution is a cause for the Worship, like the Eclipse and the Greeting of the Mosque, so that he should state the Intention to perform the Two *Rak'as* of the Ablution. So it is absurd that he should state the Intention to perform the Worship of the Ablution. Rather he states the Intention by the ablution, and what kind of an arrangement is it for him to say in his ablution, 'I do the ablution for the sake of my Worship', and then also in his Worship say,

'I perform the Worship for the sake of my ablution?' Rather, let him who desires to guard his ablution from becoming unused in a disliked time state the Intention of a Substitution performance, if, by any possibility, there should be incumbent upon him some Worship to which some defect has found its way from some cause or other, for the Substitution performances of the Worship in the disliked times is not disliked.

But as for the stating of the Intention of a *tatawwu'*, Voluntary, Worship: this has no consideration, for in the prohibition against the Worship in the disliked times, there are three important points. One of them is guarding against the resemblance of the worshippers of the sun. The second is guarding against the
(427) satans' dispersal, since the Messenger of Allah said, 'Verily the sun rises, and the horn of Satan is with it, for whenever the sun rises, he is in conjunction with it, and then, when it is high, he leaves it, and then when it is at meridian, he is in conjunction with it, and then when it passes the meridian, he leaves it, and then when it is near its setting he is in conjunction with it, and then, when it sets, he leaves it'. So there is prohibition against the Worship in those times, and attention is drawn by the prohibition to the underlying cause. The third is that those walking the way of the next abode do not cease to continue in the Worship at all times. Continuance in one sort of religious service is what brings on weariness. Whenever one is kept away from it for a time, alacrity increases and incitements spring up,
(428) seeing that 'man is covetous of what is forbidden'.

So in not using these times for the Worship there is increase of incitement and of instigation to await the end of the time. For these times are especially appointed for Praise and Seeking Forgiveness, guarding against weariness that comes through perseverance in one kind of Worship, and seeking relief by changing from one kind of religious service to another, for, in finding a thing to be new and in seeking a new thing there is pleasure and alacrity, while in continuance upon one thing there is heaviness and weariness. For that reason the Worship is not Prostration solely and not Bowing solely, and not Standing solely, but the religious services are organized from a variety of acts and dissimilar forms of Invocations, for the heart secures from each of them a new pleasure upon changing to it. But were it to continue upon one thing, weariness would quickly come upon it. Now if these are matters important in the prohibition against the disliked times, and there are other mysteries, which it is not in the power of man to gaze into, although Allah and His Messenger know better about them, these important things are not to be abandoned except for causes important in the religious law, such as the Substitute performance of the Worship and the Worship of the Request for Rain and of the Eclipse and of the Greeting of the Mosque. As for what is weaker than these, it is not fitting that one should thwart the purpose of the prohibition by them. This is the more regarded opinion, and Allah knows better than anyone else what is correct.

APPENDICES

APPENDIX I

TABLE OF THE NUMPER OF *RAK'AS* IN THE DIFFERFNT WORSHIPS

I. DAILY:

(*a*) The *farḍ* Prescribed Worships and the *râtiba* Fixed Worships connected with them

	rawâtib before the Prescribed; *mu'akkada*, Confirmed	*mustaḥabb*, Liked	Prescribed	*rawâtib* after the Prescribed; Confirmed	Liked
Morning		2 (or after)	2		
Noon	2		4	2	
Afternoon	4		4		
Sunset		2 (or after)	2		
Evening			4		4

(*b*) Other Daily *nâfl*, Supererogatory, Worships, all Confirmed:

Witr, Odd	1 to 13
Forenoon	4, 6 or 8
Between the Two Evening Worships	6

II. WEEKLY:	Sunday	Monday	Tuesday	Wednesday	Thursday	Friday	Saturday
(*a*) Daytime	4	2 or 12	10	12	2	2, 4, 8, or 12	4
(*b*) Night	20	4	2	2, 16 or 6	2	12 or 10	12

III. YEARLY:	Feasts of *al-Fiṭr*	and *al-Aḍḥâ*	Ramaḍân	Rajab	Sha'bân
Confirmed	2	2	20		
Liked				12	100

IV. OCCASIONAL:	Eclipse	Request for Rain	Funeral	Greeting of Mosque	Ablution	Entering House, etc	Prospering	Need	Praise
	2	2		2	2	2	2	12	4

APPENDIX II

BIBLIOGRAPHY

I. Encyclopedias.

1. Leyden: The *Encyclopedia of Islam.* A Dictionary of the Geography, Ethnography, and Biography of the Muhammadan Peoples, prepared by a Number of Leading Orientalists. Leyden, 1913.
2. Hughes: *Dictionary of Islam*, being a Cyclopedia of the Doctrines, Rites, Ceremonies and Customs, together with the Technical Terms and Theological Terms of the Muhammadan Religion. By Thomas Patrick Hughes, London, 1885.
3. Brockelmann: *Geschichte der Arabischen Litteratur*, von Karl Brockelmann, Zwei Bande, Weimar, 1898, 1902.
4. Nicholson: *A Literary History of the Arabs*, by Reynold A. Nicholson, London, 1907.

II. Lexicons.

5. Lane: *An Arabic-English Lexicon*, by Edward William Lane, 1863.
6. *Dictionary of the Technical Terms*, used in the Sciences of the Musalmans, edited under superintendence of A. Sprenger and W. Nassau Lees, Calcutta, 1862.
7. Jurjání: *Defitionitiones viri meritissimi Sejjid Scherif Ali ben Mohammed Dschordschani*, edidit Gustavus Flügel, Lipsiae, 1845, MDCCCXLV.
8. Dozy: *Supplément aux Dictionnaires Arabes*, par R. Dozy, Leyde, 1881.
9. Sharḥ al-Qámús al-Musammá *Táj al-'Arús*, lil-Saiyid Muḥammad Murtaḍá, Miṣr, 1306.
10. *Qámús al-Múhít*, Muḥammad bin Ya'qúb al-Fairúzábádí, Cairo, 1301.
11. *Kitáb al-Fá'iq*, Abú Qásim Maḥmúd bin 'Umar al-Zamakhsharí, Cairo, 1324.
12. *Ad-Damírí's Hayát al-Hayawán*, a Zoological Lexicon, A. S. G. Jayakar, London, 1908.
13. *Aramäisch-Neuhebräisches Wörterbuch*, von Gustaf H. Dalman, Frankfurt A.M., 1901.
14. *Thesaurus Syriacus*, R. Payne Smith, Oxford, MDCCCCI.
15. *Lisán al-'Arab.*

III. GRAMMARS.

16. *Al-Mufaṣṣal*, Opus de re Grammatico Arabicum, auctore Abú'l Ḳásim Maḥmúd bin 'Omar Zamahsário, edidit J. P. Broch, editio altera, Christianiae, 1840.
17. De Sacy: *Anthologie Grammaticale Arabe*, par M. le Baron Silvestre De Sacy, Paris, 1829.
18. Mehren: *Die Rhetorik der Araber*, von A. F. Mehren, Kopenhagen, 1853.
19. *Arabische Syntax*, von H. Rechendorf, Heidelberg, 1921.

IV. THEOLOGY.

20. *Development of Muslim Theology, Jurisprudence and Constitutional Theory*, by Duncan B. Macdonald, New York, 1903.
21. *The Religious Attitude and Life in Islam*, by D. B. Macdonald, Chicago, 1909.
22. *The Faith of Islam*, by E. Sell, London, 1896.
23. *Commentary of Ibráhím al-Bájúrí*, on the Text of Abú Shujá', Al-'Amíra al-Sharqiya Press, Cairo, 1303.

V. COMMENTARIES ON QUR'AN AND TRADITIONS.

24. *Chrestomathia Baidawiana*, the commentary of El-Baidawi on Súra III, by D. S. Margoliouth, London, 1894.
25. *Anwár al-Tanzíl wa Asrár al-Ta'wíl.* Abú Sa'íd 'Abdalláh bin 'Umar al-Baiḍáwí, edidit H. O. Fleischer, 2 vols., Lipsiae, 1846-48.
26. *Tafsír al-Fátiḥa*, by Muḥammad 'Abduh, Cairo, 1330.
27. *Kitáb al-Miṣbáḥ al-Munír fí Gharíb al-Sharḥ al-Kabír*, lil Ráfi'í, ta'líf Aḥmad bin Muḥammad al-Faiúmí, 2 vols., 1315, 1316.
28. *Irshád al-Sárí ilá Sharḥ Ṣaḥíḥ al-Bukhárí*, Aḥmad bin Muḥammad al-Qasṭallání, Cairo, 1304-5.
29. *Mishkát al-Maṣabíḥ*, of Muḥammad bin 'Abdalláh al-Khatíb al-Tibrízí, Cairo, 1309.

VI. HISTORY.

30. *The Caliphate, its Rise, Decline and Fall*, by Sir William Muir, New and Revised Edition, by T. H. Weir, Edinburgh, 1915.
31. *Sketches from Eastern History*, by Theodor Nöldeke, Translated by J. S. Black and Revised by the Author, London, 1892.
32. *Annales* Quos Scripsit Abu Djafar Mohammed Ibn Djarir *at-Tabari*, cum aliis edidit M. J. De Goeje, Ludg. Bat., 1879-1901.

VII. Biographies.

33. *Tajrid Asmá' al-Ṣaḥába*, of Abú al-Ḥasan 'Alí *bin al-Athír*, Haidarabad, Deccan, 1315.

34. The Irshád al-Aríb ila Ma'rifat al-Adíb, or *Dictionary of Learned Men of Yáqút*, Edited by D. S. Margoliouth, Leyden, 1907-13.

35. *Ibn Coteiba's* Handbuch der Geschichte, herausgegeben von Ferdinand Wüstenfeld, Gottingen, 1850.

36. Abu Bekr Muhammed ben el-Hasan *Ibn Doreid's genealogisch-etymologisches Handbuch*, herausgegeben von Ferdinand Wüstenfeld, Gottingen, 1854.

37. *Biographien* von Gewährsmannern *des Ibn Isḥuq*, hauptsachlich aus *aḍ-Ḍahabí*, herausgegeben von A. Fischer, Leiden, 1890.

38. *Liber Classium Virorum* (Kitáb Ṭabaqát al-Ḥaffáẓ), auctore Abu Abdalla *Dahabio*, in epitomen coegit et continuavit Sujuti, Wüstenfeld, Gottingae, MDCCCXXXIIII.

39. *Al-Moschtabih*, auctore Schamso'd-din Abu Abdallah Mohammed ibn Ahmed *Ad-Dhahabi*, Editus a, P. De Jong, Lugduni Batavorum, 1881.

40. *Kitab al-Fihrist*, herausgegeben von Gustav Flügel, Leipzig, 1871-72.

41. *A Biographical Dictionary of Persons who knew Mohammed*, by Ibn Hajar, Çalcutta, 1856, 4 vols.

42. *Ajá'ib al-Âthár fí 'l-Tarájim wa 'l-Akhbár*, 'Abdalraḥmán bin al-Shaikh Ḥasan al-Jabartí, Búláq, 1297, 4 vols.

43. *Jacut's Moschtarik:* Lexicon geographischer Homonyme, herausgegeben von Ferdinand Wüstenfeld, Gottingen, 1846.

44. *Lexicon Bibliographicum et Encyclopaedicum* a Mustafa ben 'Abdallah Katib Jelebi dicto et nomine *Hají Khalfa*, edidit Gustavus Fluegel, in VII Tomos Leipzig, London, MDCCCXXXV, MDCCCLVIII.

45. *Ibn Khallikan's Biographical Dictionary*, translated from the Arabic by Bn Mac Guckin *De Slane*, 4 vols, Paris, 1842, 1871.

46. (*Táj al-Tarájim fí Ṭabaqát al-Ḥanafiya*) Die Krone der Lebensbeschreibungen enthaltend die Classen der Hanefiten von Zein-ad-dín Kásim *Ibn Kuṭlúbugá*, herausgegeben von Gustav Flügel, Leipzig, 1862.

47. *Abú l-Maḥásin Ibn Ṭagri Bardii Annales*, quibus Titulus est al-Najum al-Záhira fí Mulúk Miṣr wa 'l-Qáhira, ediderunt, T. G. J. Juynboll et B.F. Matthes, Lugduni Batavorum, MDCCCLV, MDCCCLXI.

48. *Ueber das Leben und die Schriften* des Scheich Abu Zakarija Jahja *el-Nawawi*, von Ferd. Wüstenfeld, Gottingen, 1849.

49. *Ibn Saad Biographien Muhammeds, Seiner Gefahrten und der Spateren Trager des Islams,* herausgegeben von Eduard Sachau, Leiden, 1904-9.

50. Supplementum Annotationis in Librum *As-Sojutii de Nominibus Relativis,* inscriptum Lubb al-Lubáb, Scripsit Petrus Johannes Veth, Lugduni Batavorum, MDCCCLI.

51. *Tusy's Index* (Fihris Túsí) *of Shi'ah Books,* edited by A. Sprenger and Mawlawi Abd al-Haqq, Calcutta, 1853.

VIII. GENERAL.

52. *The Thousand and One Nights,* commonly called in England 'The Arabian Nights' Entertainments', by Edward William Lane, in 3 vols., London, MDCCCXXXXIX.

53. *The Manners and Customs of the Modern Egyptians,* by E. W. Lane, London (Everyman's Library).

54. *Personal Narrative of a Pilgrimage to al-Madinah and Mecca,* by Captain Sir R. H. Burton, London, MDCCCXCIII.

55. *Die Keilinschriften und das alte Testament,* von Eberhard Schrader, dritte auflage, Berlin, 1903.

56. *La Passion d' al-Hallaj,* Martyr Mystique de l' Islam, par L. Massignon, Paris, 1922.

57. *Ueber die Eulogien der Muhammedaner,* von I. Goldziher, in *Zeitschrift der Deutschen Morgenländischen Gesellschaft,* vol. I. Leipzig, 1896.

IX. AL-GHAZZALI.

58. *The Life of al-Ghazzali,* with especial reference to his religious experience and opinions, by Duncan B. Macdonald, in *Journal of the American Oriental Society,* vol. XX. MDCCCXCIX.

59. *Al-Ghazali,* by W. R. W. Gardner, Madras, 1919.

60. *A Moslem Seeker after God:* showing Islam at its Best, in the Life and Teaching of Al-Ghazali, by Samuel M. Zwemer, New York, 1920.

61. *Ad-Dourra al-Fâkhira la Perle Précieuse de Ghazâlî,* par L. Gautier, Geneve, 1878.

62. *Über Intention, Reine Absicht und Wahrhaftigkeit,* von Hans Bauer, Halle, 1916.

INDEX